WE
ARE
HOME

ALSO BY RAY SUAREZ

The Old Neighborhood: What We Lost in the Great Suburban Migration

The Holy Vote: The Politics of Faith in America

Latino Americans: The 500-Year Legacy That Shaped a Nation

With Ray Suarez

Truth Has a Power of Its Own: Conversations about A People's History

What We See: Advancing the Observations of Jane Jacobs

Brooklyn: A State of Mind

How I Learned English: 55 Accomplished Latinos Recall Lessons in Language and Life

WE
ARE
HOME

Becoming American in the
21st Century: An Oral History

RAY SUAREZ

Little, Brown and Company
New York Boston London

Little, Brown and Company
Hachette Book Group
1290 Avenue of the Americas
New York
NY 10104

littlebrown.com

First Edition: April 2024

Little, Brown and Company is a division of Hachette Book Group, Inc. The Little, Brown name and logo are trademarks of Hachette Book Group, Inc.

The publisher is not responsible for websites (or their content) that are not owned by the publisher.

The Hachette Speakers Bureau provides a wide range of authors for speaking events. To find out more, go to hachettespeakersbureau.com or email hachettespeakers@hbgusa.com.

Little, Brown and Company books may be purchased in bulk for business, educational, or promotional use. For information, please contact your local bookseller or the Hachette Book Group Special Markets Department at special.markets@hbgusa.com.

Book interior design by Marie Mundaca

ISBN 9780316353762

LCCN is available at the Library of Congress

Printing 1, 2024

LSC-C

Printed in the United States of America

TABLE OF CONTENTS

WE
ARE
HOME

PROLOGUE

The bosom of America is open to receive not only the
Opulent and respected Stranger, but the oppressed and
persecuted of all Nations and Religions; whom we shall
welcome to a participation of all our rights and
privileges.

— George Washington, December 1783

I finished much of this book while teaching in Shanghai, China, the
seaside gigantopolis of southeast China. It is, depending on the year, one
of the largest, or, *the* largest city in the world.

From the desk where I wrote, I could see construction cranes and hear
the hammering and pile-driving from construction sites, forests of apartment towers in the near distance, and soaring skyscrapers busily rewriting the rules for what a modern office building should look like.

Shanghai has a big and growing stock exchange. The city has a subway
system of staggering size and efficiency. It has shopping streets that
would be the envy of most world capitals, broad boulevards, and horren-
dous traffic. When you use the word "immigrant" here, you would have
to be referring, perhaps ironically, to the people who flood in from distant
parts of China to work. Being one of those workers is a tough road to

walk. The newcomer lured by the promise of work and life in an exciting, dynamic city is denied social benefits by various layers of government, unless he or she holds a permit to reside here. Those permits are very hard to come by.

That doesn't stop millions from going where they find opportunity in China. However, the central government fears what would happen if there was suddenly freedom of movement. Some cities would be swamped by ambitious hustlers. Some rural provinces would likely empty out. The millions who have flooded in from China's rural provinces account for all this megacity's population growth, as it has one of the lowest fertility rates of any city in the world.

Unlike New York, Los Angeles, Chicago, Johannesburg, London, Paris, Berlin, Singapore, Madrid, and Rome, Shanghai has not become a home to many foreigners even during the years it was getting rich. An astonishing 98.2 percent of Shanghai's population is from China's predominant ethnic group, the Han. Despite its low number of childbirths and breakneck economic growth, China is not an immigrant magnet. I thought about that a lot as I wrote, and as I taught an international student body in New York University's audacious attempt to create a multicultural, multinational university in this amazing city, sticking with the project even in the midst of a global pandemic. The very existence of the school speaks to one idea about the future of humankind, while rising nationalism in China and around the world speaks loudly about a very different vision.

In the largest country on earth, the word "foreigner" carries a nasty and suspicious connotation. When monkeypox rose as a potential infectious threat, Chinese health officials advised their vast public that one way to avoid getting the disease was to avoid touching foreigners. I joked with friends that the new directive might help me get a seat on the subway.

As China has not laid out the welcome mat for foreigners (the hoops you have to leap through to work here are fearsome), countries around the world are now reckoning with the very idea of nationhood itself. What does it mean to be "us"? Is it strictly a geographical designation? A product of birthplace? Is it a feeling, or something more like a legal arrangement? When we draw lines around places and call them borders, would we also say everybody inside the line is "us," and everybody on the other side, "them"?

In recent years, gunmen have headed to shopping centers in El Paso, Texas, and Buffalo, New York, to shoot up stores where Black and Latino shoppers gather. Other gunmen headed to a synagogue in Pittsburgh and a Black church in Charleston, enraged in various ways by the way they think America is changing. In 2017, a torchlit parade snaked through Thomas Jefferson's hometown of Charlottesville, Virginia, to rally around a statue of Confederate general Robert E. Lee and chant, "You will not replace us."

The idea that dark forces are engineering demographic change in the United States to the detriment of whites of European origin — by encouraging high rates of immigration to shift the balance of political power in the US — has moved from the fringes of American ideological battles to somewhere much closer to the emotional center. As Tucker Carlson climbed the greasy pole at Fox News Channel, he frequently told his audience, among the largest in cable television history, that the Democratic Party was "trying to replace the current US electorate," with "new people, more obedient voters from the Third World."

It's not true. But if you're still not grasping Carlson's zero-sum calculations around political power, he goes further to make it plain: "Every time they import a new voter, I become disenfranchised as a current voter. I have less political power because they are importing a brand-new electorate." Carlson calls people like himself — here he means white people, not rich heirs to frozen food fortunes, though he is that, too — "legacy Americans," and his former bosses, led by an immigrant family named Murdoch, did not stop him.

If you look at the division and rancor created by debates over American identity, changing demographics, and shared notions of citizenship around which we might build a similarly shared notion of nationhood or common good, you might get a nagging thought in the back of your mind. Is China's policy of universalizing Han identity, of building a shared notion of what it means to be Chinese around the norms set by the ethnic majority, a sound policy for an increasingly pluralistic 21st century? What choices face an increasingly plural America?

Even the most casual observer knows the United States chose a different way, and chose it a long time ago. While it marginalized and killed Indigenous people and enslaved Africans from the start of settlement until the Civil War, and it continued to marginalize Black and Indigenous people long after, the young nation also took in immigrants from a wider and wider set of places. The borders of the United States were wide-open for the nation's first century. The country put economic growth at the center of its national goals, and over time changed its laws to match its broadening definitions of shared humanity, shared citizenship, and shared contribution to the common good. Both things were true at the same time: the United States was a country disfigured by historic devotion to racial hierarchy and unequal treatment under law, and it was at the very same moment a nation of immigrants, on a long march to greater equality.

The main federal courthouse in Philadelphia is symbolically and spectacularly located on Independence Mall. From an office on the upper floors you can look left and see the National Constitution Center, a modern museum dedicated to that document, walking the visitor through its drafting and its meaning. When you turn right, you see the visitors' center, orienting people from all over the world for their wanderings through the historic core of the 340-year-old city. Just a little farther right, the modern structure housing the Liberty Bell fills with visitors from across America and the world, even during the pandemic. Just beyond the bell is Independence Hall, the chamber that served as the petri dish for the momentous decision to break up with the British empire and as the place where fifty-five men drew up an operator's manual for running the young country.

On a cloudy day in May 2019, after I got through the complex post–9/11 security, I welcomed eighty men, women, and children from thirty-seven countries to their new lives as US citizens. It felt like a day for idealism. It felt like a day for looking at the coming years with hope. I told them:

The United States, from its very first days as a country, had created a nationality, a people, out of shared *values* instead of shared religion, shared clan, shared land. For 240 years, yes, with some exceptions along the way, we have opened the door and made a promise, if you share with us values around the rule of law, personal freedom, around your individual ambition getting expressed inside a community... you can be us. All of us are countrymen, and countrywomen. That was always the ideal: join with us in pursuing a set of ideas, and you're in. Now granted...this country has not always lived up to its ideals. The Constitution acknowledged and allowed the continuation of slavery. For a long time, in practice, the American Dream was largely open to people of European origin, and not others. Immigrants from China were specifically barred by national law for decades. But the great genius of our country, yours and mine, is that while we don't always get it right, right away, we are always moving toward a national goal, of more freedom, of more equality, of more justice under law. Our Constitution, a brilliant document when it was written, has been amended almost thirty times. Over the centuries we opened the definition of full citizenship wider and wider, included more and more people in the definition of being a full partner in this work of building a better place to live.

You are proof, sitting here today, that we still hold a radically different idea about what it means to belong. Your children will be Americans...your grandchildren will not only be Americans; they may not even know more than a few words of your native tongue, those of you who come from non–English speaking countries.

Now that you're American citizens, what does your new home-land want from you?

We want you to work hard.

We want you to dream big.

We want you to make this country richer, fairer, more peaceful, more just.

We want you to join the rest of us as the work to make a more perfect union, as it says in the Constitution, continues always, for-ever. It's a goal we never reach. Our country, your country, is always a work in progress...never standing still...never fully satisfied... never quite finished. There's always more work to do.

In recent years, sadly, that creed has been challenged. What had once seemed like settled law, questions long since asked and answered, have become part of our national life again.

Should we count noncitizens in the US Census?

Should we automatically grant citizenship to anyone born in this country?

Should US policy discourage further immigration from poorer, non-white countries, and favor it from richer, whiter ones?

The questions, and the arguments that follow from it, are at once con-temporary and very old, with antecedents stretching back to the earliest days of self-government and the forging of a national identity.

The arrival of tens of millions from Ireland and Germany, Italy, and the czarist empire in the roughly seventy-five years from the revolutions of 1848 until the 1920s, when the US Congress slammed the door shut, was one of the greatest mass migrations in human history. This surge tide of people fleeing Europe changed the histories of not only the US, but Canada, Brazil, Mexico, and Argentina as well. In this country, many scorned the new arrivals as illiterate, filthy, diseased, unintelligent, cling-ing to foreign religions and ideas, and unfit for the responsibilities of American citizenship.

Scientists and pseudoscientists from America's greatest research universities, in concert and competition with European scholars, were frantically measuring the bridges of noses, cranium sizes, and the prominence of jaws, creating new and utterly bogus categories of human origin to back up their coalescing ideas about the differences between an immigrant from the Balkans and one from Britain. It may not surprise you to read that northern and western Europeans were found to be superior stock.

Today's version of this resistance has taken new forms, depending less on racist pseudo-biology and more on racist cultural arguments. The "America First" manifesto, seeking to establish a new congressional caucus, invokes history as evidence that "social trust and political unity are threatened" by immigrants "imported en masse into a country," who will also need the support of an "expansive welfare state" to "bail them out should they fail."

It isn't hard to see why the old backlash has risen again in new form. It's been more than fifty years since the Immigration and Nationality Act of 1965 opened the US to Africans, Asians, and Latin Americans "yearning to breathe free." We will never again have the open borders of the early 19th century, but for the past sixty years we have been far more open to chain migration from Asia, Latin America, and Africa, and the percentage of immigrants swelling the total US population has steadily climbed. It isn't at 19th-century levels, but it's large, and from the most diverse points of origin ever in our history. In 1910, almost all the top birth countries of immigrants were in Europe, and the lone exception, Canada, sent descendants of European immigrants. A century later, all the main birth countries were in Asia and Latin America. The highest percentages of foreign-born residents in our history were counted in the 1870, 1890, and 1910 census tabulations, 14.4, 14.8, and 14.7 percent, respectively. In the most recent count in 2020, the foreign-born totaled 44.1 million people, or 13 percent of the total population.

America's demographic cake is baked.

At some point in the mid-21st century, the number of Americans who trace their ancestry primarily to Africa, Asia, and Latin America will surpass the number of those whose forebears came here from Europe. Americans of European ancestry will cease to be the majority here, even if they remain the largest single racial group in the United States for many decades after that.

In 2010, for the first time in centuries (but in every year since, and for a long time to come), a majority of the children born in the US were not of European ancestry. Today those kids are in middle school. In a few years they'll head into military recruitment offices and to college fairs. Not long after that, they will constitute a majority of the workforce, supporting tens of millions of white Americans through the FICA deductions that fund Social Security checks. That intergenerational dependence is not enough, yet, to create solidarity.

The messaging, in the America First declaration of principles, and night after night in conservative media outlets, is loud and clear: these new people aren't like us. The messages confidently assert that newer arrivals are changing the country you thought you knew in ways you don't like. And, perhaps worst of all, the new people won't pull their weight. And when that happens, who'll have to support them? *You.*

We simply can't take any more striving, struggling, ambitious, hardworking people. Especially if they aren't like us already.

That idea turned out to be wrong in 1871.

It turned out to be wrong half a century later in 1921, when the nativists were rewriting immigration law.

And it's wrong today. Immigrants to America have always faced resistance, and have always, over time, assimilated and become vital parts of America. They join our communities. Their children speak flawless American English. They intermarry. This is a process as old as the nation itself, and it can't be stopped no matter how many, or how few, new immigrants arrive every year.

Where are we Americans in the first half of the 21st century, approaching our 250th anniversary as an independent country?

PROLOGUE

We are unstoppably, irresistibly *both, and.*

We are *both* the place where a Black man bounded onto a stage in Grant Park in Chicago in 2008 to accept the ovation of a cheering crowd for becoming the country's first Black chief executive *and* the country that watched—again and again—a police officer snuff the life from a Black man with the weight of his body pressing on that man's neck. We are *both* the country where a Turkish Kurdish immigrant named Hamdi Ulukaya became a billionaire in less than twenty years, *and* the country that sent secret agents into mosques in the years after the 2001 terrorist attacks to spy and root out radicalism. We are *both* the country that prides itself on being a "nation of immigrants" *and* the country openly wondering whether we still want to be. We are *both* the country that proudly declares its openness to people regardless of race, religion, and national origin *and* the country openly wondering whether this will still be America if the majority of people are no longer Christian, white, and of European descent.

The story of the coming changes in who lives here, in what a typical American looks like and when her family got here, starts in 1965 with the reform act that scrapped the old quota system and opened America up to the rest of the world. That was a milepost, a marker on a long timeline toward our present population, that begins during the Lyndon Johnson administration with a US senator from Michigan named Philip Hart, and a US representative from New York named Emanuel Celler.

What did they help create? Who are we, today?

CHAPTER ONE

"A NATION OF STRANGERS"

Men of needed skill and talent were denied entrance because they came from southern or eastern Europe or from one of the developing continents. This system violated the basic principle of American democracy — the principle that values and rewards each man on the basis of his merit as a man. It has been un-American in the highest sense, because it has been untrue to the faith that brought thousands to these shores even before we were a country.

Today, with my signature, this system is abolished. We can now believe that it will never again shadow the gate to the American Nation with the twin barriers of prejudice and privilege.

—Lyndon B. Johnson, October 3, 1965

A Marine helicopter brought Lyndon B. Johnson, the President of the United States, to Ellis Island in New York Harbor on a bright October day. There, as the President put it, "under the monument which has welcomed so many to our shores," he signed the Immigration and Nationality Act of 1965. It was a sweeping rewrite of the framework governing immigration to the United States since 1924, when Congress worried about the origin of the "huddled masses" making their way here almost entirely from Europe.

Johnson was flanked by House and Senate leaders, Vice President Hubert Humphrey, and the two surviving brothers of Johnson's murdered predecessor, Senators Robert F. Kennedy and Edward M. Kennedy; former New York governor, ambassador, and cabinet secretary Averell Harriman; and the new law's chief sponsors, Senator Philip Hart of Michigan and Rep. Emanuel Celler of New York. The President gave the crowd a moving and uplifting justification for the new law. He told the gathering that the bill repaired "a deep and painful flaw in the fabric of American justice. It corrects a cruel and enduring wrong in the conduct of the American Nation."

He was right about that.

The President went on to say that the new law "does not affect the lives of millions. It will not reshape the structure of our daily lives, or really add importantly to either our wealth or power."

He was wrong about that. Time, and events, prove that statement utterly and totally wrong.

I wonder if he knew it was wrong when he said it. LBJ was a man who understood the mechanics of legislation and getting new laws across the finish line better than any human being alive. He knew who had to be placated, who had to be enticed, and what went into the vat for the sausage-making of legislation. Reassuring everyone that they would hardly notice the effects of the new law may have been a smart political move.

In the main, it was the idealistic Johnson of the Civil Rights Act speeches and signing ceremonies who was on display at the foot of the Statue of Liberty. He told his audience the system he was ending by signing the bill "violated the basic principle of American democracy, the principle that values and rewards each man on the basis of his merit as a man. It has been un-American in the highest sense, because it has been untrue to the faith that brought thousands to these shores even before we were a country."

This is strong stuff from the Southerner shepherding civil rights laws to passage. From the Texan who taught impoverished children in a segregated Mexican American school during the Depression. Johnson used a phrase that has stuck with me for years. He said, "Our beautiful America was built by *a nation of strangers*. From a hundred different places or more they have poured forth into an empty land, joining and blending in one mighty and irresistible tide."

Many Americans might object, accurately, to the denial of native Americans inherent in that phrase, "an empty land." That is a foundation stone of our national myth, and beyond the scope of this book. Let's at least give credit to LBJ for holding that myth up to its own mirror.

Lyndon Johnson, a man from the Hill Country of central Texas, whose ancestors came from Scotland long before there was a United States, demonstrated a grasp of a subtle thing about coming here from elsewhere in the world. We arrive as strangers. We build community. We make common cause with our neighbors and fellow citizens once we are rooted here. A persistent motif in American debates over immigration goes directly to the heart of this idea.

As a people, we seem reluctant to give ourselves much credit for being able to make neighbors from strangers. We have always tried hard to shape the arrivals to make it easier for *us* to get used to *them*. The Chinese Exclusion Act barred entry and naturalization of Chinese migrants from the 1880s until the 1940s. The 1924 Johnson-Reed Act barred the Japanese from entering the US. The intent of the 68th Congress, and its successors, was to maintain homogeneity in the US, preferably by allowing immigration from the northern and western regions of Europe, and then, reluctantly, from eastern Europe.

* * *

From 1924—when the Johnson-Reed Act tried to slam the "golden door" to the people of much of the world by explicitly favoring immigration from northern and western Europe, and only then, in greatly reduced numbers—until the 1965 Act was signed, the world was a pretty complicated place. It was a world of new borders, new countries carved from old empires, a global economic depression, followed by another calamitous world war, followed by a new thing called the Cold War, and the rapid decolonization of more than half a billion subject peoples around the world.

As the dust cleared, millions were refugees, millions more were politically vulnerable, or permanently stigmatized in their own homelands. The postwar revolution of rising expectations left yet more millions of ambitious people dissatisfied and longing for a place in an America that offered hope that was in too little supply at home.

Conversely, the slots reserved for people from increasingly prosperous *Wirtschaftswunder* West Germany; from the *treinte glorieuses,* thirty years of postwar glory in France; and from a new "Golden Age" in postwar Britain, went unused. Plenty of people wanted to get here. Just not from the places for which a long-ago Congress put their thumb on the scale.

The restrictions of the 1920s combined with the tumult of the next forty years created an American population of family lore and albums of sepia photographs, but one almost entirely born in the US, even though the early 20th century saw the final chapters of one of the greatest surge tides of human migration in the history of the world. In roughly a century from 1820 to 1924, an estimated 37 million Europeans came to the United States.

In 1900, 13.6 percent of the residents of the US were born outside its borders. After restrictions, and decades of assimilation, in 1960 the population of foreign-born Americans was down to just 5.6 percent. That same year Americans went to the polls and elected John Kennedy president, a Roman Catholic whose great-grandparents came from Ireland.

By the 1960s, there were still some tens of millions of Americans who were descendants of recent waves of European immigrants, or, in the phrase of the Census Bureau, "of immigrant stock." Family heirlooms from Europe had pride of place in living rooms, instructions to novice cooks were delivered in English, but with thick accents as grandchildren often knew little more than a few words of an ancestral tongue. Twentieth-century popular culture was flush with the output of people whose imaginations were shaped by immigrant memory but, crucially, were not immigrants themselves.

Chico Marx, the New York–born son of immigrants from Germany and the Franco-German Alsace region of France, played wisecracking immigrant hustlers named Panello, Rivelli, and Fiorello. Baseball Hall of Famer Yogi Berra, grinning from advertisements for soft drinks and cigarettes, was raised by early-20th-century Italian immigrants. One of the kings of early television, Sid Caesar, clowned with customers as a boy at the New York diner owned by his Polish immigrant parents. Born John Feeney to Irish immigrants in Maine, John Ford thrilled movie fans with his mastery of that most American of genres, the Western, decade after decade.

By the 1960s the explicit pro-European bias in the 1924 immigration law — 70 percent of visas were reserved for immigrants from Ireland, the United Kingdom, and Germany — had been softened somewhat by laws passed in the 1950s. Masters of the Congress were pressed to act by LBJ, and they assured him they would, even if they were not always transparent about their motives.

Despite his own formidable skill and power as a legislator, and despite big Democratic majorities in the House and Senate, Johnson's battle for the Immigration and Nationality Act was tough. The struggles inside the Democratic majorities illustrated the deep incoherence of the party's wings.

Southern Democrats represented states the Ellis Island era had simply passed by. The former states of the Confederacy comprised the most uniformly native-born region in the country. Northeastern and Great Lakes Democrats were shaped by two mass migrations: of Blacks fleeing the South, and whites quitting Europe. Chicago's mayor Anton Cermak was born in the Austro-Hungarian empire, New York mayors Abraham Beame and Anthony Impelliteri, and Cleveland's Anthony Celebrezze all immigrated from Europe.

Senator Sam Ervin of North Carolina, in a debate on provisions in the proposed immigration reform bill, said, "The people of Ethiopia have the same right to come to the United States under this bill as the people from England, the people of France, the people of Germany, the people of Holland. With all due respect to Ethiopia, I don't know of any contributions that Ethiopia has made to the making of America." In the America of Ervin's imagination, just as it was for the US Congress in the 1920s, the country's immigrant past should remain a reliable guide to the future.

Rep. Michael Feighan of Ohio was another of the Democrats favoring reform who wanted to maintain America's racial structure, while couching it in terms of protecting American-born workers and national security. Feighan wanted to thread the needle. If a course could be found that would ease pressure from the President, allow him to get a bill passed, and assure that immigrants would not change the ethnic and racial character of the United States, he would find it. Feighan emphasized family reunification over job qualifications, believing that the profile of already settled immigrants could dictate the nationality of future ones. This "chain migration" would prove enormously consequential, but not in the manner he expected.

Like many politicians of his era, Feighan contained elements of character that made for an uneasy mix. The chairman of the House Immigration and Naturalization Committee, he cherished his own Irish immigrant heritage. He opposed the plain language of Hart-Celler ("No person shall receive any preference or priority or be discriminated against in the issuance of an immigrant visa because of his race, sex, nationality, place of birth, or place of residence") and pushed back against the President. In the 1964 election, Feighan had limped past the finish line to reelection while Johnson won one of the greatest landslides in presidential history. Feighan was strongly anti-Communist, but that did not keep his 1964 primary, against a Czech American who wanted to scrap the quota system to help more eastern Europeans get to the US, from becoming a political near-death experience. To further spice the legislative stew, Feighan and the bill's cosponsor Emanuel Celler, a fellow Democrat and chair of the powerful Judiciary Committee, disliked each other intensely.

Coming back to Washington in 1965, Feighan gave to get. He gave in on the desire to keep the quota system, and inserted family unification, one of his strongest legislative priorities. Once Feighan was on board, thanks in no small part to LBJ's intense pressure (known as "the treatment"), the 1965 Act steamed toward passage.

More than a quarter century later, when the silver-haired Ohioan died, the *New York Times* called Feighan an "Immigration Reformer" in his obituary headline.

It is easy to forget from today's distance how much of this legislative battle was carried on in the shadow of the Cold War. Hundreds of thousands of American men were headed to Southeast Asia to defend the sovereignty of South Vietnam. South Florida had absorbed thousands of Cuban refugees in the first years after Fidel Castro's victory in the Cuban Revolution. Some thirty thousand Hungarians came to the US in the years after the abortive 1956 uprising against Soviet domination. The USSR was countering the US across the world in newly decolonized countries in Africa and Asia, in a propaganda blitz that pushed photos and newsreel footage from the Southern states of police dogs menacing civil rights protestors, and local officers opening firehoses on marchers.

In the battle to win hearts and minds in the newly independent developing world, a preference for white immigrants isn't a great opening card to play. Taking down the Eurocentric quotas was, in the end, not a hard call. It may be that the country's elites were so accustomed to a modest trickle of newcomers from the world outside Europe that they did not understand the full extent of the desire to come here. Political instability, civil war, the failed promises of independence, and the large numbers of foreign students would make getting to America not only desirable but achievable.

The thumping Democratic majorities in both House and Senate

should not obscure the bipartisan nature of support for immigration reform in those long-ago days. It passed the House by a margin unimaginable in modern politics, 318–95. The Senate passed the measure by a lopsided 76–18, sending it to the base of the State of Liberty and the celebratory presidential signature. It is almost impossible to imagine today, but the opening (or, rather, reopening) of America's gates was a hugely popular decision, with hugely bipartisan support.

And those gates have proven to be floodgates. Since 1965, immigrants have accounted for 55 percent of all population growth in the United States. Some seventy million people have come to the US from every corner of the globe in the last half century. Add immigrants and their US-born children together into a single number, and you have more than a quarter of all Americans, in every corner of the country. They are us.

INTERLUDE

Samir

born in Mombasa, Kenya

I was already 20, and it was like you had won the Golden
Ticket, right? I had family and cousins here, so I kind of
knew a bit about it, like it wasn't "the streets were paved
with gold" type of thing. You'll have to work.

My parents were born in Kenya and Tanzania during the colonial
time, the British colonial time, so we were, I guess, second or third generation, and we were originally from Yemen. So growing up I was already
an immigrant from birth. The way they spoke about Yemen, and especially their parents, my grandparents, it was always as if one day we'll go
back. So you felt Kenyan by upbringing, but sometimes, you know, going
to school they tell you you're an Arab. Go back home, right?" Figuring
out just where home was would become the puzzle he would spend the
next decades of his life solving.

Settlers and traders from the Arabian Peninsula have been moving
south along Africa's Indian Ocean coast for centuries. There are Arab

settlements and towns from the Red Sea all the way down to what is today Mozambique. Swahili, the lingua franca of much of East Africa, is shot through with Arabic words and linguistic structures.

Samir, now in his forties, trim, compact, brown-skinned, brown-haired, brown-eyed, would look at home walking down countless streets in the Global South. From his youngest days he navigated multiple cultures and nationalities. After early childhood in the Kenyan coastal city of Mombasa, he moved to Saudi Arabia when his father got a job there, and then returned to Kenya at eleven. The reentry, he recalls, was not so easy. His Swahili was now accented after years abroad. His Arabic was shaped by the particular dialect of Saudi Arabia. "So I remember they teased me, even the other Arab kids did. I remember trying to fit in again."

As Samir was trying to find his feet back home in Kenya, life took an unexpected turn. His parents divorced. His father returned to Saudi Arabia. An aunt, his mother's sister, had moved to the United States and had entered Samir's mother and the children into the lottery system for a so-called diversity visa. Unlike the other increasingly exacting parts of American immigration statutes, the diversity visa, created by a 1990 immigration law, is literally a game of chance. Every year the US government awards fifty thousand visas to applicants selected at random from countries with low rates of immigration to the US. Most applicants, and most winners, come from Africa.

Millions apply for diversity visas every year. As with state lotteries, the odds of a life-changing win are minuscule.

Samir's mother won. She packed up her kids and headed to Maryland to live with her sister.

Samir knew he would have to work hard. And that it wouldn't be easy.

"When I came here, even though I spoke English and I had a network, and support, I was really surprised how homesick I was for Kenya. There, I knew how to get around. I was popular. Now, I went to the suburbs of Columbia, Maryland, and it really felt like I was in a desert, very lonely.

No cafés. People didn't even know the neighbor's name and stuff like that."

Even in the midst of winning that lottery, there was heartbreak, and a difficult decision to be made. "One thing that broke my mom's heart coming here was my brother was over twenty-one. He was in university in Kenya. My older brother. I'm the second out of five. And they told him that with the diversity visas she could only move with four out of her five kids. The oldest one had to be issued a separate green card.

"She cried a lot because it was the second time she left my older brother. When we moved to Saudi Arabia, my dad had left my older brother behind because he had already started school and was learning English. None of us (younger siblings) had started school when we moved. Now, all these years later, my mom was like, 'I'm doing this again. I'm leaving him for the second time.' She had never forgiven herself for the first one, so she was really torn about it. Then my aunt said, 'Oh, it's only going to take a year to get his green card.' So we thought. It actually took fifteen years."

Samir reassured his mother, telling her she had done the right thing. He had just finished high school. A younger brother was in high school, a sister was in middle school. The family crowded into a townhouse in Columbia, Maryland, with Samir's aunt and her family, until the five of them could rent a townhouse of their own nearby. It must have been head-spinning. Mombasa is a picturesque old port city melding Arabic, African, and British colonial influences. Warm breezes from the Indian Ocean waft aromas from spice markets and open-air food stalls. Through the day the muezzin's call to prayer ricochets through the ancient streets.

Seven time zones away, Columbia, Maryland, was a planned development, a model city meant to pioneer a new kind of medium-density urbanism for America's metropolitan areas. Developer James Rouse wanted to demonstrate a kind of development that would combat sprawl, while making room for employment, housing, recreation, and medical care all within easy distance. It is hard to think of two places less alike than Mombasa and Columbia. To hear Samir tell it, he took it all in stride.

"It wasn't hard to assimilate quickly. Get a job. I worked at McDonald's and Wawa. One of my first jobs at Wawa was at the deli counter. I spoke with a Kenyan accent. Most people when they move here, they think Americans speak fast. You almost don't hear half the words. They're saying what? But all you hear is *wa, wa, wa,* right?

"I didn't know all the different cheeses! And people were very particular. They want tuna on rye, with this, but not that. I thought, 'Oh my God, how many cheeses do these people have? These are the things that stick with me. I remember, you know, the guy's watching me. It's kind of like a Subway setup. He's watching me make his sandwich and I'm panicking. And what the hell is relish?"

In the United States for just a few weeks, Samir was working two full-time jobs at two very American businesses, Wawa, the mid-Atlantic convenience store chain, and McDonald's. He wanted to enroll in college, but hesitated, even as he worked those crushing hours. His aunt offered to lend him the money to register. "But I felt very restless. And I was scared that I was going to squander the money. That I wasn't going to be a good student, because the college was right across the street. And that wasn't college how I envisioned it. I wanted to go to *Animal House* college. But this was a community college. I was going to be living at home. Taking the bus. It was not fun."

We were sitting in a Cuban-style coffee shop in Maryland's District of Columbia suburbs as he told me his story, full of gentle self-deprecation and frequent references to American pop culture...television, movies, music. Yet even when the family had just unpacked in its new home, the young Kenyan did something audacious.

He joined the United States Army.

"I got into this country in May. By August first I had already signed up to go into the military. I was watching reruns of *Seinfeld* or something at night, and they were showing the recruiting commercial 'Be All That

You Can Be.' And make college money! I was like, 'Oh, what is this?' I told my aunt to take me to the recruiting station.

"A few years earlier I had seen *A Few Good Men,* and I really liked that uniform. You know, I fancied myself as Tom Cruise, so I walked into the Marine section, it was a joint recruitment station, and I think not a lot of people just walk in because they were kind of surprised to see me.

"I was like, 'Is it okay if I come in?' And they're like 'Oh yeah, sure! Come in!' And then I talked to them about what jobs they had. I told them I want college money. But I think back, and a couple of things were driving me. We were comfortable, middle class, in Kenya. We had house help. We had maids. We had stuff, and coming here and seeing my mother take the bus to go to the mall, Columbia Mall, really killed me. She worked at JCPenney. She sold shoes. It's like, 'Oh my God, she's going and fetching shoes for people.' To me, it felt beneath her. But I knew we needed the money.

"I thought, 'What am I doing? I can't go to college?' And at that point I had wanted to go to law school. I thought, 'My God, I've got to go to four years of university, and then three years of law school, and all that time my mom's going to measure people's feet and touch their feet?' It just killed me.

"I didn't tell her this, because I didn't want her to feel bad. And she didn't seem to mind. She was happy. She had always been a housewife and stuff, and here she learned how to drive. She was taking computer classes. She enjoyed it.

"One of the reasons I went into the military was this: I was like, okay, I'm going to help provide. I'm killing two birds with one stone. I'll make school money. I'll get out of the suburbs. And help my mom."

As Samir tells the story now, in his forties, he is recalling a time when he was still, in many ways, a kid. Both sides of him came through: emotions that are unusually wise, self-possessed, and forward-thinking, as well as his younger, fresh-off-the-plane self. He remembers sitting at the recruiting station waiting for his aunt to circle back and pick him up. An

Army recruiter mentioned that he saw Samir talking to the other branches, slipped him a business card, and invited him to chat.

"I had done the ASVAB test [the Armed Services Vocational Aptitude Battery], and I scored high. I was kind of seeing who had the best deal. The Air Force was like, well, we can send you to school and teach you a technical job, but it's going to take nine months. But I had found the suburbs were very suffocating. I wanted to get out now! I had no car. I had nothing. I was like, this sucked."

The Army pounced. "The Army guy's like, 'We can ship you out sooner!' And I was like, 'Hell yes, let's sign up.' Because I was not a citizen, there were some jobs I was precluded from. I think I picked fuel logistics because I was thinking about what I could do after I got out and still make money."

It set up an interesting argument between Samir's seasoned immigrant aunt and his newly arrived mother. "My aunt says, 'Yeah! Do this!' because she had been in America for years. But my mom was crying. She was like, 'I didn't bring you here to die! How can they even take you? You just got here!' At that point I wanted to say, 'Look, if you're willing to take a bullet, they'll take you.' But I didn't."

In recent years, when I have had long talks with people who immigrated to the United States, I always ask about patriotism, love of country, alliance, and allegiance. I didn't have to ask Samir about his motivations as he got ready to go to basic training. He told me. "It was really transactional. It was not like flag or patriotism or anything." Enlisting offered a faster track to citizenship, but that wasn't what closed the deal. "Instead of waiting five years to become a citizen, it's three years. But if they mentioned it, I don't even remember it. Because to me, whether I had a green card or citizenship, it was kind of the same." Mainly, he just wanted to get out of Columbia, and out of the drive-through window, while helping to support the family.

"So I'm ready to ship out. I'm desperate to go now. I'm ready. You know, I'm doing these dead-end jobs. I was doing two shifts a day, at Wawa and McDonald's. And McDonald's paid me extra to open the store.

So I would be there at five in the morning. I take the bus back home. That took an hour in the suburbs. At three o'clock in the afternoon I would go to my other shift at Wawa. But I was twenty. Even so, after a few weeks I remember, I couldn't even think straight because basically I went home, showered, at eleven o'clock at night. I'd barely eat. Then I had to wake up at four, four thirty, shower, and call a cab to take me to McDonald's.

"I remember being so resentful of people waiting in the line, the drive-through, before we even opened. I was like, 'Goddamnit, where the hell are you Americans going?' After a while, you kind of started figuring it out. People are very predictable. They order the same thing every day. Hey, I'm helping to pay rent, so I'm ready to go."

Grow up in Kenya and Saudi Arabia. Get a quick coat of finish from American convenience and fast food. Then put on the uniform and head to basic training at Fort Jackson in South Carolina. "I was still Kenyan. I met somebody at basic from an Indian reservation, and then what I found was a common theme. We were all poor. And nobody had really joined for any higher ideals. It was just to get out."

Even after a delay in beginning basic training caused by a government shutdown, Samir had been in the US less than a year. His American journey started to get even stranger. "They sent me to Korea for my first duty station. It was really interesting, because I barely know America, and I'm wearing the uniform, and I'm out of the country. They asked us, after boot camp and technical training, whether we wanted to jump out of an airplane or drive a truck." They promised a commercial driver's license and training in logistics. He drove a truck.

I pointed out what Samir already knew. That he had been born and raised in societies with high degrees of tribal and racial consciousness. Kenya was home to Indigenous Africans, a small population of European descent, and families with deep roots and long-standing contacts with the Arabian Peninsula. He had grown up reminded of his identity at every turn. Now, as a young adult serving in Korea, he was dropped into a society with its own racial history and an identity forged by conflict with its much larger neighbors, China and Japan. After only a few months in Maryland, sworn to defend his new home and its constitution against all enemies, wearing a uniform with an American flag on the shoulder, he was living in a country where he was, once again, a racial outlier. As it turned out, Samir said, he was marked as an American simply by not being Korean.

"I think from a young age you hone a skill of trying to blend in and not stick out. Even within the Yemeni community in Kenya, there's a social hierarchy because I know my family would not marry into certain families based on what we had in Yemen.

"In my dad's generation, Yemenis married into Yemeni families. Once in a while, somebody would marry somebody Swahili, who's dark, who looks Black like a Black American. There's a lot of people of Omani descent, from Zanzibar and Oman, who we could not marry. We're both Arabs. Both Muslim. We live in the same neighborhoods." But for some Yemeni and Omani parents, it was a bridge too far. America, by contrast, seemed much more fluid to Samir. "I never felt the weight of my identity in the US. In Saudi Arabia what rubbed me the wrong way was that people size you up. They want to know if you're a citizen because if you're not a citizen they treat you a whole 'nother way.

"So I went to Korea, and just kind of blended in there." Most Koreans are not very welcoming of Americans, or at least it felt that way. So Samir just put his head down and pushed through. Boot camp. Truck driving school. Getting along in a new country. All while the US was a country he was still trying to get to know, but now from the other side of the planet.

"When I went to Korea I just kind of stayed in the base. The base was like a mini-America. You've got your bowling alley, you've got your movies and stuff. I really missed home. Again, that's Kenya.

"I missed my mom, but I didn't miss Columbia, Maryland." That's not a Kenyan thing. It's not an immigrant thing. It could very well be a "twenty-year-old in a strange environment and far away from home" thing. Samir's time in Korea ended with a transfer back to the US. At this point he had been a legal resident of the United States for a few years and had spent almost all that time outside the country. His next duty station was Fort Lee, Virginia, just south of Richmond and a few hours south of Columbia.

Now able to use his GI benefits to buy his family a home, he wandered into a real estate agent's office near the base. His mother was now an assistant manager at JCPenney and was able to request a transfer to a store close to Samir. "I found an agent who was the spouse of a military commander. She asked why a twenty-two-year-old was trying to buy a house. I was single. I told her it was for my mom and my siblings and she liked that."

His mother drove down from Maryland to accompany Samir on the house hunt. "The second home we looked at, as we were leaving, on the top of the door there was a small sticker that said, in Arabic, 'In the Name of God.' My mom said, 'This is a sign. This is the one.'

At the time, he had all of $300 in a checking account. "I remember we were going to closing, and the company asked, 'How much money are you bringing to the closing?' I was like, 'What do you mean? You said zero down!' They said yeah, but people usually bring some money to the closing to lower their payment. I answered, 'You said zero down. That's literally what I have. Zero.' I was twenty-two and signing a document for a thirty-year mortgage. Thirty years!"

For a young enlisted man, Samir had adult responsibilities. He had bought his family a house just two years after they all moved from Kenya. Now he had to figure out if he could live in it, too. "I went and talked to my commander and told him I had legal guardianship of all my younger siblings, and asked permission to move out of the barracks, which was also financially advantageous because you get a housing allowance. I wasn't sure they were going to let me, but because I was a legal guardian and my platoon leader kind of put in a good word for me they let me.

"I lived with my mom and my siblings in a nice home and my mom was very proud. It's one of my proudest achievements, that I bought a house for my mom when I was twenty-two. It had trees in the front. It had trees in the back. It felt very good that I wasn't a screw-up. The funny thing was slightly embarrassing. We only had one car. So my mom would drop me off at Fort Lee in the morning, like I'm going to school." She would drop him off at the base, and at the end of the day Samir would meet her at the mall for the drive home.

He had arrived in the States less than three years before. He was gaining rank and responsibility as an enlisted man in the United States Army. His mother was getting promotions at JCPenney. His siblings were succeeding in school. The family owned a house in a leafy suburb in Virginia. That's many people's version of the American Dream. Did he feel American?

Samir's answer to that question took a turn that echoed with countless other stories immigrants have told me over the years, about the realization that no matter how much they had embraced America, or held her at arm's length, they no longer really belonged back home, either. "On my second trip to Kenya, I went to Mombasa where I grew up, and now this is maybe fifteen years after I left.

"I felt very sad because physically it looked the same, but I didn't know anybody in the neighborhood. Everybody I grew up with left because it's very hard. Kenya is like the rest of the world. There's a lot of income inequality and it's quite stunning. I have family who have properties in London, they drive special-ordered Mercedes from Germany. And I have family who can't send their kids to school and we have to donate money for them to go.

"Anybody of means left. They're in Dubai. They're in Saudi Arabia. Some even went back to Yemen when Yemen was reunited and we thought the economics prospects would be better. I was in Kenya, standing on the street corner where I used to hang out with my friends, and I stood there for what seemed like ages and I didn't recognize anybody who walked by.

"And it dawned on me. This doesn't feel like home anymore. My friends were all over the world. So, I don't feel at home anywhere. I enjoy living here now, and I'm established and stuff like that. But I struggle with that." He says he doesn't share those misgivings with his now teen-aged children.

Samir became somber as he reflected on recent years. During the 2016 US presidential campaign, he said, he never believed Donald Trump could become president. He dismissed the television star as "a circus act," and was confident that even if Trump did win, American institutions would rein him in. He recalled the years in Kenya under the authoritarian president Daniel Arap Moi, and how resisting the Moi government awakened his own teenage political consciousness. He showed me a picture of himself at fifteen, at the front of a line of marchers in an anti-Moi protest in Mombasa. The photo was taken by the security services and given to Samir's father as a kind of warning to cool it.

His younger brother inquired about taking flying lessons in Richmond in the late 1990s, which resulted in a visit from the FBI after 9/11. Agents asked Samir's mother about their local mosque, and her children's activities there. Now in middle age, he is aware of anti-Muslim bias and exclusion. In response to a Facebook post he headed down to Dulles International Airport with his sons to protest the Trump policy excluding visitors from several Muslim majority countries that came to be known as the Muslim ban.

"One thing I noticed was, there's more than just Muslims. It was really, really encouraging. When I went back to my own community I said, 'Look, you guys have to start showing up for other people's causes.' I remember there was a guy carrying a sign that said 'Jews for Muslims.' It wasn't the number of people at the protest, it was the solidarity.

"I think we had gone through grief stages of denial, of crying. But now he had won, and we have to survive. Now it's defiance, you know?

"I've lived through 9/11. I've seen the anti-Muslim stuff. Most people might not realize how many supported that. So I doubled my effort to tell the kids, 'You are an American. You're Muslim. You're Arab. You're everything, you know? And you can be everything.'" But he added, "Even though I didn't really feel so American myself."

* * *

"Plucky immigrant takes his chances in America" is a four-hundred-year-old story. Plug in the specifics of visas and enlistments and passports and crossing the globe, however, and Samir's becomes more of a "21st-Century American Life." After his time in Virginia, he was sent to duty in Saudi Arabia, in a base not far from where he lived as a boy. An American military presence on Saudi soil dated from the First Gulf War to liberate Kuwait. A permanent American presence in the land of Islam's holiest sites fired the anger of young men across the Muslim world, many of whom rallied to the small and growing "Base," the translation of the Arabic name al Qaida.

Samir's instinct was interesting. Rather than lean into his familiarity with the country and its culture, and his Arabic-language skills, Samir rarely brought it up. In his shape-shifting life of just pushing through and getting ahead, he decided to avoid the attention these rare attributes might bring. Occasionally, when negotiating the completion of truck loading and fuel deliveries, paperwork and delays, he would drop the mask. But rarely. Whenever possible, he conducted his business with the Saudis in English.

The Army knew of his skills. He had scored high enough on a language proficiency test for the military to offer training to become an Arabic interrogator. Samir said, "Of course, this is before the War on Terror, this is before September 11, and it was very attractive because the school is in Monterey, California. I was really tempted."

Samir called it "a fork in the road." It was, all told, a six-year program of training and deployment. At the end of the six years, he would have spent a total of eleven years in the Army, "and nobody spends eleven years in the Army. You either get out after you do your service, or you do twenty."

In the end, to be closer to his family and shorten his commitment, Samir accepted a transfer to Texas, where he was trained as an animal research technician, before transfer to the military's biological and chemical research lab at Fort Detrick, Maryland. During our time together Samir mentioned feeling like Forrest Gump sometimes, just ending up in places to be a witness to critical times. He arrived just as Fort Detrick was the center of an investigation into the source of anthrax being sent to politicians through the mail.

After the September 11 attacks, Samir was glad he had not chosen to work as an interrogator. He got out of the military and spent more time with his mother in what unexpectedly turned out to be the last years of her life. His army experience with animals led to a job at the National Institutes of Health. He even took a shot at an almost stereotypical American immigrant experience: he opened a restaurant across from a military base and hired a bunch of family members — nuclear and extended — to work there. "That's another lesson I learned. Never hire someone you can't fire."

He lost money, sold the restaurant, and kept on working at NIH. During a visit to Montgomery County Community College, the manager of the biotechnology lab noted that NIH was the county's largest employer, and the two men agreed that not enough students apply to the plentiful entry-level jobs from the local college. Today he sits on the advisory board for Montgomery College, and gives career development workshops around the county. Word got around, he said, and those sessions brought more invitations, now for displaced midcareer workers trying to reboot their work lives, get more training, and get rehired.

Is this a story with a happy ending? Samir pauses, reflects, and looks back on the kids he grew up with in Kenya, people he can now stay in touch with through social media platforms like WhatsApp. "Some of them were way better students than me. Were way better kids than me. Across the board. And life has not been kind to them."

He remembers how young he was when he felt he had to pick up his family and carry them on his shoulders. "That really drove me. America. I'm very aware of the opportunities. They're overwhelming, the opportunities. For all its flaws, and there's no country without flaws, it's been very good to me."

With his first wife, the daughter of immigrants from Egypt, Samir is raising two boys, now teenagers. Remarried to a woman from the Arabian Peninsula Sultanate of Oman, he also has a baby boy. In the middle of 2023, we spoke for the first time in more than a year. Now approaching fifty, Samir is reflective and philosophical, seeing America through his boys' eyes.

"I take them with me to drop off food donations at a county homeless shelter and food pantry. I want to humanize these people for them. Sometimes it's just the luck of the draw that we're not in that shelter.

"One of the things I told them is, 'I am your safety net. I didn't have a safety net. When I was young I saw my friends, and other families. They didn't have to worry about sending money home. They didn't have to worry about helping their mom, or helping their siblings.'

"'For me at your age,' I tell them, 'life was a high-wire act. If I fell there was no one to catch me. I am here to catch you. So think big. I want you to take risks.' A lot of the choices I made were made because of my need to provide. There were things I could not pursue because I had to support my mom and my siblings. Maybe if I was American and I didn't have to provide for my family I would have been able to make different choices. I would have sought out those adventures. I want my kids to be able to do that."

His oldest son, Hazim, finished high school and decided not to go right on to college. Samir took him to the local recruiter for the Maryland National Guard to discuss a four-year commitment. Did he feel a sense of déjà vu? "The first thing he asked when I suggested the National Guard was 'Am I in trouble?' I told him I learned a lot from the military. I gained a lot from going, from testing myself, from accomplishing difficult things. And it gave me confidence that I carried with me for the rest of my life.

"He's looking for a dash of excitement. To do some service. For something bigger than himself. He's still a baby in my eyes. You think, 'Oh my God, he's going out into the world. This will help him become a man.' I'm happy with the idea."

Samir said his sons, US-born, American from first breath, are adept at "code-switching," changing the way they communicate and handle themselves in response to their environment. "They act differently depending on who they're around. They slip in Islamic phrases when they're talking to Muslim immigrants, or they're at the mosque. They say, 'Dad, you speak differently when you speak to Kenyans.' They mimic what I do more than what I tell them to do."

I was curious about the differences between the way his older sons, one finishing high school, the other finishing middle school, experienced Maryland as brown kids, as Arab Americans, as the offspring of recent immigrants. And the Maryland suburbs are far more diverse than when he arrived thirty years ago from Kenya. Will it be easier still for his baby boy?

"I'm much more aware of my identity. I came from the Old World. And really, I was always an outsider, no matter where I was. When I was in Saudi, no one there was going to consider me Saudi no matter how long I stayed there. I spoke the language, played with my Saudi friends, lived in the culture.

"I'm from Kenya, and I was Kenyan culturally, but not African. You'd hear, 'Go back to where you came from,' that sort of thing. I'm Yemeni, but at the same time I'm not Yemeni, either, and I wouldn't fit in there. So you're never quite home. You might have an affinity for a place, but every now and then someone will remind you, 'You are not from here.' It's an element of the human condition.

"What I am trying to do is give back as much as I can." He teaches first-generation community college students what he calls "soft skills," not academics, but what they will need to know to apply for jobs, how to handle themselves in interviews, how to negotiate salaries, or for a raise. "I tell them, 'You don't get what you deserve. You get what you ask for.'"

As the Taliban completed its takeover of Afghanistan and the US withdrew after twenty years, Samir helped the most recent wave of Afghan arrivals to the US, filling out the necessary paperwork for asylum claims and requests for transitional benefits as they resettled. He explained his drive to help others is spurred in part by a kind of "survivor's guilt."

"Here I think I can speak for myself and other immigrants. It's something like guilt. You made it out. I'm in contact online with a group of high school and primary school friends. When I look at them I see they've aged significantly, much more than me, because their lives have been so hard.

"The people back in Kenya who did everything right, worked hard in school, did well in their exams, but never made it out? They are in bad shape. From luck, nothing but luck, I got to come here. I have to make the most of this. I have to help out, because I've been given this opportunity.

"My dad worked in Saudi Arabia for years, but he could only rise to a certain level because he is not Saudi. In Kenya, there are unwritten rules about people from which tribes get to do certain jobs. Coming here, you can re-create yourself. And that's not true everywhere in the world. I tell my sons, 'If you want to be an astronaut, you can be one. You can go toward that path.' "

Looking back at his life so far, Samir does not credit all of his success to America's transformative power. He said his outsider status forced him to be adaptable in ways other people may not be. "You could have dropped me off in Shanghai, and if you came back in ten years I would have made it somehow. You have to be flexible. You have to do whatever it takes."

Samir, and his growing family, are in part the face of "The Next America."

CHAPTER TWO

WHY WE LEFT, HOW WE CAME

Talk to people who started life somewhere else in the world about why they came to the United States, and common themes emerge: economic privation, political, religious, or ethnic persecution, search for opportunity, family unity. At the very same time, every story is as individual as a thumbprint. They can be funny, amazing, frightening, inspiring, and heartbreaking. Sometimes, all those things.

During the second George W. Bush administration, the Congressional Budget Office (CBO) issued an extensive report on US immigration policy. Like the Roman god Janus, the paper tried to look backward into history, and into the coming years at the same time. Without question, that report would not read the same way if it were written today. It is worth parsing it, one step at a time.

The lengthy document began with a basic statement of principles, laying out the goals of US immigration law. "First, it serves to reunite families by admitting immigrants who already have family members living in the United States." That proposition, that family reunification came first of all priorities, reflected the political reality: that this aspect of the law was one of few that all sides in raging immigration debates could agree on. Or, at least it was. For decades.

Nelson Castillo is a successful immigration attorney, born in El Salvador. His English is accented, elegant, and expressive. It turns out he did not want to move to the US at all. "My mother left me in El Salvador when I was four years old. She came to the United States with a non-immigrant visa, with a tourist visa. She overstayed her visa and proceeded to work as a housekeeper." Nelson recalls his mother's original intention was simply to make enough money to build a home back in El Salvador. Immigrant plans that change once they get marinated in American life is another common part of these stories. Imagined sojourns, quick chapters in life meant to improve life back home, instead end up being long-term investments in becoming American.

Nelson's mother worked for a prominent, wealthy, and politically connected family. Phone calls were impossible in a tiny rural town where few residents had telephones. The boy grew up with letters and the occasional gift from a faraway mother, while he lived with his grandmother, and then his schoolteacher father.

His mother was sponsored for legal residence by her employers but couldn't leave the US during the years her status was pending. Nelson did not see his mother for six formative years. He remembered an encounter one day after school: "I saw from a distance this beautiful, beautiful woman. She was wearing a hat. Somebody said to me, 'That is your mother.' But as I interacted with her, I really didn't know my mother. We had rarely connected because of the way I was raised.

"It's not like today with social media and telephones and many other things. You got a letter once in a while. You got a photo once in a while." His mother had come back, and now wanted to bring Nelson to the US. He was eleven years old. "But when my mother came, I didn't want to come to the United States. I didn't feel a need to come to the United States.

"My mother was a stranger to me even though she was this beautiful woman who had been writing to me and periodically would send me things, clothes or money, like many immigrant parents do to help their children." He changed his mind, and not long after he had told his father that he was leaving his grandmother's house to live with him, Nelson now looked north. He arrived just before Christmas in 1981. Though her sponsoring family had helped her become legalized, they weren't ready to have Nelson and his sister in their house. So the young Salvadoran found himself in his first American home, on New York's Long Island, just outside New York City.

The Immigration and Nationality Act of 1965 included family unification procedures that made it possible for hundreds of thousands of families to reunite with their relatives, sometimes one by one, as passage could be paid for, with certain US specification.

Samir's older brother, a university student already over twenty-one at the time the family won their visas in a US government lottery, was required to make his own application to enter. It would be more than a decade before he would join the family in Virginia. He was happy to be in America, but his relationship to the family had been changed by the long separation. As I spoke to dozens of families like Samir's, whether they were playing by the rules or looking for a way to get around them, the constant struggle for them was figuring out what the law said, where their own situation fit in it, and how politics, circumstances, and world events drove their decisions.

The 2006 CBO report said the second priority of US immigration law was to "admit workers with specific skills and to fill positions in occupations deemed to be experiencing labor shortages." That remains a priority for the government, and every year, many thousands of immigrants depend upon sponsorship from American companies.

Javad Maher, born and raised in Iran, and his wife, Margaret, a Scot who met her husband in Iran, watched with rising concern in 1979 as the Shah Reza Pahlavi went into a wandering exile, and the Iranian Revolution tightened its grip on daily life in the country. Javad recalls, "We were very disappointed in how the revolution ended up. We were not happy with the Shah's politics, with his dictatorship, but we were expecting that a liberal democratic leader would replace him. Unfortunately, theocracy was what we got."

Margaret Maher picked up the story. "My daughter went to public school in Tehran. And before the Revolution, kids were integrated. First, they separated girls and boys. Then they said she had to pray four times a day. And of course, none of us knew how to do it. My husband had no idea, either."

Javad shot back. "I knew how. But I didn't do it." He had been born and raised a Muslim in the city of Yazd, a historic and religious cross-roads home to Jews, Zoroastrians, and Muslims. When Javad was a teen-ager, an aunt worked at the hospital operated by the Church Missionary Society, a centuries-old British charity. He was attracted by Christianity and baptized. He married Margaret in an Anglican church, and by the time of the Revolution, he was completely secular. Normally, that would not have mattered to very many people, but in Khomeini's Iran, it carried the potential to make life increasingly uncomfortable.

Javad remembers how the new government, day by day, pushed more and more religious restriction and regulation into daily life. Still regarded as a Muslim by the government, despite his conversion and marriage in a church wedding to a non-Muslim foreigner and working as a librarian for the United States Information Agency, he said he worried "that it really counted, to the point that we'd be under a microscope."

The Mahers left Iran. First, for Scotland, where they found their prospects as bleak as the weather. Margaret was a trained nurse. Javad, a librarian with an advanced degree in library science. They could not find work in Scotland. They next set their sights on Canada. "At the time the American hostages were still hostages, so they [Canadians] weren't welcoming to Iranians. At first I thought, 'Okay, a Commonwealth country. I'm a nurse. No problem.' But they refused. Even though there were Canadian hospitals that came to England recruiting nurses."

Canada wasn't the only "way out." Hospitals in Texas and California invited Margaret to come to America. Even in the midst of the hostage crisis, when hostility and suspicion of Iran were on the rise, the family packed up and moved to Texas. They knew it was for good, that Iran would never again be a place comfortable for a family like theirs. "We got an American visa about a month after the hostages were released."

Margaret Maher was now at home in her third country. Until the Islamic Revolution and the tumultuous departure of the Shah, she said, "I had made up my mind that I was going to be in Iran for the rest of my life. But after everything that happened, I laughed. It was hard, because I had been there for eleven, twelve years. It was hard, but it had to be done."

Looking back at those hectic first years of the Revolution, Javad said he and his wife knew the move to America was permanent. "I knew the Revolution was not going to be a temporary thing. And things were going to get worse."

Margaret had been invited to the US by another Texas hospital, many years before, when she was single and just out of nursing school. "I decided I didn't want to go to Houston, so I went to the United Nations Volunteer Corps. And they sent me to a village in Kurdistan, near Sanandaj.

"Sanandaj was the capital of Iranian Kurdistan. Kind of up in the mountains. They had one street with asphalt, and we had electricity for three hours at night. There was an English nurse there who married an Iranian, and he was working there. And he was friends with Javad. He came to visit the husband for his birthday, and that's where we met."

I asked Margaret whether right there, in a village in Iran's Kurdish region, she knew this young librarian was *the* guy. "Yeah. He was very good-looking."

"And she was very pretty. And she is still." Javad didn't travel to see his friend with finding a wife in mind. "I was not thinking of getting married, period. But when I met her, we — you know. I changed my mind and I thought, 'Yeah, that's her.' "

Margaret got pushback from her mother, who said marriage might be all right for her and Javad, "'but think of your half-caste babies' is what she said." Javad's family had a different objection. At twenty-two, the Scottish nurse was simply too old for their young man. "Girls used to get married at fifteen, sixteen…eighteen maximum. After eighteen every-body would say…"

Margaret immediately jumped in, "What's wrong with her?"

"Yeah!" Javad echoed. "What's wrong with her?!" But he added, "Really, the only thing was the age. They loved her. They still call to talk to her. They very genuinely love her."

The third priority for American immigration law spelled out by the CBO report said the US "attempts to provide a refuge for people who face the risk of political, racial, or religious persecution in their country of origin."

Jaime Contreras was born in El Salvador in 1974. He grew up in the care of his maternal grandmother, after his mother left the family and his father found work in another city. "We were extremely poor. When I was a kid I almost died. In El Salvador, at least back in those times, you could die from little things. Like a simple illness. For lack of Tylenol or whatever.

"My grandma couldn't afford medication when there was something wrong with my skin. She took me to my father and said, 'You got to take your son, because if you don't get him healthier, he's going to die.' So I left that little town when I was seven years old, and that's when I actually started going to school, because I never went to school in the little town. The civil war had started, and you had to walk miles to school, so she didn't let me go.

"But also, my grandfather on my mom's side was very involved with the guerrillas in El Salvador during the civil war. So the other reason we fled that little town was because we were going to get killed if we didn't leave."

There are many skeptics in the US today who, upon hearing stories like these, wonder whether refugees are exaggerating what the refugee statutes call a "well-founded fear of persecution" if they remain in their homeland. Are they really in that much danger? El Salvador is a tiny country and had a population of fewer than five million at the time of the war. An estimated seventy-five thousand civilians died in the thirteen years of the war, from 1979 until the peace settlement in 1992, a number much greater than that of all the American service people who died in the Vietnam War, in a country one fortieth the size.

"I remember when my grandfather got killed. I remember him being carried on a stretcher with blood falling from the stretcher. He was shot in the back. My grandma said, 'Well, you're going to die if you stay here regardless, from some illness or a gunshot from the war.' So we fled the little town.

"In San Miguel, where my dad lived, it was dangerous, too. He worked as an ambulance driver. He told me the reason we fled to America is a lot of the intellectuals like doctors were supporting the FMLN and their guerrillas [the Farabundo Marti National Liberation Front, the main guerrilla army]. They would fill my dad's ambulance with medications to take to the fighters. He got caught once, and after that he had a target on his back.

"So he came here in 1983. There were six of us, five boys and my sister, and he brought us up in pairs. So my older brothers first, then my sister and another brother, then me and the youngest brother. I didn't come until 1988, and we came in undocumented. My dad had filed for asylum, but the process was taking forever. And he was scared we were going to get killed in El Salvador, so he decided to bring us all here.

"And it was getting really dangerous down there. I remember going to school after a shoot-out between the army and the guerrillas and walking past dead people in the street as I headed to school. It was terrible, to say the least."

At the time Contreras's family made its way north in the 1980s, the Central American population in the United States was relatively small, less than half a million. Today, after decades when the region has been wracked by serial wars, oppressive governments, collapsing economies, and natural disasters, that population numbers more than 3.7 million. More than half of them live in just four states: California, Texas, Florida, and New York.

Contreras's family headed to another heavy concentration of Central American immigrants: Washington, DC. Never known as a port of entry for newcomers to the US the way the New York, Miami, or Los Angeles have been, the capital's metro area has nonetheless become an immigrant magnet in recent decades, home to large populations of Latin Americans, South Asians, and East Africans. As Washington, DC, became one of the most expensive places in the country to buy real estate, those populations have headed out to the far-flung suburbs of Maryland and Northern Virginia. Today, Prince George's County, Maryland, has the fifth largest Central American population of all counties in the United States.

Inside the District, the Adams Morgan and Columbia Heights neighborhoods became Central American enclaves, and Contreras's new home. There was just one hiccup between the coyotes shepherding the two youngest Contreras boys through Mexico and their arrival in the US. His little brother, just twelve years old, left the Mexico City hotel room where the immigrant smuggler had stashed Contreras, his brother, and his cousin on their way to a Tijuana crossing. When he came to check on the boys and found one missing, risking his payday, a frantic search commenced through the streets of the giant Mexican capital. The coyote put his entire human cargo to work, rousting them out of hotel rooms to comb the streets for the boy — only to find him alone in his hotel room after he returned on his own.

The angry smuggler spanked the boys. After a heated telephone argument with Contreras's father, the coyote put them on a plane to Washington after they crossed the border, without telling their father in which one of the three DC-area airports the boys' flight would land. The father ran from airport to airport, but it was already too late. The flight from San Diego had landed at Dulles International Airport, where the

Contreras brothers and their cousin were picked up by immigration authorities who found them wandering the concourses.

The boys gave Immigration and Naturalization Service agents the father's contact information, and all were eventually united. Because the father was already an asylum applicant, there was no danger of deportation for the boys. "They were not going to send us back because by the late '80s it was a full-fledged war."

You can trace a modern history of the world by watching where people are fleeing, where they are going, and when. The United States is different from former colonial powers like Britain and France. In London and Paris, Birmingham and Marseilles, ties of history, labor shortages for the colonizer, and crises among the colonized, all combined to create immigrant neighborhoods after World War II, with unprecedented diversity. In the 1980s, "Two-Tone" bands mixed Jamaican rhythms and instrumentation with British rock and roll and created exciting new music. In the 2010s, Idris Elba, a son of immigrants from former British colonies in West Africa, born in London, won rave notices as Deputy Chief Inspector John Luther in the British TV series *Luther* and was speculated about as the new James Bond. In the 2020s, Rishi Sunak, a Hindu son of immigrants, became Britain's prime minister.

In France, Franco-Algerian detectives work cases in crime mysteries, Zinedine Zidane led France to victory in the World Cup, and before Carlos Ghosn became one of the world's most sought-after fugitives and highest profile criminal defendants, the Brazilian-Lebanese Frenchman was one of the world's most celebrated business executives.

The US has always been more of a stealth empire. While large numbers of Filipinos and Puerto Ricans, Samoans and Guamanians have made their way to the fifty states, what drives most refugees here is neither historic links nor American sovereignty in their countries.

Nelly Der Kiureghian's family was a comfortable and secure member of the Lebanese merchant class. Lebanon was becoming more violent, more complicated, and more threatening year after year. "We owned a business in downtown Beirut that was demolished by a bombing during the civil war, and my mom started thinking about coming to the United States. She was a widow, my father had passed away very young, and she had an uncle living in Los Angeles."

After their business was destroyed, Der Kiureghian's mother was reluctant to rebuild. "She didn't want to start again in Lebanon. My grandparents had settled in Lebanon after the Armenian Genocide as refugees in the 1920s. In 1976 everything we had built was taken away overnight. She thought, 'If I'm going to start again, I want to start in a country where there is a future for peace and advancement.'

"My great uncle applied to bring his sister to the United States. That's my maternal grandmother. Through that process, within a year, my mother, my older brother, and I entered the United States as immigrants from Lebanon." Der Kiureghian was seventeen and finishing high school, enough of an adult to understand what was going on, and enough of a child to not have much of a say in the matter.

"The whole downtown area of Beirut had been bombed. We felt totally vulnerable because that was our only source of income. My brother was a medical student at the time. My mother was carrying my dad's legacy running the store. There were two options. One was to come to the United States, which was my mother's first choice, and the second option was to go to Canada.

"Being a Francophile, and a Francophone [a French speaker] in Lebanon — I attended a French school in Lebanon which was still a Francophone country — my first choice was to go to Canada. I knew there would be no problem with having to learn a new language there. Our relatives lived in Montreal, and Canada had special provisions at the time for Lebanese refugees who wanted to move there."

Her mother, and, in a sense, Mother Nature, won. Der Kiureghian's mother said emigrating and starting someplace else from scratch was already hard enough. Moving to frigid Quebec from balmy, Mediterranean Beirut would only make everything harder. In addition, her mother had concluded the US was a better bet economically. Southern California it was going to be. Der Kiureghian enrolled in a Los Angeles high school.

It is not often discussed when Americans talk about immigration that a surprisingly large share of immigrants to the United States, even during what some historians call the Age of Mass Migration, 1850–1913, returned to their home countries to live. It is still happening today. The move to America becomes just a chapter in their lives when they were trying something new or had a goal in mind, like making money for a specific purpose. Some find the country is not to their liking or find it just too hard to resettle or make a living. From a quarter to a third of immigrants to the US return home. American film audiences pulled out their handkerchiefs to watch the struggles of a Norwegian immigrant family in San Francisco in *I Remember Mama*. Yet the Norwegians who decided to pack up and go home found their time in America made them even more competitive in the Norwegian job market. Across the decades, large numbers of Irish, Polish, Italian, and Mexican immigrants have headed home after a time in the US. There was an Italian saying in the 19th century, "He who crosses the ocean can buy a house."

Before long, Der Kiureghian's family was back in Beirut. The fighting had stopped. Her brother went back to his medical studies. Maybe the family could make a future in Lebanon after all.

"What we had believed was the end of the war only turned out to be a break to reload. In 1978 the war started again, and it last for another ten or fifteen years. And the destruction was much more severe the next time." The status that had allowed the family to move to Los Angeles in the first place also allowed them to return. Der Kiureghian was back in the twelfth grade after finishing high school in Lebanon. She spoke Armenian, Arabic, and French, but didn't have much English. "I had strong command of French. I understood all the Latin roots, so I did well on paper. I was able to take tests and do well. But a conversation was very difficult for me. Socially, it was pretty much a desert for me."

After ping-ponging back and forth between California and the Middle East, there would be no new moves. She found Los Angeles, sprawling, auto-dependent, anonymizing, a difficult place after Beirut. "Unless you came with a circle of friends or a family from your native country with whom you can continue your interactions, Los Angeles is not an easy place for an immigrant. Making new friends, for me, was very difficult."

You might think the presence of a very old Armenian diaspora in California would have smoothed the way. Novelist William Saroyan was a product of that earlier Armenian wave. He was born in Fresno to parents who had come from Ottoman Turkey in 1905. By the late 1970s, those Armenians were settled, assimilated, and dispersed. "The Armenian immigration from Lebanon and Iran had just started. The Armenian community in Los Angeles had been living there a long time. Their mentality was entirely different."

Der Kiureghian's husband, Armen, is also Armenian, from Iran. He was part of the great wave of Iranian students who headed to American universities before the Islamic Revolution. From graduate education at the University of Illinois in Champaign, he moved on to a career in higher education as a professor and administrator at the University of Southern California and the University of California, Berkeley. He went on to be a cofounder of the American University of Armenia, now more than thirty years old.

He was early in his academic career, and weighing whether to return to Iran, when the country was rocked by political tumult. "I was debating whether I should go back or not and then the Islamic Republic made up my mind for me."

Not everyone who sought and received refugee status in those years was fleeing convulsive violence and the threat of sudden death. As the Cold War recedes into America's rearview mirror, the Jackson-Vanik Amendment, signed into law by President Gerald Ford at the beginning of 1975, isn't talked about much. That law, stuck onto a bill setting the ground rules for trade with the Eastern Bloc, enticed the Soviet Union to let Jews who wanted to emigrate leave the country. It created new immigrant neighborhoods in Brooklyn, Queens, New Jersey, Florida, and Los Angeles.

"Most Favored Nation Trading Status," a designation which set the terms for bilateral trade relations, brought all kinds of benefits to exporting nations. The Jackson-Vanik law denied the possibility of MFN status to countries that restricted their citizens' right to leave the country, long considered a human right in international law. Initially hundreds of thousands, eventually millions of American journeys began when the law picked the locks keeping people in the USSR, Czechoslovakia, Poland, Hungary, Vietnam, the People's Republic of China, East Germany, Laos, Cambodia, and elsewhere.

On October 29, 2019, a US Army lieutenant colonel raised his right hand on Capitol Hill and swore to tell the truth, the whole truth, and nothing but the truth in the House of Representatives' impeachment inquiry. The officer, in his dress blues, wore his résumé on his chest. Among his decorations were the Purple Heart given for wounds suffered in combat, the Defense Meritorious Service Medal, the Combat Infantryman's Badge, a Ranger tab signifying completed training as an elite combat infantryman, and a Parachutist's Badge. Lt. Col. Alexander Vindman was about to give testimony in one of the most solemn and high-stakes congressional proceedings of all, the impeachment of a sitting president. In his twenty-year army career, Vindman became a foreign area officer while in uniform, and in his capacity as director for European Affairs for the National Security Council he had been listening on an extension when President Donald Trump had a phone conference with the newly elected president of Ukraine, Volodymyr Zelenskyy.

Vindman was born in Ukraine in 1975 and came to New York as part of the Jackson-Vanik wave of Soviet immigration. He was four years old, arriving in New York with his twin brother, Yevgeny. Along with British-born Fiona Hill, the National Security Council's specialist on Russia, and Ambassador Marie Yovanovitch, born in Canada to Russian immigrants, Vindman became one of a trio of immigrant star witnesses giving evidence that bore the potential to bring down an American president.

In 1979, more modest concerns were pushing the Vindman family west. The twins' mother had died. Their father, a civil engineer, was stuck in his career because of the casual antisemitism shot through the Soviet system. There were unofficial quotas limiting the promotion of Jews in various fields, government work was really the only game in town in Odessa, and he had concluded he would rise no further.

More than forty years later his son had traded his uniform for a well-tailored silver-gray suit. I talked with the man whose face was, for a time, on the cover of every American newspaper, about his unlikely journey from Kyiv to Brighton Beach. "According to family lore, and there's some data to substantiate this, we were on the very last flight out of Ukraine before the Soviet Union halted traffic, halted these refugee flights out.

"The Soviets had invaded Afghanistan and the US boycotted the Moscow Olympics, and this was a kind of diplomatic tit for tat, and we were on the last flight out of Kyiv. We had other family members that were not that fortunate and were supposed to come behind us, and they didn't."

Vindman and his brother began their journey just before their fourth birthdays, stopping in Vienna and Italy before finally arriving in the United States. "Initially we settled in the Brighton Beach area, and there was a yearlong period during which we went to a kind of pre-K at a YMCA, and then went to first grade at a yeshiva [Jewish religious school] with a bunch of other refugee kids. Then, relatively quickly, my father didn't want us to grow up in an ethnic enclave speaking Russian to peers. He wanted us to acculturate, assimilate a little into American society. So he made it a point to move us deeper into the city. And as you know, if you move neighborhoods, you're in a different country. We moved to Borough Park and started public school at P.S. 105."

I started laughing at the very idea. We were two Brooklyn kids sitting on a bench on a leafy street near the State Department and the World Bank in eerily empty pandemic-era Washington, DC. An immigrant kid had just told me his father, who wanted to take his boys out of an ethnic enclave, moved him to one of the densest concentrations of Orthodox Jews in the world, the Brooklyn neighborhood of Borough Park. It was a place that moved to the rhythms of changing sunset times for sabbath observance, where women pushing strollers built for multiple babies got into traffic jams at kosher groceries, where men wore the satin breeches, fur hats, and ritual clothing of cities and towns in pre-Holocaust Eastern Europe as they hustled down 21st-century streets to meet other men for prayer. There are times when a walk through Borough Park might leave you feeling you could just as easily be in Jerusalem, or that you've stepped through a time-travel portal to a 19th-century market town in Lithuania, as on the streets of America's biggest city.

"The Soviet Union discouraged the practice of faith and discouraged it in ways that would have a direct impact on career progression. One of the reasons my father brought us over as refugees is because he recognized that we would not have even the same opportunities he had. There were quotas limiting Jews, folks that were ethnically identified as Jewish, from attending higher education.

"But my father did have a strong Jewish identity and he made it a point to introduce us to Judaism through an orthodox group called the Lubavitchers. They had an organization they established around refugee kids that came over, and that's how we were exposed to Judaism. Multiple times a month we'd go to this organization called Friends and Refugees of Eastern Europe, go to a Lubavitch synagogue, and study the faith and practice the faith."

In Brooklyn, at forty-seven years old, the elder Vindman and his five-year-old twins marked the covenantal bond of Jewish men dating back to Abraham. They were all circumcised. Normally the ritual removal of the foreskin takes place on the eighth day of life. For many Soviet Jews, it came much later. "We remember it, so I imagine he remembers it," Vindman said. "It's definitely not something that could easily be forgotten. I think it's a pretty keen sign of commitment."

Now a PhD candidate and writer, Vindman has no doubt "a lot of the things I've managed to accomplish I wouldn't be able to do in any other place in the world. There are other thriving democracies, but they're much more rigid and hierarchical, in terms of societal castes. I got it through a combination of street smarts from New York and hard work, and some other traits that were a combination of nature and nurture passed down from my family."

So far we have met some people who came almost by luck rather than intention, like Samir, whose mother won a visa lottery she didn't even know she had entered. Or Nelson Castillo, who by the luck of circumstance was able to easily come to America as a teenager under family unification statutes. Some came, like the Mahers, when they saw history and circumstance threatening to disrupt their lives and bring government scrutiny and pressure. Jaime Contreras was growing up as his country descended into chaos and murder, which you might call the luck of bad circumstance. Alexander Vindman's father was handed an opportunity to give his sons a better life by the accident of Cold War politics.

Millions of Americans begin their time in the US not as recognized immigrants, refugees, or skilled professionals. Instead they live in the shadows, building American lives while struggling to remain one step ahead of the Immigration and Naturalization Service, the Social Security administration, and the Internal Revenue Service. Some are able to shake off their undocumented status over time, others still face the reality of it every day.

"A lot of my family was already in the States," said Jesus Contreras, a Houston emergency medical technician. "Like many others, I come from a mixed-status family. A lot of my aunts and uncles came over during the Bracero era, picking strawberries, following the migration through the States picking fruit, field work, and they had the opportunity to become citizens that way. My cousins and a lot of my family were born US citizens. A lot of my family had the ability to become legal residents and citizens."

Contreras was born, and started growing up in, the Mexican border regions. In Spanish a *bracero* is a laborer. The Bracero Program, begun during the Second World War, filled gaps in the US farm workforce brought on by the draft. The US government signed an agreement with Mexican counterparts to guarantee decent working conditions, sanitation, food, and shelter, along with a guaranteed minimum wage of thirty cents an hour. It strengthened a 20th-century immigrant flow that began with the Mexican Revolution in 1910 and continues to this day. Of the more than forty million US residents born in another country, a quarter come from Mexico alone. Depending on prevailing US law and economic conditions on both sides of the fourteen-hundred-mile border, that boundary can be almost impenetrable. For Mexicans, *la frontera* created a byzantine set of allowances and restrictions, along with innumerable mixed-status families.

Jesus Contreras said his mother watched with horror as violent crime rose in Mexico's border cities. Criminal gangs fought each other for control of the trade in illegal drugs to satisfy American users' appetites, and over the lucrative side businesses of smuggling guns south, and migrants north. The illicit enterprises often mixed and mingled and made the international border—an imaginary line economists often talked about as an abstraction—into one very real and dangerous place.

"She thought the safest thing for us to do would be to come to the US. We actually ended up leaving my dad. It was a spur of the moment decision. When we've talked about it in later years, she said she had me in mind, and the long term. She actually had a pretty good job in Mexico, and she had retirement benefits built up at her job. She pulled that retirement money and used it to move to the States."

I put it to the young EMT, now well established in a career with the Houston Fire Department, that many undocumented immigrants, living and working illegally in the United States, spent much of their formative years blissfully unaware of the constantly looming threat of deportation. Even when he arrived at six years old, Jesus knew he was different from his US-born cousins. "My mom has always been a very honest and blunt person with me. I don't mean in a harsh way. For me, that meant being able to talk about things and digest things in the way people should. I knew from a very young age my mom didn't have a social security number, that my mom couldn't get certain jobs or certain careers because she didn't have the opportunity. So, I was aware as early as I could understand what immigration and undocumented status was, that we were in that boat.

"I realized that there were a lot of doors that were going to be closed to me specifically in the work sector. I couldn't work because I didn't have a social and proper identification security number. I couldn't get a driver's license because I didn't have a passport or US birth certificate. I just knew the same way my mom had overcome a lot of these issues, I could overcome them, too. But it was tough."

"I remember the conversation my mom and I had the night before I left. My sister had no idea what was going on," Socorro Castañeda said, recalling a conversation now four decades old. "My mom told me, 'Both of you are going to go now and join your aunts and uncles and your *abuelita* and *abuelito*. You're the oldest, so you've got to take care of your sister.' I always say it was at that age that I took on the role of a caregiver."

Castañeda was nine years old. Her mother had come up with a way to get her daughters into the United States that first makes you shake your head in wonder, curious about how many other people have tried it over the years, and then, makes you contemplate how many have succeeded. Her mother's *comadre,* Socorro's godmother, had two daughters roughly the ages of Castañeda and her sister. The *comadre* crossed on foot from El Paso, Texas, to the other half of the sprawling binational metropolitan area, Ciudad Juarez, in the state of Chihuahua. In her purse, she carried her own daughters' US visas, the identification documents needed to cross back into the States.

It sounded almost far-fetched. Didn't the visas have photos attached? "They did have photos!" Castañeda exclaimed. "What's really interesting is that we did not look anything like these girls. Very different." Her *madrina,* her godmother, came to Juarez, took the girls in hand, and headed back across the Bridge of the Americas to walk back into the US. Her godmother was joined by her husband and began to walk Socorro and her sister into a new life in the US. "I remember while we approached the bridge when they were going to do the first checkpoint, my godmother said, 'Okay, now is the time to pray.' She takes out her *Virgen de Guadalupe* [a portrayal of Jesus's mother, Mary, as Our Lady of Guadalupe, the Patron Saint of Mexico] that she carried in her purse, and she put it under the visa cards of her daughters, and she told me, 'Start praying that She protects us.'

"We get to the immigration officer. He looked at the visas. He looked at us. He looked at the visas again. I'll never forget, he had this smirk, kind of like, 'Are you kidding me?' He just laughed. And he said, 'Okay, go.' And he let us go."

The family had taken an enormous risk. By presenting her own daughters' visas, her godmother had put her own right to stay in the US on the line as well as her husband's, and by extension, that of her daughters. Of course, Castañeda and her sister would have been barred from entry, and an attempted illegal entry would be held against the girls if they tried to legally migrate later. Yet the gamble worked. The four of them got in the car and began the long drive to San Jose, California. "We didn't know the magnitude of what we were doing. One of the reasons we came to the US is that my sister and I were sick. My mom took us to the doctor and the doctor did several blood tests. We were both anemic. We had parasites in our stomachs."

Though her father was working six days a week, there wasn't always enough to eat at home. Castañeda said that even as a little girl she was given black coffee to supplement a meager breakfast. A schoolmate once asked Castañeda's mother why she gave the girls coffee. "And my mom said, 'Oh, it's because they like it.' But it wasn't that. She kind of had to wake us up to be ready for the day if we didn't have enough food."

So far, so good. The audacious plan was working. Once over the border and onto the interstate highways, the scheme still carried risk. The

Border Patrol had installed checkpoints farther into the US, well away from the international line, to intercept illegal crossers who had arranged pickups after making their way over on foot. "At every checkpoint my godmother would say, 'Okay, cover yourself up and pretend to be asleep. If you're awake they're going to ask you questions, and they're going to ask them in English because we're telling them you're our daughters. If you don't speak a word of English, they're not going to believe us.'

"At every checkpoint I would cover myself with a thick yellow blanket and I wouldn't breathe. I was so scared that I wasn't breathing so I wouldn't make any noise. Even now when I close my eyes it takes me back to that very moment. It was scary. Even if my sister thought it was a game."

The girls made it to San Jose, and the embrace of extended family. That is when Castañeda's big-sister duties really kicked in. Her sister began to ask her questions about going home, and their mother's whereabouts. "She was sick. And she would cry and cry." It took their mother three tries to get across the border, by crossing the Rio Grande into Texas. Their father could not make it across for another year. The girls started San Jose schools, fourth grade and kindergarten, and started work in the fields.

"Sometimes, when we think of field workers, we automatically assume they live near the fields. But we lived in the city and commuted to work in the fields. I worked alongside my mom. We picked plums. I would get so tired. 'Ay mami, yo no quiero.' Oh Mommy, I don't want to, and she'd answer 'Ay m'hija, each one is a penny!' I knew it was going to take a lot of pennies to make a dollar.

"But that's how we were able to sustain ourselves. We lived at one of my aunts' house, since that was the only income we had and little by little we would save. Finally, my dad crossed the desert in July of the following year." The US agencies working to stop illegal migration have made crossing near major metropolitan areas, like San Diego and El Paso, much harder, forcing would-be migrants to more forbidding landscapes. Desert crossings have killed growing numbers of migrants over the years.

US Customs and Border Protection, an arm of the US Department of Homeland Security, estimates more than seventy-five hundred border crossers have died in the deserts of the southern border in the last twenty years alone.

Decades later she recalled her father's painful, swollen, blistered feet after the long walk from Mexico into the US. He had worn cowboy boots, not the best footwear for the trek over mountains, through scrub, and across scorching sands in July. The family was reunited, and Castañeda and her sister still needed medical attention, along with supplements to address her anemia, and medication to control her intestinal parasites. "We used one of our cousin's medical cards to go to the clinic to get checked. I remember them telling me, 'You just tell them your name is so-and-so. It's best if you remain quiet, or else they're going to ask you questions. You let me answer the questions for you.' I knew we were doing something that we were not supposed to do. I knew that we had to be careful.

"In the '80s the immigration raids were very bad here in San Jose. It got to the point that they would park buses outside the churches to wait for people to leave church and check their documents as they tried to head home. So we lived with that fear. We lived in a little converted garage, and during that time my mother would cover the windows with blankets to make it seem like no one lived there. My aunts and uncles who did have documents bought groceries for us. I remember my mom crying and crying because she didn't know if my dad was going to make it back home from work."

Castañeda said she lived in fear from the age of nine until fourteen, especially about the possibility of her father being caught by immigration enforcement, since he traveled far afield to find work as a laborer. To this day, she can be traumatized by the sight of officers wearing green similar to the Border Patrol colors. "I'm fifty-one. When I even see a park ranger dressed in those colors it automatically takes me back to when I was nine and ten years old. I get reactions in my stomach. I can't help it. It still happens every time I see someone dressed in those colors."

She was rescued from a life of permanent hiding during the second Reagan administration with the passage of the Immigration Reform and Control Act (IRCA) of 1986, which offered amnesty to illegally resident people who could prove they had been in the country for five years and had been law-abiding. Applicants to the amnesty offered by the act had to admit they had broken the law when they immigrated, and to pay back taxes and fines. It was more complicated than it might sound at first. The life of people living undocumented lives involved all kinds of dodges, subterfuges, assumed names, and fake documents. Finding documentary proof of the very things you had spent years hiding was demanding for many families.

Some of the most challenging documents to acquire needed to come from employers. The IRCA contained stiff enforcement measures for companies employing undocumented workers, and those same workers were now asking bosses for documentary evidence they had been working for years. Afraid they would be exposing themselves to immediate jeopardy and prying eyes down the road, some employers simply refused to sign any such document, which might also demonstrate they had been paying workers off the books, skirting requirements for workers' compensation and unemployment tax payments to their states.

The amnesty provided to millions of undocumented people, making them legal permanent residents, and putting many on the road to US citizenship was supposed to be politically palatable to reluctant members of Congress because of the enforcement provisions. The US would radically reduce its undocumented population, the idea went, and use new teeth in employment law to keep a new flood of undocumented immigrants from growing in its place. Employer fines were supposed to grow with each subsequent violation, to deter businesses from hiring unauthorized workers.

Over the years, industries and their lobbyists pressured Congress to lay off, especially during times of labor shortages and strong economic growth. As a result, enforcement was never strong enough to act as the deterrent intended in the law. The many employer penalties called for in the statute were unevenly applied, or often not enforced at all, and the flood tide of undocumented immigrants kept rising. Estimates of the undocumented population grew from five million in 1986 to more than eleven million in 2013, with some reports putting the number closer to twenty million by 2022.

The plain language of the 1986 law makes it a violation to employ, recruit, or refer workers *you know to be in the country illegally.* The word "knowingly" (which also appeared in the statute) in the statute has set off an epidemic of calculated employer obliviousness that lasts to this day. While the new law brought in a raft of new record-keeping requirements meant to verify a person's right to work, the burden for the legitimacy of the documents subtly shifted from boss to worker, and an already busy marketplace in fake and forged documents was kicked into higher gear. Workplace raids found plenty of undocumented workers, along with large numbers of workers suspected of being undocumented because of their appearance or English-language skills.

Thus immigration authorities took fire from left and right, from employers trying to harvest perishable crops, get meat to market, and finish subdivisions on time and on budget, and from immigrant rights advocates offended by the possibility that an office cleaner with an accent was going to be required to prove his or her bona fides in a way someone assumed to be native-born would not.

Not all the workers who slipped through the cracks after the IRCA's amnesty were from Latin America. Deborah (who asked me not to use her last name) does have an accent. Maybe, after more than thirty years, we might call it the trace of accent: the distinctive Antipodean vowels of a New Zealander. "I feel like America did a really good marketing job about itself in the 1980s. Living on an island out at the bottom of the world looking at America, everything was big and bright, people were doing fun things, kids were going to high school and the prom." Deborah's American Dreams were nurtured by movies, television shows, and regular copies of the American edition of *Seventeen* checked out of the local library by her mom.

"We thought America was the Holy Grail of places. I went and lived in London for three years, and a friend of mine had gone to New York and said it was amazing. And I became fixated on New York as my next destination. I really kind of foolishly expected to be able to work out of great white privilege.

"I had already gone to London, and there's such an infrastructure for people to work there [British law at the time made it very easy for New Zealanders and Australians to work temporarily in the United Kingdom] and lots of Kiwis there. I'd gotten jobs and friends and apartments and it was all super easy.

"I was just like, well, yeah, New York. I really hadn't given much consideration to the thought that I would not have legal status there. I thought, 'Ah, it'll be fine.' It really wasn't fine. I made it work. But it was not really fine."

Deborah's parents had been immigrants to New Zealand from Scotland, which would have made it simple for her to become a permanent legal resident of the UK and make her adult life there. There just wasn't enough Holy Grail in London.

"I wanted to be cool. I wanted people in New Zealand to think I was cool. They all went to London and I did the same. And I was like, 'No, no, no. I'm cooler than you. I'm going to go to fucking New York. And then you're going to think I'm cooler than you."

She was twenty-four years old. How hard could this be? "I had come from working in a bank in London. It was a peak time for foreign exchange trading. I had been making pretty good money over there, and just pranced over to New York, thinking it would be the same. Somebody at a bank in London set me up with an interview at Dean Witter in New York, at the World Trade Center.

"I got all the way to HR and somebody asked, 'Do you have a green card?' I told them I didn't and they said, 'We don't sponsor.' Now I'm so savvy. But then? The only jobs we could get were under the table. We couldn't get bank accounts. It all just became really hard.

"I got really sick. I had bronchitis, and no money. It all started coming in on me." Deborah was trying to get started in New York during the first years after the Immigration Reform and Control Act came into force, and many employers were taking its provisions seriously out of caution and fear of the significant fines. "I was a nanny. I remember meeting another nanny who was French and had just gotten her green card in that amnesty. I was so jealous. I had just missed the boat. I could have lived in New Zealand or Australia or anywhere in Europe [as a legal resident of the pre-Brexit UK], but, nope, she wants to live in America! I was going to put up with whatever suffering came my way."

Deborah told me going back to New Zealand was out of the question. She said it was never going to feel like home, that she didn't feel like she fit in. "I just fell in love with New York, honestly. And I had the energy back then to deal with all the bullshit. It became a quest." She had come to the US with a high school classmate from back home in New Zealand and met another man from back home also trying to make it in New York. The trio became a Kiwi support network. "So I wasn't alone in my predicament. I didn't want to go back to New Zealand. I felt like I would have failed. Once I lived in America, everything seemed possible. Growing up in New Zealand, nothing seemed possible."

Life in America continued to be a struggle, she said, until 1998, when she moved to Los Angeles, green card in hand, and found an apartment. She had gotten the green card the way a lot of undocumented people do, by marrying a citizen. "I was waitressing and getting paid under the table. This amazing guy was a chef at the restaurant, and we became boyfriend and girlfriend. We had kind of a tumultuous relationship. I basically just begged him to marry me." She had been working for another New Zealander who was helping her get lawful permanent resident (LPR) status, a green card. The boss hired another New Zealander, an immigration attorney, to help get Deborah papers, but he wanted too much money.

"I persuaded Ray to marry me, and that's how I got the green card. We had a wedding at City Hall, and made it look real, and we had this amazing immigration lawyer friends of mine had used. When my high school friend married her gay roommate, she found this lawyer. Total New

Yorker. Knew all the tricks." The lawyer advised them to make everything look as legitimate as possible. Deborah's new Puerto Rican husband took her down to the island, where the couple took enough pictures to make a honeymoon album. Her lawyer read her transcripts of immigration interviews so she knew exactly what to expect, and knew how to answer key questions. The two did have a legitimate connection. They had been in a relationship, after all. "I felt like we could have answered those questions quite easily. He wasn't a stranger. I wasn't paying him."

Her lawyer joined her at her immigration interview and surveyed the government officers working that day. He told his client he hoped they got one particular screener: "There's a very old lady here, and if we get her, we're home free. She doesn't care. She's going to retire in like two weeks. Then she comes out, calls my name, and the lawyer said, 'Yes! We're good.' She was great. And that's it."

Now a legal resident of the US, Deborah could have marched right into the above-ground, fully legal economy and gone to work. She even could have gone back to Dean Witter. Instead, almost out of habit, she stayed in the black economy, getting paid off the books for years to come. Working in restaurants, she realized the world of the undocumented is stratified, riddled with the same race and class differences as other parts of the economy.

"I have the greatest respect for people who did not have the white privilege I had. I worked in many restaurants with busboys, with people who fucking walked with the coyotes, the smugglers, through the desert. I did not have to do that.

"I'm a sassy Kiwi. I have an accent. I'm blond. I was very conscious of the difference between me and other undocumented people, especially in the restaurant industry." Swimming in the ocean of hustling immigrants in New York, Deborah got a glimpse of what undocumented people who are not blond can face. "My friend Donna was British. Her family's from Guyana. She couldn't get work. She was beautiful, sassy, maybe a little quieter. She could only get a job mopping floors. And she was like, 'I didn't come here to mop floors.'" Donna went back to Britain.

Over the course of our long conversation it occurred to me that Deborah had fallen in love with the idea of making it in America, but not just any America. It was the America of her dreams, an urban, hustling, complicated, connected America. "I met a guy on the very early beta version of the internet. He lived in Omaha, Nebraska. I was an adventurous person. I figured, 'Let me go to Omaha and see what this is about.' It soon became very clear to me that my American experience was not going to be satisfied living in Omaha, potentially behind a white picket fence. It was definitely all tied up with New York City."

We talked about how the two places she's spent most of her adult life, New York and Los Angeles, are the two biggest homes of undocumented people in the United States, accounting for a wildly disproportionate share of the country's immigrants in the shadows. After thirty years, now deeply rooted in Los Angeles, having watched America's star fall in much of the world in her view, did it all work out? Getting on a plane and jumping feetfirst into Undocumented New York? "The people in New Zealand who thought I was fucking cool for living here now think I'm fucking dumb for living here."

Both her parents are now dead. She was an only child, so there is no family waiting for her in New Zealand. There is money her parents have left her, sitting in New Zealand. It won't go far in Los Angeles. I asked if she would recommend coming to America to someone contemplating the move today. Her own goddaughter in New Zealand, now twenty-seven, wants to do just that. "I'm actually stunned that somebody has the same stars in their eyes about living in the United States now that I had back then.

"You're obviously not paying attention to politics if you think it could be okay to come live here. But I wasn't paying attention back then, either. First of all, we're in the middle of a fucking pandemic that does not seem to be going away. Second of all, have you been paying attention for the last four years? She doesn't care. She wants to come to LA, West Hollywood, and meet famous people."

As I crisscrossed the country speaking with immigrants, one thing I heard over and over again was mention of how hard Americans work. The stress. The pressure. Of course, people worked hard in the places they come from, and too often get paid too little for doing it. Nevertheless, hard work is deeply ingrained in their expectations. You can do well in the US. Very well. But you'll have to work. Deborah was no exception. "The guy who does my yard work, Emilio, is from Oaxaca in Mexico. He came before the amnesty, so he got his green card in 1986. He and I talk about the immigrant experience a lot. He doesn't even really care about gardens. When he came here, around seventeen, it was just the job that he could get. Then he built a business around it. And now he makes really good money."

There are millions of native-born Americans who worry that the forty million people living in the US who were born somewhere else on the planet are changing their country in ways they can't define, can't control, and can't be comfortable with. What those people don't understand, or seem not to want to understand, is that, along with changes to the country, something else is going on. America is transformative. It makes those who come here into something new, a new people. We give too little credit to the immigrants for being open to that transformation, and too little credit to America for making that alchemy happen.

But it isn't easy. There are Rules. And they change frequently.

CHAPTER THREE

PLAYING BY THE RULES

Americans are split on "The Rules."

We extol the people who "play by the rules." The way we use the term in everyday speech evokes one great big society, one of the largest on earth, where stability and order are valued, and following those rules is, or should be, rewarded.

We also, from time to time, celebrate and admire the renegade, the rule breaker. There is plenty of affection for the people who, if they follow rules at all, are particularly fond of the ones they wrote for themselves. The admiration expressed by many for the rule follower is grudging. For the rule-breaker? Delight, amusement, and sometimes (if we are honest), a little envy that we don't have the nerve to flout them ourselves, because of worries about consequences.

These rules exist in written and unwritten form. There is encourage-ment to keep your nose clean, avoid brushes with the law, and stay in school, and a professed revulsion for borrowing more money than you can pay back. Those prescriptions live side by side with defenses of Donald Trump's bankruptcies among some, Bill Clinton's sexual dalliances among others. Barack Obama's adolescent weed habit as a member of the "Choom Gang" drew giggles from some Americans, and scornful judgment from others.

Now imagine being an immigrant trying to navigate the extensive and mysterious codes, both written and unwritten. The rules for coming to the United States are challenging, sure, but also confusing, byzantine, and daunting enough to encourage people to seek a way around them. I sat down to dinner with a California family that news stories might blandly call "mixed status," but that pat phrase obscured just how bizarre the law could be. The Hernandez family had come from Mexico to work in Southern California, working on construction sites and cleaning houses. They had two children, both American citizens. When economic conditions changed in both countries they returned to Mexico.

During the subsequent years back in Mexico, the couple had two more children. In response to hard times in Mexico and a blazing hot California economy, in the late 1990s, the growing family returned to California. And had another kid.

When Barack Obama introduced "Deferred Action for Childhood Arrivals," or DACA, it was opened to young adults and children who had been brought to California by parents coming to the US without following immigration law. The argument was that minors have little choice in whether they come to America with migrating parents, so the US government would put very low priority on their apprehension, prosecution, and deportation. Congress had narrowly failed to pass the "DREAM Act," which would have offered undocumented young people a path not only to legal residence, but eventual citizenship. Instead, DACA would have to do until the White House and Capitol Hill could see eye-to-eye on how to help the DREAMers.

However, even DACA did not offer something for nothing. Even the act of following the rules means you have to tell us how you have been breaking them for years. DACA applicants were required to tell the federal government where they had gone to school, where they lived, and where they worked. There was an age cutoff beyond which an adult could not apply for protection. Leaving the country and returning in recent years would mean disqualification.

Back to the dinner table in Southern California. The two oldest children were just fine. Born American citizens, though they had spent much of their formative years in Mexico, they were able to simply pick up with their American lives when the family returned to the States. Things were more complicated for their kid brother and sister. The brother, Javier, had become an immigrant rights activist, urging other childhood arrivals to take advantage of the legal residence, taxpayer identification number, and protection from deportation that DACA offered. Yet one person he could not advise to take advantage of the program was his own sister, Sonia, who was brought to the US under the age limit. Now just ten months past her thirty-first birthday — she was too old to apply. She had lived in the US for most of her life, she worked for a real estate brokerage, drove a car, and she had raised her American-born children, all while legally vulnerable to deportation.

It is common during debates to hear people frustrated with the current state of play, with millions living and working long term against the law, to demand that undocumented people "go home, and get on the back of the line."

The problem? There is no line. Not a line that is relevant to people's real lives anyway. Sonia, a few months older than the DACA threshold, would like to "get legal" through her husband, Cesar. When we met, he had already been "in line" more than fifteen years. Had he followed the advice to go back to Mexico and get on the back of the line, that would have meant taking his citizen children out of school and raising them in Mexico, a country they do not know at all.

Just after the introduction of DACA in 2012, I met Carlos Batara, a lawyer in Riverside County, California, with a large immigration practice. When young people came to Batara asking for advice, or for help filling out the DACA application, his advice was simple: Don't do it. Batara was wary of a process that required people who had been living in the country long term, and out of status, to tell the government every-thing about themselves. "If you're willing to risk and assume [that] they will never come back and use the information you have given them against you to bring removal proceedings, and if you assume the DREAM Act is going to pass, that's fine. Go to another attorney. I think that almost borders on malpractice."

Over a decade later, I checked in with Batara to see if his thinking about DACA, the rules and the risks, had changed. The program is now in its third presidency, but the vulnerabilities and exposure to risk have not changed much. "There are four possibilities. DACA could continue with no changes. DACA could be revised with new dates or some other provisions. The DREAM Act could be passed. Or DACA could be killed, terminated altogether.

"With new clients I go through the four scenarios. As before, it's their choice. But I warn them that if it's terminated and terminated harshly, you are subject to deportation." Batara concedes that for governments of either party, the optics of mass deportations would be so bad there would likely be restraint. The program participants would end up where many of them started. In limbo.

Today, Batara is a little less wary of the downsides of deferred action. When potential clients raise the possibility of a DACA application, "I tell them you have to make an informed choice." The legislative deadlock that defeated the DREAM Act and kept DACA protections from being guaranteed by law has persisted for more than a decade, and Batara thinks one side of the equation has gotten too much attention, the other too little. "There was too much advertising on the internet and in the community about DACA getting you work permitted, and deferred deportation. The longer-term possibility of one day the program ending and potential deportation facing them wasn't discussed as thoroughly as it should have been."

Throughout the years a network of DACA recipients across the coun-try has been using social media to keep in touch with, and keep tabs on, each other, as they shelter under the relatively flimsy umbrella of presidential whim. A resident physician at San Francisco General Hospital from Thailand, a Venezuelan immigration activist in Washington, a custom auto designer in Los Angeles, a medical resident in Boston, a lawyer protected by DACA who helped prepare the legal case that blocked its repeal, and an emergency medical technician (EMT) in Houston.

Jesus Contreras is blunt, almost matter-of-fact about his tenuous grip on the American Dream. "I knew from a very young age that my mom didn't have a Social Security number, that my mom couldn't get certain jobs or certain careers because she didn't have the opportunity or the ability to do so."

Contreras was not an infant in arms when his mother brought him across the border, but a young schoolboy. Quite apart from the enduring stereotype of unskilled, rural "border-jumpers," she was leaving behind a white-collar job and life in a metropolitan area. She cashed in her chips back home to launch her start in the US, joining established family members and beginning the shadow life of undocumented workers, eyes fully open, to "figure things out" as Contreras calls it. And we just ended up staying here since then."

His extended family straddled the US-Mexico border. "Half of my family was already in the States," having come as agricultural workers. "So a lot of my family were born US citizens and residents of the country." Contreras said his reputation in the family was the kid who was always asking questions, "and I learned that way, very quickly. I learned English enough to go into full English classes in a summer, and I was out of ESL classes within my first semester of elementary school in the United States."

Talk to people who grew up undocumented, and they will often say they were not conscious of their immigration status during their elementary and middle school years. As adulthood draws closer, so do the realities of their status. Contreras said he knew "it was now up to me to start making decisions for my future and start thinking about how I was going to pay for school and do life and start a career and get a job." These were all things made at least more complicated, for some impossible, to pull off without legal residence.

"I realized there were a lot of doors that were going to be closed for me in the work sector. I couldn't work because I didn't have proper identification. I couldn't get a driver's license because I didn't have a passport or US birth certificate. I understood these things. I was very aware of them. I just knew the same way my mom had overcome a lot of these issues I could overcome them the same way.

"But it was tough."

Complicating Contreras's road ahead was being a Texas resident. It was one of the states that required undocumented students, no matter how long they had lived in Texas, to be considered out-of-state or international students for the purpose of setting tuition at public institutions of higher education. While a graduate of a Texas high school would pay $6,000 per semester at the University of Houston, the tuition doubled for international students. "It was an insane amount of money and I remember at the time not wanting to stress out my mom or my family. It was just the fact of the matter. I can't sit here and pout about it. But it just sucks that I can't go where I want to go because it's a lot of money." His mother promised to help to come up with the money or borrow from family. Then fate intervened.

"I was very, very lucky to have an athletic scout for a cross-country team from a junior college in North Texas come out and see me run. He saw the numbers I put up on the mile and other events. And he offered a full-ride scholarship for my first year." Contreras ran with other immigrants. "The majority of my teammates were foreigners as well. Ethiopians, other undocumented Latino teammates. I was very fortunate to qualify for that and have the opportunity there. I put in the hard work for that, but if it wasn't for that I'd be tens of thousands of dollars in debt from school still."

Late in high school Contreras had taken a year-long course training emergency medical technicians. He remembered being excited about the work and seeing a possible career path. Though he scored well on the state qualifying exam, his immigration status kept him from being certified. A year of college study paid for by college athletics passed before fate intervened again. President Obama unveiled DACA, Contreras was cleared for work, and the door to work as an EMT was pushed open again.

"It changed my life. It changed a lot of people's lives. I successfully completed the paramedic program. And became a paramedic at a local service in Houston. I've been doing that ever since." Contreras can sound older than his thirty years. He has seen a lot on the job. He has seen a lot on the political front as DACA became an interparty controversy. "It hit the peak really early on in the Trump administration when there was a lot of hateful, uneducated, disgusting rhetoric thrown at immigrants and young people like me. The big thing was that we were criminals. Bad people. People prone to crime, to kill, murder, rape, we're gang members.

"I'm thankful we're in a country where we can fight and defend ourselves with facts and with numbers. With the truth, and with the justice system. In the end, that justice system's what really held us up these years. The Supreme Court, the lower courts, they're the ones that really held up our program [when] we got attacked without any factual evidence [and it was said] that we were detrimental to the country.

"That's the American Dream right there. It's just to keep fighting, keep working, and pushing forward." As Contreras looked back over more than a decade since DACA, he saw Hurricane Harvey, which ravaged the Gulf Coast in 2017, as an important milestone in his own development as an outspoken advocate for young undocumented people. Undocumented people have generally shied away from the limelight. Hiding becomes second nature. After days of near round-the-clock emergency work in the aftermath of the hurricane, Contreras got a call from an immigration attorney who encouraged him to talk to the press about his time as an undocumented first responder in the midst of natural disaster. "I used my experience as a paramedic to really show people the kind of individuals we DACA recipients truly are, which is productive, successful, good-hearted, willing to give back to the community."

Jesus Contreras is a trained professional, doing vital work in his hometown. He makes a decent living. He calls himself "an American at heart.

As American as you can be." Yet for all that outward success there are regular reminders he is not like his neighbors, or colleagues at work. "I couldn't go see my dad when he was buried in Mexico. I couldn't go see my grandpa when he got buried in Mexico. You can't say your last good-byes to dying relatives in other countries." He called those family duties "a basic right." He told me he and his girlfriend would love to get far away from the intensity of the job during his annual vacations. "Something as simple as being able to pick up a passport, take a flight. To maybe Mexico, or Europe, or an island somewhere in the middle of nowhere." He cannot leave the country until the question of his status is settled one way or another. Leaving for any reason could make it difficult, or impossible, to return.

During our long conversation about his American story, it came through loud and clear that Contreras was very willing to argue for his legitimate place in the only country he has known since he was six years old and wishes he did not have to do it. "You really shouldn't have to prove yourself to other people to say that you belong in this country. You really shouldn't have to be a paramedic killing yourself, working fifty-six hours a week to tell other folks that you deserve to be in this country. You shouldn't have to do something heroic every single day over hundreds of thousands of other people just to say that you belong in this country. I'm a first responder. I've saved lives. I've been part of huge disasters. I always want to say that there are people that aren't doing this, that deserve it just as much, if not more, than I do."

Contreras is proud of his work. His belief that he has already punched his American ticket is strong and unapologetic. His work during the pandemic testified to his value to Houston. Among undocumented people, Contreras said, "there's a mistrust for the health care community. There's a mistrust for law enforcement. There's a mistrust for any government official because immigrants know they're more likely to be betrayed by some sort of authority figure than any other person in this country, and they're in a place of vulnerability." This meant people infected with the coronavirus waited too long, too often, to call for help. "It tends to be pretty late in their disease process." Extracting desperately ill people from their apartments, Contreras said his language skills became as vital a tool as a gurney or a stethoscope.

"I was just at a scene of a crash where a mom and her two daughters got into a car wreck and she was there with nothing but English-speaking officers. I was there to translate for her. It's not part of my job, or my duty, but I'm there to translate and help folks that can't speak up for themselves. She was crashed into, it wasn't her fault. But she was scared and she was worried because she's a non-English speaker, with white officers, with people who are not like her, with people who may not understand her.

"My partner's also Latino. He's also Mexican. So we showed up and we wanted to make sure that she was spoken for. That she got her point across, and she could say what she needed to say. Small things like that.

"You get a patient that's Mexican, or Latino, and you have to reassure them that it's okay for them to be where they are and it's okay for them to ask for help." Contreras is determined, and disappointed. He had thought by now the fight for protection for DACA recipients would have been over as part of a comprehensive immigration reform. "We're still here in the same fight.

"I've been a part of this fight long enough now that I can't always get my hopes up, but I'm always there to fight regardless. I'm like Rocky, you know? You put me in a fight, I may not win, but I'll be in there to take some hits and fight back."

Even as the historical process of taking in immigrants and putting obstacles in their paths has repeated itself for generations, the "rules" keep changing. New Americans become students, observers, dissectors, striving to understand social customs, manners and mores, styles of interaction. They bring their heads, and the already built worlds living between their ears, to a place they may even think they already know a little, and find they still have more to learn.

* * *

Imam Ossama Bahloul recalled his early impressions of American culture that he gained from close observation. "I grew up in a society where you cannot call anyone older than you by their first name. Then I saw people here calling all people by their first name. I thought it was disrespect, but I learned it was absolutely fine."

Younger immigrants have their eyes wide-open all the time, constantly gauging what it means to belong, to fit in, to the already complicated world of young people. When are you Black, and not Black, at the same time? Solomon Kibriye told me about an uncomfortable lesson on his morning bus ride to his parochial high school. He had only been in the US a short time.

"I think at the time, out of a school population of maybe four hundred students, maybe ten of us were Black. And I was African, an immigrant. So I was doubly different. And I was the only Black kid on my school bus.

"Kids were very friendly. I made friends easily. I guess you'd say I was one of the nerdy crowd, but I had lots of friends from all the different groups in a very cliquey school.

"Every day we drove through a town [in southern New Jersey] that was predominantly Black. And the public high school in that town and our Catholic school had a long history of bad interactions.

"I don't know if it's still done now, but they used to have these weird experiments in school where they gave you an egg and you had to pretend it was your baby. You had to take care of it. So all of these kids on my bus had these eggs. We were passing through this town, and they thought it would be a really funny idea to throw these eggs at the passing public school kids on the street.

"Then on the return trip the public school kids pelted our bus with bananas. Mushed-up bananas.

"There was a kid on my bus. He was a year behind me in school, and he was actually someone I thought was a friend. Like a good friend. We sat near each other on the bus all the time. We talked. We hung outside of school.

"He opened the window and screamed the N-word at those students. And he got back in his seat, and I'll never forget this because it was so weird. I was shocked, but because he was friendly, I didn't expect that to come out of his mouth.

"A girl on the bus started screaming at him. She said, 'That's very rude of you to say that in front of Solomon.'" What followed was a teenage immigrant's impromptu lesson in the American way of race. Solomon's erstwhile friend turned to his accuser and explained, "Solomon isn't an N-word. He's Ethiopian. He's from Africa. He's not an N-word. Those people out there are N-words."

The girl agreed. Kibriye recounted the incident like it happened yesterday, instead of more than thirty years ago. "She said, 'You're right. Those are Ns out there. Solomon is not an N. But it's still rude to say that in front of him.' They got into a serious fight and the bus driver had to stop the bus to calm us all down. They got into a fight over the issue. Not that the N-word was not a word that should be used. It just shouldn't be used in front of me because it wasn't polite.

"I realized that they liked me, right? But that's just because they knew me. If they didn't know me, they would not like me.

"And that really shocked me because I thought, 'These guys are good people. They're my friends,' you know? High school kids. They are learning it somewhere. It changed my perception of the whole community. It was a big step in getting me to learn what it was to be Black in American society. Before that, I didn't have the whole picture."

What Kibriye experienced was a one-on-one version of the particularism Americans often bring to their interactions and mental maps concerning immigrants, and racial, ethnic, and religious minorities. Too many people unapologetically perform a strange kind of calculus as they look out their front door (or at their screens) at a changing country.

They may look with dismay at the gross numbers nationwide, in their state or community, and draw unhappy conclusions about the looming future and their place in it. Many will tell public opinion researchers they are worried about the status of native-born white Americans, while stoutly denying an ounce of animus toward immigrants, or Black and brown people.

Why? Because Begum and Osman live two doors down, and in a pinch are always happy to help out with school pickup when a parent is running late or to bring an interesting dish to a block event. Because Francisco, a peer, a project manager at work, is competent, and seems to be an involved parent. Because Aisha kindly picked up your shift on Christmas Eve so you could attend a family event since she does not celebrate the holiday.

In the decades I have covered changing American demographics, and interracial and interethnic shoving matches over political power and influence about how resources are deployed in this society, this pattern has emerged again and again. The big, brown, undifferentiated mass is dangerous. This massive mob of strangers is changing your way of life, without your permission. Even while the individual brown people you happen to know are people you like, and live and work with fairly easily.

The conclusion these Americans make is a traditional, historical one, and one that is deeply un-American at the same time. Throughout America's long history, as immigrants have arrived from new points of origin, they have faced prejudice yet eventually assimilated. And those very same groups have joined their older-resident citizens in bestowing harsh new obstacles on the next wave. Somehow, being in the place where Osman, Francisco, and Aisha do well means they must do worse. They see a country that is "ours" and not "theirs." The tiny grace notes of American life, the cake Alejandra brought for the office to share on Three Kings Day, the pride Vikram expressed when his son became an Eagle Scout, the joy Minh shared at lunch over taking the citizenship oath, may reinforce an inescapable conclusion — "these people are a lot like me" — while leaving undisturbed the conviction that something threatening and out of control is happening.

* * *

For all the changes wrought by the 1965 Immigration and Nationality Act, a small but steady flow of European immigrants began well before the law and has continued long after. The Cold War had created a bifurcated Europe, one part with rapid reindustrialization and rising affluence to the west of the "Iron Curtain," the other part, to its east, with what the US regarded as "Captive Nations." Poles, Serbs, Croatians, and Russians continued to make their way to Pennsylvania, Ohio, Illinois, and elsewhere. The growing cracks in Communism's impregnable facade, the breakup of Yugoslavia, and the unraveling of the Soviet empire created a Bosnian Muslim settlement in St. Louis, Uzbek nightclubs in Brooklyn, and Sunday masses in Polish in Chicago.

Zoltan Boka was eleven years old when his parents abruptly announced the family was leaving Budapest — for Philadelphia. "It wasn't like we were all going to sit down and start talking about it happening one day. It was basically 'Okay, pack your bags!'

"I didn't speak English because back then Hungary had mandatory Russian classes, which we ignored, and English class in the afternoon. But my English was bad. I mean, I spoke three sentences.

"There are groups that could move into their own niche, like Chinatown. Hungarians are not numerous enough to have their own place. So it was like, 'You're going to learn English. You're going to hang out with the Americans. And that was that.' So there was no preparation period. It was just, 'We're doing this. Now.'"

It was 1988. Hungary had forged its own path inside the Warsaw Pact, looking for ways to loosen up the system while still a one-party state showing its loyalty to the Soviet system. So-called Goulash Communism was fundamentally as restrictive and authoritarian for Hungarians as daily life was in Poland, Czechoslovakia, and Bulgaria.

Boka is frank about how difficult the whole move was. "Kids, much more than adults, crave stability to the point of boredom. Most kids want to eat the same food every day. So it was like that.

"When we came here, we were supposed to stay with my uncle. And my uncle had an angina attack and died two days before we flew out. Not good timing, you know? Communism was ending, but they didn't want people to leave. We were supposed to stay with my uncle's kid, and his kid really didn't want us there. And we moved around a lot in Philadelphia, probably six or seven places before I went to high school."

Boka's parents were doctors. The US did not accept their accreditation. While the pair studied for American board certification exams, they worked as nurses, and at a pharmaceutical company. "They worked 'in the vicinity of medicine' until they got their paperwork and passed their boards. They had to do their internship and residency again, which is not a whole lot of fun when you're like forty years old.

"You hear all this talk in America about how they want legal immigrants. They want everyone to have their papers. No, not really. While my parents were doing their residency, the chief resident's idea of a good time was that he would line them up, walk up and down, and yell in their faces. 'One word from me and it's back to India!' because so many of them were visa holders. My parents had green cards." During the process back in Hungary, having immediate family in the US made a big difference. Yet once family tragedy struck, the Bokas were on their own.

"I started going to school like two weeks after we got there. After we left my uncle's house we moved to a dicey part of Philadelphia." His new neighborhood, Olney, felt severe impact from white flight in the 1960s. The long-settled European-descended families had headed to the suburbs and were replaced by Black Americans leaving cratering neighborhoods elsewhere in Philadelphia, and immigrants from Korea, Vietnam, the Dominican Republic, Mexico, and Colombia. He called his new school, Finletter Elementary, "very chill." It was only when his parents moved him to a suburban school that he found out Finletter was so easygoing he was not properly prepared academically to be promoted. He had no way of knowing he was falling behind. "In Hungary we had school uniforms. We had to sit on our hands. It was not, you know, 'Do you want to go to class today?' If you had to live in that part of the world at that time, Hungary was not a bad pick." He felt he learned more in his Hungarian schools than at Finletter.

Boka has a slightly distanced, wry view of America, its attributes, and its faults. Looking on as his parents struggled to restart their careers, moving to different parts of the country as he learned "The Rules," I asked him directly whether he had any regrets about leaving Hungary just before the fall of the Soviet Union. "That's a loaded question. I mean, you're never really going to be able to answer what it would have been if I'd stayed behind.

"There's more breathing room here than there would have been over there. You can understand why we did what we did." As a young adult, he was diagnosed with a slight neurological disorder and a learning disability. "One of the reasons I live in New York is there are more civil rights here, more disability rights, more everything. I think the US is in some ways more open, and more willing to be open. Every country has its prejudices. Every country has its hangups. It's just different here than it is over there.

"I mean, over there [back in Hungary] two years ago a leader of the ruling party said, 'I want to put together a list of Jews.' Why? No reason, just to keep track. I don't really see something like that going far here, but you never know." I asked him if he had been given an unusual vantage point for understanding America, being an immigrant during an era of high levels of immigration, but a white immigrant. "I remember when I lived in the South. Most of my friends were African American. Most white people wouldn't give me the time of day. This girl told me once, a Black girl from Mississippi, 'Remember, you're not white. You're Jewish.' And I'm like, okay, if that's what we're doing now, okay, fine.

"The white guy thing is a social thing. Tucker Carlson's the ultimate white guy, right? Then there's the Hispanic group: some of them are moving toward being like the Italians, just white people with funny names. Race is a flexible thing, you know?" A trained anthropologist might not explain it in exactly that way, but I knew what he was getting at. He had learned the American way of race not as someone born to it, but on the fly, by trial and error.

"I never met a Black person until I was eleven years old. When I was growing up in Hungary, we called Black people a word that now I know they don't like very much. It was just a word, no different from microphone or suit or whatever. Then I come here and use the word, and this is not going over well. My English is not great, but I am getting the sense from the tone of this conversation they're not liking it. Every society has their own inside and outside people and it can change very quickly. You could be inside one day and then not inside the next day."

Could Boka remember a time when he felt he was getting the hang of life in America? A time when he felt he finally understood the country? "No. Because the US is not one thing. We moved around a lot. In high school we moved to a small town in Pennsylvania, about an hour south of Scranton. It was not my idea of a good time. I don't want to go into sob stories, but let's just say they would give me the Hitler salute in class. This was not ideal." I mentioned that this part of Pennsylvania had long been settled by immigrants from Europe. Boka replied, "Chris Rock had this routine about how everybody's treated like crap by the people who got here before them. I could become a 'white guy,' theoretically, you know.

"I could move to New Mexico. I could change my name! You know, that was an option when I got my citizenship, they asked if I wanted to change my name. I could change my name to Bob Smith. Get some relaxer for my hair. Maybe take some classes, modulate my accent a little bit. And just, be Bob Smith." There we were, sitting on a bench in Lower Manhattan, choked traffic slowly flowing by, and a fella from Budapest was spinning out the self-transformational dream of millions of Americans. Issur Danielovitch could become Kirk Douglas. Margarita Cansino could become Rita Hayworth. This short, curly-haired guy with the hard-to-place accent could see very clearly the shape-shifting privilege offered by his new home. Yet he was comfortable remaining Zoltan Boka.

"My grandmother, for example, her family changed their name. Their family name was Lichtmann. That's not going to get you any applause in

Budapest. So they changed it to Lakatos. She still got deported to Auschwitz.

"I remember Jeff Sessions was going on about immigration" — Sessions was the US Attorney General from 2017 to 2018 — "and at some point he said something about the Irish being drunks. [A memoir by FBI deputy director Andrew McCabe quoted Sessions to this effect.] I was like, are you really, in 2018, talking about drunken Irishmen? That's weird to me. That's like we're going backward.

"So even though I could shave and change my name and be Bob Smith in Arizona. I could also not become that." One transformation Boka could not pull off was speaking unaccented English. Many people who come to the US as young as eleven manage to speak English with a fluent accent of their new home region. Boka told me his English as a Second Language teacher in the Philadelphia public schools was "a Hispanic gentleman with an extravagant mustache" who spoke heavily accented English. The young Hungarian would learn English from a man who apologized to the class for the quality of his English. Boka says he really learned the language on the streets, "on the fly. I never really had sustained formal instruction. You're just going to have to learn it. There's no Hungarytown in Philadelphia."

This was one immigrant who, largely by accident and happenstance, had seen more of the country than most native-born people. After his parents recertified as physicians, they looked for work in states with persistent physician shortages, states that would offer high salaries and recruitment bonuses to move. The two middle-aged Hungarian physicians moved to McAlester, Oklahoma, roughly midway between the Arkansas border and Oklahoma City. Boka headed to university in Memphis, a seven-hour drive away. He later worked at the Tennessee State Legislature in Nashville, and his American education continued.

"I'd go in every day, and they had a statue of the guy who founded the KKK in the lobby, Nathan Bedford Forrest. They had a statue of the guy in the lobby. They had a giant statue of Forrest in the middle of the

Interstate [Interstate 65, near Nashville, since removed] and I was like, guys, this is not working out for me.

"I think New York is as close to home as I'm going to be in the US. Because what I love about New York is that they don't give a damn about you. They don't care what you look like. They don't care what you sound like. They don't care where you're from. In New York, there's only one acceptable prejudice, and that's against poor people. Which is not nice. But what I'm saying is that all the other things that you might get in Pennsylvania or Tennessee, here it's not on the table. There's something to be said for that.

"I live in a city that's mostly immigrant. I live in a city that's mostly not white. I live in a city that has a large Jewish presence. That has strong helping professions. It's comfy."

And if someone asks Boka if he's an American?

"I'm a New Yorker. How's that?"

Jaime Contreras's story of learning the written and unwritten rules involves no long-term plans, no grand schemes, no ultimate goal. After arriving behind his refugee father and getting legal status, he had to respond to the challenge of the day. He told me he was doing well in high school, even thought about trying to go to college and become a lawyer. "In my family, once you're old enough to get a work permit, you're going to get a work permit and go to work to help pay the bills. So my dad got me a work permit. At that time the minimum wage was $4.75 an hour, so you could work at McDonald's to make $4.75, or you can go to work cleaning and make 5 bucks an hour.

"So I went to clean buildings." He met an organizer who introduced herself in Spanish and said she was from "El Union," using a Spanglish term in place of *sindicato*. It caught Contreras's ear because back in El Salvador, loose talk about organizing labor unions, *sindicatos,* could get you killed. In Washington, the pitch went, El Union would get you a raise instead. And health benefits. And a pension.

That night over dinner he told his father about the encounter, and got encouragement to join, and help organize the cleaning staff at his office building. "We had seventy workers. Half Black. Half Latino. And I was this bilingual kid. The union kind of helped me focus, to help them put the building on strike. We won the union a couple of months later, and I became shop steward." Contreras's American education was well under way, and his union saw him as a kid with a future.

"The union asked me to come to work for them as a part-time union rep, and I did that. Then the guy who was in charge at the time said, 'Hey, when you graduate from high school you can come work for the union full-time and go to school on the weekends.'

"I graduated in May of 1994 and they said, 'If we have the money in August, we'll bring you in full-time.'" For a teenager in a hurry, helping to support his family, three months seems like a long time. "I decided to join the Navy instead."

The organizing director for the local was angry when she heard about it. "She said, 'Why didn't you talk to me? You could have worked for the national union!' I said, 'I'm a kid! I don't know about union politics!'

"Six months before I got out of the Navy, she and other folks were calling me to come back and work for the union. I became an organizer, then a union rep. Then in 2001 the president of the union asked me to run with her to be the treasurer. By then I was twenty-six or twenty-seven." Contreras's local merged with the powerful 32BJ of the Service Employees International Union (SEIU). "Then I became a district chair, and then a vice president." No big deal, right? I kidded Contreras about being a young man in a hurry: from being smuggled across the border by a coyote to a high school diploma to the US Navy to a senior position with a major American labor union.

Looking back on his choices, the leader of more than twenty thousand organized workers in the Washington, DC, region credits both drive and luck. He said if he had skipped the Navy and gone straight into full-time union work, he likely would have quit in frustration, so great were the tensions between native-born Black and Latino immigrant workers. The teenager was urged by his teachers to apply for scholarships and start a college career, urged by his family to go to work, and urged by the union to start organizing full-time while starting higher education.

He recalls with satisfaction that by picking "none of the above" and heading into the service, he saved his union career. "I would have gotten fired, or I would have quit out of frustration with everything going on in the union." When I told Contreras how many immigrants mentioned uniformed service as a transformative experience in their American journey, he quickly agreed. "It helped me mature. The Navy paid for my education through the GI Bill. By the time I came back, I had learned so many leadership skills. About taking and giving direction. Respecting the discipline. It's priceless to me.

"Look, in the military you can go in and come out a better person, you can go in and come out really screwed up. I'm glad I came out as a better person. The things I learned about leadership and discipline and how to run a tight ship are still with me and help me through life and in my current position in the union."

A citizen. A union official. A veteran. A college graduate. Contreras is very conscious of the person his own journey has made him, and he has listened over the past twenty years as the national conversation around immigration and immigrants has become tougher, more shrill, less open to compromise. He called it "a disgusting way of looking at the world, offensive, unpatriotic, and un-American."

"I came here undocumented. I served. I'm an immigrant. How dare you call out people like me and my family and generations of other people from around the world; how dare you insult people like that?

"You know, immigrants carried this economy for the last two and a half years through COVID. We were the people that had to show up to work every day. We couldn't work from home. Pick the crops in the field and serve the food, and work at the grocery stores. Clean the buildings. Sanitize the buildings. You have to show up!

"At the airports now, it's just like the United Nations. It's all immigrants, and not just Latino immigrants. It's especially immigrants of color who are the ones being demonized. I'm not in any way, shape, or form minimizing what's going on in Ukraine. But those folks are being received with open arms because they're white.

"Nobody wants to leave their homeland. I wish things were different and I could have had the opportunities I had here in El Salvador. But I didn't. People are forced to leave their homelands for a variety of reasons." From his union's work in providing literacy and citizenship classes, he sees the zeal new Americans bring to learning the ropes, trying to play by the rules. When the rules are not working, he asked, and the Congress will not fix them, what then?

"Back when we were having the actual debate on immigration reform" — during the Bush and Obama years — "undocumented immigrants contributed something like $90 billion net per year to the economy. And rarely do they get anything back in the form of benefits because they can't apply. They don't qualify for anything. They don't even get much of the money they paid on Social Security, even if they have a taxpayer identification number, they don't. Most of them don't reap the benefits of the taxes they pay."

A kid picked up by the INS at a Washington airport now knows labor law inside and out. He understands the mechanics of crafting contracts, and how a line of small type in a multi-hundred-page immigration bill could change the futures of thousands of his members who want to become US citizens. When he looks at the life he has lived, and the lives of his members, where does he come down on America's promises to its people?

"I consider myself a patriot. A true patriot, not a fake patriot, like the folks waving the flag. I don't have to wave a flag to show that I'm being a union organizer and putting money in people's pockets and helping the poor. To me, that's being a patriot. Doing good things for people is for me being a patriot.

"I do appreciate the opportunity I have been given in this country as an immigrant." Contreras was now on a roll, and sketched out with vigor and emotion what he sees as the road ahead, requiring "both sides, the two main political parties in this country have to change the direction we're headed in general.

"With the big issues, like immigration, gun control, health care, education, they're just going to have to remember why they were elected to those congressional positions, which was to do good things for the country.

"The American promise is not what it used to be, even when I came here in the 1980s. It is for some people. It depends on your skin color." He described the Republican Party as increasingly hostile to immigrants, and the Democrats as "asleep at the wheel." He knows his five children, teenagers and young adults, will live out their lives in a different America from the one he came up in. He worries about the state of the planet, the international scene, and the intractable nature of the US debate over immigration. After running down the litany of problems he sees, Contreras still called himself an optimist. "I think more and more people are paying attention to the fact that we can't keep going in this direction that we're headed right now. Young people are also paying attention, and that, to me, is important because they are going to inherit whatever mess we leave for them. So I hope to leave it a better place for them."

Martha Lagace is an anthropologist who has long studied African immigrant communities in the United States, and now works as the director of research for African Communities Together (ACT), an organization that helps individuals and communities find their footing and get started in the US. Lagace keeps a close eye on immigrant communities, legal status, ESL and job training, and civic engagement among Africans now living in America. ACT is a 21st-century version of the immigrant aid organizations that helped Irish, Italian, and Eastern European Jewish arrivals start their American journeys at the height of European migration to the US.

Like those immigrants of old, newly arrived Africans are gravitating to the country's biggest metropolitan areas. The service sectors in the big metros are huge, diverse, and constantly hungry for low-wage workers. At the same time they are complicated places to live. "People are dealing with rising rents, while making minimum wage. They are doubling up, because people can't afford the rents.

"Many African immigrants don't have health insurance, and this is especially a problem for women of reproductive age. There's so much diversity in African communities. Some people are doing pretty well, South Africans, Nigerians. But other people, especially from the French-speaking countries, are really having a hard time both in housing and health care."

While Americans are regularly told by news outlets about the "crisis on the southern border," they are rarely given a detailed picture of what is going on there. Now people from all over the world make their way to Mexico in order to try to cross the border into the US. In recent years, law enforcement at the border has expanded beyond intercepting Mexians and Central Americans trying to work on American farms and construction sites. Border agents are apprehending Cubans who no longer try to float across the Florida Straits but instead make their way to Nicaragua and try to enter the US over land. Ukrainian and Syrian refugees fleeing war and chaos, and Asians unsuccessful in their efforts to get visas try to enter through Mexico. Lagace said there are now increasing numbers of Africans in detention, and it is hard to find out "how many people are actually locked up by ICE. And their families can't do anything about it. Others already here face the sorts of problems that people who are undocumented have, for instance, if they've overstayed their visa: They can't leave, and they really can't work." To Lagace, American bounty is not so much a pull factor, as episodic crises in Africa's sending countries becomes a push factor. Even with all the daunting challenges of negotiating life in America, she said, Africans will continue to take their chances in the US.

However, pluck, ambition, and hard work cannot simply propel families past the real troubles of urban America. African immigrants are exposed to all the regular trials of immigration, and then add the challenges of Black residential areas in New York, Washington, DC, and

Chicago. "Many Africans do send their children back to the old country during their teenage years, in the hope they'll avoid some of the problems. Especially with the criminal justice system. In a way it's safer for them. There's also a long tradition of children being raised by grandparents, so it's not that unusual.

"We don't know exactly to what extent African children are shuttled into special ed. If they come to this country when they are already ten or twelve years old, speak with an accent, they are too often put into special ed. There's a stigma around anything that's perceived as a disability.

"For many parents there's a kind of bewilderment that the American school system tends to want parents to be involved in everything. To come to meetings and work with the PTA and volunteer on Saturdays and things like that. It's not really common in many places in Africa." In common with many immigrant families, both parents are working very long hours at low-wage jobs, and the expectation that they be available to come to school presents an added burden made heavier by language barriers.

It is not unique to African immigrants that there is pride and fulfillment in being the person who sacrifices to make other people's lives better. "You are subjecting yourself to hardships as a way of proving your worth, and becoming a moral person in that way," Lagace explained. In a framework that does not fit neatly into American ideas about these same challenges, you might hear Africa scholars and historians refer to "home" and "bush."

"Home is your place, in your country. It's where your ancestors are from. But today that home is changing a lot, and it's not necessarily a welcoming home, or a safe home, or a place where you can meet every day. The bush is conceived of as a place where a person has to go to prove himself. With the expectations that there will be hardships. But those hardships are necessary for becoming an individual." In the 21st century, that place of testing, for hundreds of thousands of Africans, is not part of your home country, but far away in America. "You'll find them in elder care, in transportation, working as drivers and parking lot attendants.

There was a terrible story of an immigrant who found himself locked in a freezer in a bakery in Brooklyn. Accidentally locked in the freezer in the middle of the night, he perished. A man from Mali. They're doing dangerous, low-paying jobs."

As the American mood toward immigrants and immigration has bumped up and down, there is an elegant irony in the concentration of African women, of immigrants in general, in home health care. In a country where the native-born population is aging, and the immigrant population is young, more and more Americans will spend their final years in the constant company of an immigrant who will attend to their most intimate needs.

It is not hard to imagine the surprise of some elderly Americans, for a long time unsure how they feel about how the country is changing, who now have their shopping done, their medications monitored, their meals prepared, and their bodies bathed by a woman who began life in West Africa, the Caribbean, or Latin America. A person you might have been reluctant to share a neighborhood with, or see your grandchildren in school with their children, now helps you clean yourself up after a bathroom mishap, listens to your stories for hours, and will sincerely weep at your funeral. It may be one of the most surprising additions to "The Rules" Americans have had to absorb.

CHAPTER FOUR

GOD AND THE
AMERICAN DREAM

Big stories, involving the futures of millions and the daily lives of nations, can sometimes be elegantly illustrated by tiny events, involving just one person.

In 1923, the Supreme Court of the United States ruled that Bhagat Singh Thind could not become a naturalized American citizen. Thind was a Sikh from the Punjab province of British India, living in the United States as a student. He had volunteered and served in the US Army late in World War I. He even continued to wear the traditional Sikh turban, covering the long hair Sikh men traditionally avoid cutting. Possessed of a long martial tradition, India's small Sikh minority formed a pillar of the British-organized Indian Army. Thind became a sergeant, and received his US citizenship when still in uniform, as was promised at enlistment. Then things took a strange turn. The Bureau of Naturalization withdrew the grant of citizenship, overruling a federal district court.

What kept Thind from becoming a citizen even after his service was not his Sikh religion, but his race. The Bureau of Naturalization maintained Thind was not "Caucasian" under the language of the existing statute. He took his appeal to the State of Oregon, only to be opposed by the same Bureau of Naturalization that barred him the first time. This time, along with race, the bureau cited Thind's political sentiments: his support for Ghadar, a pro-independence movement organized in the Pacific Northwest by Indian migrants. Yet Thind won his appeal, and once again became an American citizen.

Undeterred, the Bureau of Naturalization continued its campaign to keep Thind a resident alien, taking the case to the US Court of Appeals for the Ninth Circuit, which passed the case on to the United States Supreme Court.

The appellate court asked the country's highest court to rule on very specific questions in this case: Is a high-caste Hindu of full Indian blood...a white person? Also, since a 1917 law — the Asian Barred Zone Act — specifically barred "Hindus," did that include people who entered lawfully before the law was passed? (Briefs continued to use "Hindu," and even "Hindoo" as catch-all names for the people of the Indian subcontinent, even though Thind was not a Hindu.)

With all the obsessive parsing of the legal precedent common to the high court, there was a lovely irony embedded in the statute: A faithful Sikh, considered suspicious because he supported evicting his birth country's colonial masters, might have been saved by a little persecution! The Barred Zone law shutting the door to Indians contained an exception for "all aliens who shall prove to the satisfaction of the proper immigration office or to the Secretary of Labor that they are seeking admission to the United States to avoid religious persecution in the country of their last permanent residence, whether such persecution be evidenced by overt acts or by laws or governmental regulations that discriminate against the alien or the race to which he belongs because of his religious faith."

The high court had already turned back a Japanese petitioner seeking naturalization in its precedent-setting ruling in *Ozawa v. United States*, citing the racial exclusion contained in the plain language of existing laws when rejecting the citizenship position of Takao Ozawa. Writing for the court, Associate Justice George Sutherland noted, "The appellant is a person of the Japanese race, born in Japan....Including the period of his residence in Hawaii appellant had continuously resided in the United States for twenty years....That he was qualified by character and education for citizenship is conceded....The appellant in the case now under consideration, however, is clearly of a race which is not Caucasian, and therefore belongs entirely outside the zone on the negative side."

Thind identified as "an Aryan," that is, a descendant of the ancient civilizations of northern India and Persia. That meant Thind was "white," according to the racial science of his day. One might have assumed, if Ozawa was not allowed citizenship because of his "not Caucasian" status, Thind would have to meet the technical definition set out by the high court. The justices had no problem contradicting themselves.

The high court ruled Thind would not be considered white in the eyes of "the common man," and his petition for naturalization was denied. The Punjabi doughboy, defeated in his attempt to become a citizen of his adopted country a third time, did not go down in defeat alone. Some fifty other Indians who had been naturalized also lost their citizenship when the nine justices unanimously ruled against Thind.

This time, in his written opinion, the very same Associate Justice Sutherland, an immigrant to the US who came as a boy from England, set out his reasoning in blunt, layman's terms. "If the applicant is a white person within the meaning of this section, he is entitled to naturalization; otherwise, not."

Associate Justice Sutherland was equally clear about the purpose of the law. "The intention was to confer the privilege of citizenship upon that class of persons whom the Fathers knew as white, and to deny it to all who could not be so classified. It is not enough to say that the Framers did not have in mind the brown or yellow races of Asia. It is necessary to go farther and be able to say that, had these particular races been suggested, the language of the act would have been so varied as to include them in its privileges."

The associate justice did not trouble himself with whether this clear racial barrier to American citizenship was right, or fair, or consistent with the values of equal justice under law (that was a task for Congress). Associate Justice Sutherland did not need to ask why he was able to move to the US from Buckinghamshire, become a citizen, a US senator, and a Supreme Court justice, while a scholar from Amritsar in Britain's Indian empire could not. Thind's quest for citizenship bumped up against the plain language of existing law. The question became "What does the statute mean?" and for the high court the answer was simple.

Rather than engage in tricky biological or historical speculation about the meaning of the term "free white persons," the opinion used the definition an average American would use for "white" or "Caucasian." In the court's estimation, racial theories and the history of Indo-Aryan Asia notwithstanding, Bhagat Singh Thind might have been a free person. He just was not white.

In much of the modern era, Americans have spoken with great affection of the country's immigrant past. They like to think that throughout the nation's history, immigration was the engine driving the country's unique diversity. To be sure, that is true. In practice, however, only white immigrants were able to become citizens of the United States for the country's first century of existence. From the signing of the Declaration of Independence until 1870, only white people who made it to the US had any hope of becoming American citizens. In 1870, with the passage of the post–Civil War amendments to the Constitution, "aliens of African nativity and persons of African descent" were added to "free white persons" to become the only two categories of people who could be naturalized under law.

Add to those statutes the Chinese Exclusion Act of 1882, and the practice of gradually raising barriers to Japanese migration and naturalization, and Sikhs, Hindus, Buddhists, and Muslims around the world were largely blocked from naturalization, not by virtue of their religion, but by virtue of the believers' races and countries of origin.

It must be noted that what people meant by commonly used terms like "race" and "white" does not match contemporary definitions. The Dillingham Commission's reports of 1911, funded by Congress in an attempt to create a framework for debate over limiting immigration from Europe, used a vast array of "racial" definitions for people who in 21st-century America are simply called white. The reports, which over the course of the commission's work ran to more than forty volumes, defined a number of distinct races, including: "Africans" (Black) and "Cubans" (separate and distinct from "West Indians"), and groups that would later simply be called "white": "Dalmatians" (from the Adriatic Coast of what would become Yugoslavia), "Ruthenians" (Eastern Slavs from Poland, the czarist empire, and Ukraine), "Scotch," and "Welsh," among others.

After decades of assimilation and acculturation, Americans would think of almost all these people as "white." The Dillingham Reports fretted about so-called New Immigrants and "the extent to which recent immigrants and their children are becoming assimilated or Americanized," as compared to the descendants of "Old Immigrants" who had "overcome" barriers to assimilation, "while the racial identity of their children was almost entirely lost and forgotten." These conclusions were no small matter as Congress looked for a way to limit immigration: Historian Katherine Benton-Cohen noted in her book *Inventing the Immigration Problem,* "Within a decade almost all of these policy initiatives (meant to reduce immigration from the 'races' of southern and eastern Europe) were implemented into law....The commission's reforms effectively ended mass immigration from 1924 to the passage of the Hart-Celler Act of 1965." Implicit in Congress's assumptions in the early 20th century was this: Some people can, over time, become just like us. Others can't.

Using race to shape immigration standards—even as the definition of the white race kept changing—ended up having a religious effect. Into the 20th century, this statutory language around race resulted in only a narrow band of the world's religions being widely and openly practiced on US soil. Though American religion was stunningly diverse and endlessly inventive, in the main it consisted of a wide range of Protestant Christianity, Catholicism, and Judaism as practiced by the immigrants of

Eastern Europe and descendants of the Iberian Jewish diaspora. Beyond that, there were tiny, vestigial Muslim communities scattered across the country.

Though it is rarely acknowledged in the way we teach history, Muslims lived in the United States from the earliest decades of the colonial period. They were West Africans, whose ancestors converted to Islam centuries earlier and were brought to the western hemisphere to work as slaves. Slaveholding Americans intensely and systematically suppressed the home languages, cultural practices, and the original religions of their human property. An indigenous Islam tied to the cultural memory of Africa could not take root in the young United States. So:

> Immigrants were white.
> Whites were from Europe.
> European immigrants were almost uniformly Christians and
> Jews.
> So, by the mid-20th century Americans were almost
> exclusively Christians and Jews.
> Almost all African slaves and their descendants were
> converted to Christianity.
> Thus, even most *non*-white Americans were Christian as
> well.

The exceptions began slowly in the last years of the 19th century and the dawn of the 20th. A tiny trickle of immigrants arrived from the Ottoman empire, from modern-day Turkey, Syria, Lebanon, and Palestine. Many of those immigrants, mostly men, were Muslims. Yet even Ottoman immigrants were mostly Christian, so that a century later the majority of Arabic speakers in the US, from Syria, Lebanon, Palestine, Turkey, and Iraq, were Christian. In an appeal similar to the *Thind* case, courts ruled in *Dow v. United States* in 1915 that immigrants from "Syria" in the Ottoman empire were white under law.

Why go to court over this? It is vital to remember that in the early

20th century, depending on the state where you lived, significant rights depended on your race: Where you could live, whom you could marry, where your children could go to school. It is no wonder so many courts were asked to determine whether people who did not always neatly fit into the binary American definitions of race—you were either white or you were not—headed to court to establish their right to claim whiteness.

Later iterations of immigration laws would remove the bar to non-white naturalization. But for a long stretch, the country's religious and racial demographics did not change very much. As John F. Kennedy and Richard M. Nixon squared off in historic, televised debates, and the downing of a U2 spy plane saw the Cold War get frostier still, the United States was 88.6 percent white, and 11 percent Black. In the 1960 Census, fewer than a million people out of roughly 180 million US residents were classified as Asian. There was no census category attempting to count the Latino population until the 1970 Census.

Muslims in the US at that time numbered fewer than a quarter million, many of whom were Black American converts of the 20th century. Hindus numbered only in the thousands, thanks to the lingering effects of the impediments to South Asian immigration. Buddhist numbers are harder to track, but in 1960 American Buddhists lived mainly in Hawaii and California, and were almost entirely Asian immigrants and their descendants, a number severely restricted for the preceding eighty years.

The 1965 immigration law reform and the larger trends away from established churches combined to take a sledgehammer to American religious practice. The declines in religious self-identification and active affiliation with a house of worship were already in full swing as the pace of immigration from Latin America, Africa, and Asia started its multi-decade rise.

Believers arrived by the millions: Roman Catholics from the Philippines and Mexico. Muslims from Egypt, Syria, Pakistan, and Senegal. Hindus from India, Trinidad, and East Africa. Jews from Israel, Brazil, South Africa, and the former Soviet Union. These new Americans crowded into established worship spaces to hear ancient teaching in their native languages and built new congregations all their own. At the same time, long-settled American families began a generations-long march away from ancestral faiths, picking up new ones or becoming completely unaffiliated. It will be fascinating to see if the newest Americans follow suit and abandon or radically redefine the traditions they bring with them.

It should be noted at this point that many of the numbers in this chapter are derived from polling and social science research. The US government does not keep religious statistics or ask new arrivals their religion. The marked changes in religious identification are as much a result of mathematics as sociology. As the number of annual legal arrivals rose from some 250,000 in the 1950s, to one million per year in the late 1990s and into the 21st century, the number of immigrants who belonged to minority religions rose as well. Younger, and more likely to have more children, these families have been driving change in religious demographics for decades.

Though the numbers of Muslims, Hindus, and Buddhists in the US rose steeply from the late 1960s on, the heavy presence of Latin Americans in the immigrant flows meant the majority of immigrants coming to the US remained Christian, even as the relative size of that majority declined. Those young Latinos have had such an enormous impact on the Catholic Church that their presence in pews and on parish rolls helps paper over the rapid decline in observance among native-born Catholics.

This was true even in what might seem the least likely places. As I headed to church one morning in Jackson, Mississippi, in the heart of the Old Confederacy, long part of the most uniformly native-born region in the country, the sign outside a stately Catholic church near the state capitol building listed multiple *Misas en Español,* masses in Spanish.

For all the impact Latinos have had on America's largest faith community, sociologists and religious scholars are watching them closely. With each succeeding generation, more Latinos are leaving the Catholic Church, heading for non-affiliation or becoming evangelical Protestants in large numbers. There are now Spanish-speaking Protestant megachurches filled with praying and swaying converts, and immigrant families who came to America *already Protestant,* in many cases converted by missionaries supported by US-based evangelical churches.

The second most frequent religious affiliation among immigrants is "none"; people with no religion make up about one of every seven new arrivals. More on that later.

No religion has seen faster growth in the United States during the modern era of immigration than Islam. The large and rising number of US-born converts have combined with decades of arrivals from West Africa, the Middle East, and South Asia particularly, creating storefront mosques in dense urban areas, and soaring suburban towers broadcasting calls to prayer outside New York, Washington, DC, and Chicago, among other cities. In the most recent three decades, Muslim immigrants have doubled as a portion of all new arrivals to 10 percent.

"There is a trend within the Muslim community that sees our well-being and protection in the civil rights movement, and an alignment with progressive, marginalized groups," said Dalia Mogahed, an Egyptian-born, US-raised scholar, and a close observer of demographic trends in Islamic America. "There is another group that sees our protection aligned with religious freedom. Therefore, more conservative groups are calling for more religious accommodation in nondiscriminatory laws that have the community nervous. Nervous around what we are now expected to do or not do within our own houses of worship.

"So I see this division between those who want to build coalitions with religious conservatives and align themselves with these groups and call for Muslim rights in the name of First Amendment religious freedom. And then those who feel that no, the protection of the community is aligned with more of the Civil Rights Act, and therefore align themselves with progressive movements. And I see this division as now the greatest source of stress for the community."

I asked Mogahed, now director of research at the Washington, DC–based Institute for Social Policy and Understanding, given the history of the last quarter century, if those tendencies have created some strange bedfellows. Conservative Muslims seeking to protect practices aligned with ancient gender-based customs are connecting with religious conservatives who have often been hostile to Islam, while other Muslims seek allies among Americans who no longer practice a religious faith or are hostile to Muslim practice in particular. "There isn't perfect alignment with either group because of these issues. Sometimes the left is hostile toward religion, and especially hostile toward some aspects of our faith that are socially conservative. There's no way around those aspects of the Muslim faith. But at the same time, they're welcoming of Muslims as a marginalized group. Then there's the other side, religious conservatives who are happy to align with Muslims when it comes to religious freedom issues tactically, but you listen to their sermons and we're all Satan worshippers."

One early winter day I killed time before an afternoon appointment in Minneapolis. I sat at a high counter looking out the window of a Starbucks in the Calhoun Square Mall. A Black man in a long overshirt, a *thobe,* and a heavy jacket to hold off the wind, his close-cropped hair topped by a knit *kufi* hat, was stopping passersby to hand them Muslim literature. He stopped all kinds of people but seemed to devote special attention to young adult men. Civil war in Somalia had sent people streaming out of that equatorial country in the 1990s, and the snowy Twin Cities became the home of the largest Somali community in the US, some one hundred thousand strong.

As I nursed my coffee and flipped through a magazine I noticed his approach change. The assignment no longer seemed to be pressing leaflets into waiting hands. The tall, broad-shouldered, and gregarious street proselytizer had convinced a small group of people to stop on windy Hennepin Avenue. He now led two short rows of men in afternoon prayer, *Asr,* one of the five appointed prayer times each day for observant Muslims.

In unison, the men touched their heads to the redbrick paving stones in front of the mall. Minnesota, long kidded affectionately on public radio's *A Prairie Home Companion* as the home of church suppers, Lutheran choirs, Midwestern reserve, and a decidedly unshowy, private flavor of religion, was now the home of something new. Some shoppers carrying bags from the mall stopped for a moment and in respectful silence watched a ritual that traveled to Minneapolis from very far away. Others politely stepped around the kneeling men lined up in short rows on the sidewalk as they headed to their next destination. This was only ten years after 9/11. I wondered how well such a scene would play in other parts of this big and complicated country.

One naturalized American has seen every side of American welcome, American shunning, and American freedom. Ossama Bahloul came to the US not long after the September 11, 2001, terrorist attacks. A graduate of one of the world's most renowned centers of Islamic scholarship, Al-Azhar University in Cairo, the imam arrived speaking no English, recruited by a congregation in Irving, Texas, a suburb of Dallas, to help with Ramadan observances.

Bahloul remembers the conversation with an American consular officer in Cairo just before the trip. "They asked me about the length of stay. I remember saying to him, forty days. And he even asked me, why forty days? I said to him, 'They asked me to be with them for one month and I thought I will give myself ten days to see America a little bit, and I will come back.' It wasn't an intention to stay in America."

Once the imam was in Irving the mosque asked him to stay another year. "They gave me an R-1 visa instead of just a tourist visa. They gave me the right to stay in America, even to work, for three years." Bahloul admits he might have been a little less aware of the controversy, the hate speech, the suspicion of Muslims in America swirling around him because he spoke so little English. He felt confident he was learning about the country and its folkways as he learned more English and learned his way around. He left Irving to serve a congregation in Corpus Christi, Texas, for three years. Then the imam was called to serve a growing congregation in Murfreesboro, Tennessee. The city was home to Middle Tennessee State University and a growing Muslim community.

"I remember a friend of mine. We used to play racquetball together. A Jewish man, very kind. And when I said to him 'I might go live in Tennessee.' He said 'A man like you—or myself—must not live in Tennessee!' I asked him why. He said, 'This is the Christian land. You will be going to the heart of the Christian land. They might give you a hard time.'"

In the 21st century, as in ancient days, there are Jewish prophets. Ossama Bahloul's American Dream was about to be put to the test by a hard time.

"I came to Tennessee. It was beautiful. I came in the spring. It was hilly and there were beautiful trees everywhere. I really like it a lot in comparison to Texas. The landscape of Tennessee is beautiful."

His congregation in Murfreesboro, with immigrants and their kids from South Asia and the Middle East, was straining against the physical limitations of a small commercial space in a strip mall. The imam had married an American-born convert to Islam in Texas and now had young children. It was a busy time at work and at home. Even as he was navigating a new hometown, a new job, and family life, his education in American life continued. "I was astonished by the diversity in the Muslim community in America. I grew up in Egypt. Very much Egyptian. Everyone in the mosque was an Egyptian.

"Then I came to America and there were people from everywhere at the Islamic Center. This was astonishing to me. I got to speak with someone from India, someone from Pakistan, Africa, Latin America. All of those people within the same place."

His congregation in Irving was large, some three thousand people. During feasts like Ramadan they came to the mosque wearing a vast array of traditional dress. "I was astonished by this. And I thought, I still believe now, this is one of the most special parts about America. It's diversity and giving its people an opportunity to interact with people from everywhere." That idealism would soon be tested.

When the Islamic Center of Murfreesboro could no longer hold its growing congregation, a benefactor donated money for land, and a capital campaign began for the construction of a purpose-built worship, education, and social space in a lightly populated, wooded area on the outskirts of town. When the congregation approached county authorities for a permit to begin construction, it set off a four-year legal battle over the site. The permit was challenged in court. There were marches and emotional town hall meetings. Televangelist Pat Roberts labeled the planned center a "mega mosque" and sought to galvanize the opposition.

I visited Murfreesboro to report on the mosque controversy and interviewed one of the leaders of the local anti-mosque movement. While I sat on her living room couch, Sally Wall, a local realtor, served me coffee and cookies and a scathing portrait of Islam, and of the plans local Muslim worshippers had for Murfreesboro. Wall told me they would eventually take over and impose Sharia law in Rutherford County. "I believe that's their purpose in life. To dominate, eventually, the government and the laws of the land, whereas we separate the government and the religion and all, and they don't." This did not stop Wall from trying to use the power of government to stop the Islamic Center of Murfreesboro from building its new home. After thirty years in a small city of one hundred thousand people, this Muslim congregation now was portrayed as a threat.

One strange aspect of the opposition was the tendency to treat the congregation as a new arrival, rather than something that had been quietly growing in their midst for three decades. At the next meeting of the county zoning board, a woman stood up to say, "Everybody knows who is trying to kill us. And it's like we can't say it." A man stood to agree. "This is my concern. Will radical ideas and violence be brought to our doorstep?" With the dismay came threats. "If construction does begin, I would also encourage contractors to boycott it. And I would encourage the boycott of any contractor associated with the project."

The sign proclaiming the center's land as its future home was set on fire. Construction equipment on the site was vandalized. In a lawsuit to try to stop the construction, the organizer of a march opposing the mosque, Kevin Fisher, said the county had failed to give adequate notice for public meetings, and that the building could endanger public safety by providing a forum for radical Islam.

Ten years after the ruins of the Pentagon and the World Trade Center smoldered in Washington and New York, the people of Rutherford County said they could be next. That's when I first met the imam. He was distressed. And hurt. And baffled by the threat of a Muslim takeover.

"The use of the term 'Sharia Law,' and that the Muslims like to sneak Sharia Law, and they don't like the Constitution. Who said this? I did not say this personally. I don't know any Muslim scholar in America who said this." We talked about the Bill of Rights, and his adopted country's traditions of religious openness. He especially appreciated the support he received from other churches in town. One particular ally was the Blackman United Methodist Church and its pastor, Bryan Brooks. The Methodists and other churches held teach-ins and clergy gave sermons, trying to cool down the heat in Murfreesboro. Rev. Brooks was dismayed by the reaction of many of his neighbors, something he had not predicted. "Wildly suspicious things were being said about people who have been in the community for decades, who are neighbors, who might be people's friends or professors or doctors."

When we met again in the 2020s, Bahloul recalled with great affection the support from Christians in town and from across the country, while vividly recalling the hatred. "I remember this guy came to my office and he was really mad. He said, 'I am here to let you know that you are going to hellfire, because you do not accept the Christ.' I had no option but to say to him, 'Why are you so excited about it? If I am going to hellfire, you should feel bad for me. Exhibit some sympathy!'

"I went to a small city where the pastor had invited me to answer questions, and this woman came up to talk. And I thought she wanted to shake my hand. I gave her my hand and she put pork sausage in my hand." Pork is forbidden food for observant Muslims.

"She said, 'You and your people are so full of hate, you even hate these animals,' meaning pigs. I said, 'Ma'am, we don't eat pigs. If any pigs are alive today, it's because of us. You guys are killing them and eating them. If anyone has a negative view of this animal, it's you! Not me.'" It sounded like Bahloul was getting the hang of being an American just fine.

The case eventually made its way to a federal court of appeal and then the Supreme Court, which refused to hear the case, allowing the lower court ruling in favor of the mosque to stand. It was over. The Islamic Center of Murfreesboro would rise, like so many modern suburban places of worship, in a small sea of parking lots.

Bahloul was a naturalized American. His children were American-born. The imam embraced the support from local churches, and spurned attempts by international Muslim organizations to turn his problems into a cause célèbre. He was gratified by the pro bono legal assistance from the Becket Fund for Religious Liberty, which saw the mosque's case through to the end. "We should all be proud of the American Constitution. We should all protect this constitution and be attached to it. Because of the American Constitution, people like me become Americans."

At the end, the mosque was built, and the congregation continued to grow. Bahloul, now working at the Islamic Center of Nashville, said the process made him even more attached to America. He still wishes it all never happened, and his tone audibly darkens when he talks about the conversations he had with his own young children, and others in his flock. "I remember a seven-year-old asking me 'Why do they hate us?' I couldn't answer him. Why do they hate a child? It hit young kids like this hard."

I parted company both times, in 2011 and 2022, touched by this immigrant's fidelity to American values. In twenty years, he has moved from a monthlong sojourn with a little sightseeing trip thrown in, to joining a new people, marrying an American, and because of his experience, testing and deepening his civic faith. He told me, "No one can say, 'I am more American than you' because of how you look or how you speak. If anyone were to claim such a position, it's a sign of foolishness because all of us came from elsewhere. This is beautiful about America."

* * *

Dalia Mogahed came to the US from Egypt as a child. Her school years were all spent in American schools, and her formidable résumé in industry and research organizations speaks to both mainstream success and her credibility as an expert on this country's Muslims. I asked her if, looking back over the arc of her life in America—from her arrival near the beginning of the Reagan years to the 2020s, from flareups of Islamophobia, suspicion of women in hijabs, FBI surveillance of mosques in the early 2000s—she felt less welcome in America.

"Two things have happened over the span of my lifetime. One is the way I dress"—Mogahed has worn a hijab since she was a teenager—"has become more normalized, right? It's on TV, it's on Gap ads, you have models on the cover of Vogue who are wearing hijabs. Things I never would have seen as a teenager. So now people are used to it. There's less of a staring factor if I'm in a place like New York City or Washington, DC, or any other urban area. If I'm in a rural area, there's still stares.

"The second thing that's happened, though, is how I have changed. You used the word 'welcome,' and I like that you used it because it gives me the chance to say, 'I'm not waiting for a welcome.' This is my home. If anyone has a problem with me being in my home, they are free to leave. But I'm not waiting for anyone's welcome because I'm not a guest."

I pushed back, noting that it is deep in people who come to a place to make their home to want to feel welcomed, accepted by a wider community, seen as part of the people who call that place home. To be one of Us, if you will, rather than Them. She stood her ground, gracefully. "I guess 'equality' is a word I would feel more comfortable striving for."

Mogahed explained she places her emphasis elsewhere. "It's almost a change in paradigm from one of striving for acceptance to one of striving for equality. I think there are going to be folks who will never like me. And I'm not waiting for them to like me. They are not my host. I think it's important I push back on Muslims who talk about not feeling welcomed because it will create a paradigm in your mind where you are forever the guest to a host, and it's an unhealthy way to think.

"We need to feel co-ownership for the well-being of our country, for the safety of the country. It's actually to the detriment of every American if folks don't feel a part of this project and have full ownership for it. I'm not saying that people are dangerous if they don't feel that way. But they're not going to invest in the same way as when they feel they are co-building their home."

Djibreel Diagne, working to further the reach of the Mouride Islamic movement from West Africa in the United States, worries about the future. He is well aware that in other religious communities, among America's Christian majority, among Jews, and others, young Americans are drifting away from the religion of their parents. Would young Muslims, in this case West African immigrants and the children of immigrants, follow the example of their native-born peers? Diagne noted that in Senegal, pious families have their sons enrolled in schools where they spend years memorizing the Koran. The mastery of all 6,236 verses, becoming a *hafiz,* a "memorizer," is a respected status in Muslim communities. Yet when a teenager, even a memorizer, arrives in the US, things change.

"He's a *hafiz,* he's a good kid. He graduated high school. But he doesn't want to go to school anymore. He doesn't even frequent the mosque. That's sad. That's a shame. And there are tons of examples of kids like that when they arrive, they change." His words are echoes of immigrant elders over the generations, lamenting that youth from their immigrant community, from Ireland, from Lithuania, from Norway, find a freedom from religious expectations in their new American home.

"We live in a community where we are a mostly immigrant community, first generation, second generation. Your second generation may not be aware that people are successful. Businessmen, a lot of people in your generation made it. Many are American now; they are very well groomed by their parents." Diagne is hoping his Mourid organization can reach out to, and hold, new Senegalese migrants making their way north from Brazil, through Central America, to the US southern border.

Holding on and worrying about keeping the youth connected to their religious heritage is a throughline uniting immigrant communities. Solomon Kibriye, a deacon in the Ethiopian Orthodox Tewahedo Church, told me he could feel the shifting of gears in the late years of the 20th century, when his "church in exile" gradually became an "immigrant church."

The difference? The exile church thinks of its presence in another country as accidental, and temporary. It keeps the flame of practice and teaching burning but makes no long-term plans to remain in a new home. "The first wave of Ethiopian immigrants were either connected to the imperial government or they were fleeing the emperor's government. Or they were fleeing the strife after the revolution.

"There was always the hope, 'We will go back. Communism will fall, and we will go back.' People worked and they bought houses and opened businesses, and they were doing well, but the churches were always churches in exile. Eventually, we were going to take this church home. That was pretty much the same with the Ethiopian mosques. There was a sense that we were not here forever."

The communists did fall, but the Ethiopians did not go home. In fact, they now took advantage of the diversity lottery and continued to come to the US, now for economic opportunity. "And now they're not renting churches, renting space from other churches, they're actually buying property and building churches. Very few still have green cards. Most people have citizenship now." Kibriye told me that that important transition brings a new mindset. The new mindset requires a new church. I put it to this ordained man that Ethiopians would hardly be the first immigrant group trying to sort out worship in America long-term, when children and grandchildren are less likely to speak the language of the old country. "We're still recent enough that we're still worshipping in Ge'ez [an ancient Ethiopian liturgical language] and Amharic [the language of the largest ethnic group in the country], and people come. Even those who might not fully understand what's going on will come because it's part of our identity and the rituals still mean something.

"There is an increased demand for English services. Some of the older, more conservative clergy are not too thrilled with that. For example, in our church all the services are in the traditional Ge'ez and Amharic, but we have TV screens above the sanctuary where the text is shown so people can follow the service and sing along." Some congregations have gone even further, Kibriye said, "There are churches that offer liturgy purely in English. In our church, every three weeks the clergy takes turns giving the sermon. When it's my turn I give my sermon in English for the young folk who don't understand Amharic."

Kibriye said some Ethiopians have moved to Egyptian Coptic churches where English is the norm. "I think what'll happen is we will be like Greeks in the US and Russian immigrants where they have assimilated into American society, but their religious practice is still their old Greek and Russian orthodoxy but in English."

So far, Kibriye said, there has not been a large migration to the American churches where most other Black Americans worship. "We have to do something in order to appeal to younger parishioners. So there's definitely more outreach to younger members of our community. There's enough of a cultural identification that will keep them in the church, but we need to do more in order to make them feel served."

The Ethiopian deacon is trying to find a way to save a faith rooted in the other side of the world, transplanted in a new country. Muslims in America have to make space for themselves in places where they had little or no history. Some immigrants find something else entirely—a new kind of tradition that blends a little of the home country with a new expression of faith offered by life in America.

Dearborn, Michigan, was founded toward the end of the 19th century and grew along with its nearby neighbor Detroit. The town was long associated with Henry Ford, his car company, the industrialist's passions and pursuits, his estate, and the museums and libraries he built there. Dearborn was a so-called Sundown Town for much of its history, that is, a place where Blacks were discouraged from being present after dark, that discouragement carrying with it the implicit threat of violence.

Christ Episcopal Church is a congregation that dates back to before the incorporation of Dearborn as a city. It sits on land donated by the Ford family. Henry Ford's wife helped break ground for the new church building in 1948. Fast-forward seventy-five years and Dearborn is a place the creator of the Model T might have a tough time recognizing.

Along with its English-speaking congregation, Christ Episcopal is also home to Mother of Our Savior Episcopal Church, a mission church of the Diocese of Michigan assigned to serve the Arabic-speaking Christians. Dearborn is about half Arab American and is the largest population center of Arabic speakers in Michigan, the state with the largest Arab population.

The ordained priest-in-charge, or "missioner" of Mother of Our Savior, is Fr. Halim Shukair, a Lebanese-born, American-trained priest of the Episcopal Church. Anglicans in Lebanon were never part of the communal tension, the rivalries, bloodletting, and civil war that has marked Lebanon's unhappy life as an independent country. There the drama was between Muslims—Sunni but now increasingly Shia—and various other Christian groups at home in this part of the world since the founding of the first Christian churches in the 1st century: Maronite Catholics aligned with the Roman Catholic Church, Orthodox, and Chaldean believers.

Decades of emigration from Lebanon have made Christians of all stripes a minority in the country. Lebanese Christians headed for France, for French-speaking communities in Canada, to Latin America, and to the United States. Holding on to the dream of ordination, and of doing his divinity studies in the US, Halim Shukair knew his options would be limited once he became a priest. There was only one Anglican congregation left in Lebanon. There was one in Damascus, Syria, but the country was embroiled in civil war and that church seemed an unlikely destination. As a Lebanese passport holder, he could not be called to serve Anglican churches in Israel proper, or in the Palestinian lands occupied by Israel since the 1967 war.

"I said, maybe God is calling me to a new thing." Just before he finished his training at the historic Virginia Theological Seminary in Arlington, Virginia, Shukair met the Bishop of Michigan, Wendell Gibbs, who asked him to come west. "He said, 'We need an Arabic-speaking priest here in the diocese. To reach out to the Arabs and the Christians. We need to know who these Christians are.'"

The following year he was ordained in the Episcopal Diocese of Michigan on behalf of the Anglican Diocese of Jerusalem. "And here I am in Dearborn." I asked him about his people. Who were they? Had they been raised Anglican Christians back in their home countries in the Arab world? Most of the congregation of Mother of Our Savior were raised Roman Catholic, Orthodox, or Maronite. They are in Fr. Shukair's pews because he reached out to them and offered them a new church to go with their new country, while also offering the American church a new way to be Episcopalian. Because the most modern version of the Book of Common Prayer has no Arabic translation, he wrote one. The resulting text is appealing and familiar, he said, to people coming in from other churches, while preserving the theology and teaching of today's Episcopal Church.

In common with the other churches of the Protestant "Main Line"—Presbyterians, Methodists, Lutherans, and Congregationalists—Episcopalians have been dwindling in number as Americans leave church and traditional family observance behind. I asked this new American whether in subsequent generations, he saw his people and their descendants migrating to the American branch of the Anglican church, or following their US-born peers into looser or, indeed, no affiliation. Would he have to make accommodations as fewer Arabic-dominant, younger parishioners became more American, and less Lebanese, Jordanian, Syrian, and Palestinian?

"I have two bulletins, one in Arabic and one in English. For my sermon, I preach in Arabic, and then I summarize it in English. I take five minutes to summarize it at the end." He was unsure about how long into the future that model would last. "In the long run, maybe we can have two Eucharists, one in Arabic, one in English. I believe even for the youth who don't understand all the Arabic, they can come into the church and listen to the Arabic hymns. I believe the model in the Maronite Church is now 50/50 Arabic and English.

"It's not only for the church to be a worshipping community, but also to be an educational community. I believe there is a lot of teaching about what it means to be an Arab and Middle Eastern Christian. When you mention the word 'Arab,' nobody thinks about Christians."

His Mother of Our Savior flock lives side by side and under the same roof with the historic Christ Church congregation. The gift he said his congregants bring these Michiganders is a living link to the lands of the Bible. "Like a lady who has lived all her life before she moved to the US, in Jerusalem, she says, 'I used to worship every Sunday at the Church of the Holy Sepulcher.' We have people from Damascus. St. Paul received his Revelation when he went to Damascus. I believe the Mother of Our Savior congregation is like a 'Fifth Gospel.' The English-speaking congregation learns from us, and we learn from the English-speaking congregation."

Far from the gray skies over Dearborn, there is a warm breeze racing across the flat landscape of Frisco, Texas, one night in winter. Rising above the ocean of subdivisions and strip malls is the striking, sandstone-colored tower of the Karya Siddhi Hanuman Temple, bathed in light as nature puts on her own light show in dusky yellows and pinks. On a weeknight, hundreds, and eventually, thousands will head for the front door, drop off their sneakers, sandals, heels, and workday dress shoes, to walk barefoot into the sanctuary.

Once inside the large worship space, the visitor and worshipper is confronted with multiple shrines, vertical rooms sheltering representations of Hindu heroes and deities. The interiors are brightly lit, and the statuary draped in garlands of flowers, mingling their own perfume with the incense-tinged air. On this night, there are joint and individual devotions. Some worshippers are content to grab a spot in the vast carpeted area before the shrines, to read, meditate, and pray. Others get closer, dropping to the floor and prostrating themselves before the shrine to begin their prayers. Others still are in constant movement, circling the shrines again and again, chanting and praying as they go.

The evening's devotions are punctuated by announcements from the priests scattered around the sanctuary that a specific cycle of prayer is about to begin in one or another of the shrines. Small knots of worshippers break away from what they were doing to join the growing cluster at a shrine door. The air is filled with chanting, singing, and whispered prayer. Priests touch babies offered on the outstretched arms of new parents, while older children assemble in a classroom off the sanctuary for instruction in Hindu scripture.

There is a corner featuring portraits of the temple's founder, Sri Ganapathy Sachchidananda Swamiji, depictions of key events in the history of the faith, and a variety of religious objects. For a small donation, a member or visitor can buy a black cord, a *thoram,* to accompany prayers and petitions to the Hindu deity Hanuman.

I stopped a priest to talk just a few minutes before he headed to one of the shrines. He wore a calf-length saffron robe that covered one shoulder then swooped across his chest to leave the other shoulder bare. His forehead was marked with dye. His wrists held various knotted cords, *katuka,* and he carried a small glass lamp with a tiny, flickering flame. I asked Vishwaksena Chandrashekera if, back when he was training to be a priest in India, he ever imagined living and working in a place like Texas. He smiled, said he had no ambition to come to America, and he was only here because his guru, the founder of the temple, asked him to come. The thirty-five-year-old told me, through an interpreter, that when he was needed somewhere else, he would gladly go.

Chandrashekera stressed his view that Hinduism was light on rules, light on coercion, and asked the believer to make up their own mind about commitment, attachment, and observance. He was very clear about his sense of purpose, and equally clear about his intention not to try to make anyone do anything. But if you come seeking the teaching, seeking instruction and ritual, it was his mission in life to supply it to any Indian who finds their way to the temple's front door.

Meanwhile, on the other side of the vast worship space a father keeps his son in his peripheral vision as the two move from shrine to shrine. At each stop the man clasps his hands in a prayer position and lifts them to his head, holding his hands over the tiny flame at each station before touching his face with both hands. The son, about three years old, watches intently, and reaches out for the flame to mimic his father, who looks on. After watching an age-appropriate attempt to mirror his movements, the father bends way down, gently grabs his son's tiny arms at the wrist, and slowly leads him in the ritual. The son tries again. Much better!

"Isn't that the way we all learn, right, by watching our parents? Parents can say whatever they want, but you learn from not only hearing them but watching what they do, and that's universal," said Laxmi Tummala, a member of the temple board, an observant Hindu, the daughter of mid-1960s immigrants from India, and a realtor who finds the bulk of her clients among the burgeoning Indian population of the Dallas–Fort Worth metro area. "Typically, in Hinduism in India, we don't have Sunday school classes. That has not been a thing typically. Kids learn from their parents. That's the way the recent modern history has been.

"Now in this country, because we understand that there are so many other influences, and that it's important to have a way for our children to learn should they so choose, or should their parents so choose to send them, we do have Sunday school classes at the temple." While Sunday school may not be traditionally Hindu, it is as Texan as barbecued brisket.

There are large and growing Indian communities in the northeastern states and on the West Coast. Grabbing a midday drink at a busy coffee shop before heading to a showing, Tummala told me the milder weather combined with one of the more affordable housing markets in Big Metro America make towns like Frisco a good bet for Indian immigrants settling down with children, migrants from other parts of the country, and the newly arrived.

There are groups of single men, of slightly older women with children in tow, and of elderly men and women. Scattered throughout the building are portraits, in a wide variety of poses and sizes, of Sri Swamiji, the founder of this temple and the spiritual leader for its members. Now Sri Ganapathy Sachchidananda Swamiji lives in India and makes episodic trips to the string of temples he has founded across the world, wherever the Indian diaspora has pooled up in communities like unlikely Frisco, Texas.

In decades traveling through and reporting from the American South I have watched the most uniformly native-born section of the country, a place that never really had an "Ellis Island" era, become a more diverse place. The South is still the place where a person you have only just met might feel free to ask where and how you pray, having already assumed you do. You might be surprised by such a question in New Hampshire, Oregon, or Washington State. In Texas, it is merely a familiar part of "getting to know you."

When I ask Tummala if assimilation and acculturation will eventually thin the crowds at this temple, whether these new Americans will go the way of even their Bible Belt neighbors, with lower rates of religious affiliation and active participation. In response she excitedly told me of the enthusiastic participation in a temple-wide project: reading or memorizing the seven hundred verses of the Bhagavad Gita in the original Sanskrit. "Decades ago, centuries ago, people used to memorize it. After the temple inauguration in 2015, Swamiji was here for forty-three days. During that time he said, 'It would be good if kids started memorizing the Bhagavad Gita again. The whole thing. And it would be good if they did it in nine months.' There was a person at the temple who had the skill to be able to take that on. Swamiji asked him to take it on that first year; in nine months, we had forty-three children who memorized the Bhagavad Gita. Now we have about three thousand people who have either memorized it or are fluently reading it."

The answer to the challenge of American secularization I heard in Frisco, Texas, was not that different from what I would hear among immigrant Muslims, Buddhists, or Roman Catholics: We will work to keep the children affiliated. "Not only are they memorizing the verses; they're actually learning the meanings of the most important ones that will help them throughout life, right? So not only are you increasing memory power, concentration, but you're also learning some of the beautiful meanings of these prayers."

The temple, as an organization, is hard at work being Hindu in a new land, and being very present in the civic sphere, in ways that would be familiar to congregations across the sprawling Dallas metroplex. There are food drives, community service projects, and "adopt a road" beautification campaigns. It is a familiar kind of outreach, even for a place and style of worship never before encountered by motorists rushing along the crowded suburban arterial roads. "We do conscientiously do that," said Tummala. "Number one, because it's the right thing to do. Give back. Be a part of the community. Number two, it's important that we have visibility in the community as a good steward, a good citizen. It's really important to us, and to Swamiji. And in general, it's important."

At the urging of her religious leader, Tummala even launched an unsuccessful run for Frisco City Council, an important milestone for a new immigrant group finding its feet in a new community. "Swamiji said, 'I want you to run. It'll be good for the community.' It was a way to show that we can do more than just be in our own space. Now we have lots of people on boards and commissions and people who run for various public offices. It's very important to be a part of the community and visible in that way."

All in all, she gave strong testimony that this corner of Texas was a good place to be welcomed as an immigrant, and a good place to be

Hindu. "Frisco has been great to us. Really, from the beginning. Welcoming and great." Holi, the Hindu festival of colors, a celebration of spring, now is a Frisco-wide observance in the public parks, mounted jointly by the temple and local government. "The city parks department has said many times that Holi is becoming their favorite because no other event can pull teenagers like this one. Teenagers have a blast at this thing." Frisco also has a city-sponsored lamp-lighting for Diwali.

The perhaps stereotypical intolerance, or suspicion of the unfamiliar, many might associate with the South, is, for Tummala, a relic from her parents' generation. Her parents came to Mississippi in the mid-1960s. The old Southern racial binary in law and custom, that you were either white or you were not, could not wrap its head around South Asians at first. "A friend I grew up with in Mississippi had somebody ask her at school when we were little, 'Are you black or white?' And she said, 'I'm neither.' The child replied, 'Well you have to be one! Which one are you?' It's been just a few decades since then, and it's some good progress.

"My parents came to this country in 1965 and '67. At that time in the South, you still had black and white restrooms in many places. They were allowed to use the white ones." As foreigners, Tummala said, they could become honorary white people.

I asked Tummala about her own sons, now young adults in college, and about the prospect that they might "marry out." Did that possibility worry her? "It's not a matter of color. It's a matter of faith. My parents were strong in their faith. And with God's grace, I'm strong in my faith. And with God's grace, my children are strong in their faith. Because they are so strong in their faith I think that marrying anybody of another faith would cause lots of marital conflicts."

She allowed that some Hindus, as members of a small faith community in an enormous country, are marrying people of other religions, or none. "I haven't yet hit the point where my kids' age group is getting married. But I can tell you that from my generation, 50 percent of my friends married outside of Indian-origin spouses, and 50 percent within. Even at the temple I see many mixed couples coming in, more and more.

The other day I saw grandparents with their grandchildren, who were definitely mixed, but they felt very comfortable there."

Frisco saw South Asian immigrants arrive in larger and larger numbers in recent decades to become a major presence in town. A similar migration took place in Lynwood, California, a small city tucked into the south end of giant Los Angeles County. It's the birthplace of Kevin Costner and Venus Williams, and the boyhood home of "Weird Al" Yankovic. Today Lynwood is about 85 percent Latino, overwhelmingly Mexican. In 2020, three-quarters of the households in Lynwood were counted in the census as primarily Spanish-speaking. Lynwood is home to one of the largest immigrant-serving congregations in the enormous Roman Catholic Archdiocese of Los Angeles: named for a 4th-century bishop, St. Emydius has some twenty thousand registered families.

My anticipation grew as I approached the church one Sunday morning. Though the church has a parking lot, I still had to park several blocks away. I walked through blocks of small, detached single-family houses, built during the rapid growth of Los Angeles County after the Second World War. Towering palm trees stood guard at the curbsides, and inside the small fences were carefully tended gardens stuffed with succulents, sitting adjacent to driveways stuffed with automobiles. When these houses were built, a car for each family was one of the whispered promises of the good life in Los Angeles. Now every member of the family, from teenage on, aspired to have one, and it showed.

The long-distance parking spot and the hike to church made me a few minutes late. In most churches in America that is a small matter. Whenever you get there, there is room. At St. Emydius, being a few minutes late meant I would stand in a side aisle at the back of the church for the entire mass. Every last spot where a human being might park their rear end, from the front pews by the altar, to the transepts at left and right of it, to the side chapels and the very last pew, was packed.

Lectors read passages from Scripture, a cantor led the congregation in prayer and song. Look around this church, built in 1948, and you see a building not all that different from the hundreds that rose in America's suburbs as the Catholic Church followed their faithful from old ethnic ghettoes and ports of entry out to new, automobile-dependent suburbs. Among the saints honored in stained-glass windows are giants of two millennia of Catholic history like Peter, Paul, and Teresa of Avila. There are also windows hinting at the congregations that built and sustained the parish in its early years, rather than the one filling the place today.

On the right side of the nave was a window honoring St. Thomas More, who served Henry VIII as Lord Chancellor of England, and who would not publicly support the king's divorce, or the proclamation of the monarch as the head of the church in England. More was executed, martyred for his defense of the Catholic faith in Britain. On the left side, across from More, was St. Patrick, the patron saint of Ireland. At the front of the sanctuary, next to the main altar, stands an enormous mosaic of the more recently added Virgin of Guadalupe, Patroness of the Americas. Mary in this form is the object of intense veneration back home in Mexico, and among Mexican Americans in Catholic churches across the US.

The parish was established in 1921, and St. Emydius's first decades saw a long line of Irish and Irish American priests. Frs. O'Donnell, O'Carroll, McGuinness, McNulty, O'Connell, and O'Neil got the church through the 20th century. As Lynwood changed, so did the church. Today the pastor is Rigoberto Rodriguez, a native of Michoacán, Mexico, who has led the congregation since 2011. During the procession to the altar Fr. Rodriguez is a warm and affectionate presence, greeting adults and blessing babies and young children, smiling his way down the long aisle to the altar.

Floating high above that altar is the baby Jesus, clad all in white, as the congregation approached the Feast of the Presentation of Our Lord in the Temple, often called Candlemas, or in Spanish, *Dia de La Candelaria.*

Projection screens on either side of the altar display prayers and responses and lyrics to hymns. In the vast throng are infants no more than a few weeks old, and tiny *abuelitas,* grandmothers at mass with children and grandchildren who tower over them. When mass ends, much of the throng fans out into waiting cars, causing local traffic delays, while another big chunk of the crowd heads to a waiting luncheon and to a lane next to the church with tables laden with goods for sale, snacks, and religious objects. The proceeds support various ministries of the church.

A short time later the only English-language mass at St. Emydius begins. The church is not full this time, even though this is the only Sunday mass in English while nine others are in Spanish, stretching across the day from six thirty in the morning until eight thirty at night. The congregants are, like the crowd that just left, almost all Latino. As I listened to families chat as they headed to pews, there were many adults who spoke to each other in Spanish and to their children in English. I figured a lot of the people who came to pray and sing and take communion would have been just fine in the Spanish mass. If you are prepared to talk to God in English instead of Spanish it is just a lot easier getting a seat.

It has long been said that the decline of church attendance and membership among the descendants of earlier immigrant groups is so large that the second largest faith identity among Americans, after Roman Catholics, is former Catholics. People who watch the church from inside and outside have credited Latinos in the recent waves of new arrivals from Central and South America, Mexico, and the Caribbean for staving off the decline seen in other Christian denominations since the beginning of this century. Close to half of all Roman Catholics in the US are Latino. A majority of the students in the nation's Catholic schools are the descendants of Spanish-speaking immigrants and long-settled Latino families.

"It's more than anecdotal. That's for sure." Fr. Allan Figueroa Deck, SJ, chatted with me at the Jesuit community house on the campus of Loyola Marymount University in Los Angeles. The Jesuit school sits on more than a hundred acres of now priceless LA County, atop a plateau offering gorgeous views of the sun-dappled Pacific in one direction and the vast city in the other. The Jesuit is a historian and sociologist and a man who is watching the trends closely for hints about the Catholic future in the US.

"About a third of those born Latino and Catholic are disaffiliated. They prefer not to identify as Catholic. Though a number of them will certainly want to baptize their child if they should have children." Even people setting aside the practice and habits of a lifetime still feel the tug of ritual and family custom. Only around 6 percent of Latinos in the United States identified with no religion in 1990. That number more than doubled by 2009 and had quintupled by the 2020s. These trends mirror those in the wider society, especially among younger Americans.

Fr. Deck said the Catholic Church could no longer rely on young adults finding their way back after major life milestones. "Traditionally one of the practices that brought people back to the institutional church was marriage. If they wanted to get married in the church, of course, but also if they wanted to have children it would occur to the couple they needed to identify a faith if they wanted to raise a child in the faith. That was our way to draw people back.

"But as you know, significant numbers of young people are not getting married. They're partnering. They're living together."

Fr. Deck's mother came to the US as a girl at the end of the Mexican Revolution. It was a series of wars and displacements stretching from 1910 into the 1920s that saw millions of Mexicans flee, both temporarily and permanently, north to the US. He reminded me that Mexicans were among the oldest inhabitants of the place where we sat, and one of the newest at the same time. Among the families at St. Emydius were families in Los Angeles County for generations, and families still finding their way in a new home.

As an academic, he watches the trends. As a Jesuit, he is understandably rooting for the home team. Moving forward, Fr. Deck sees several issues for a church challenged, fortified, and revived by immigration, not only from the Spanish-speaking nations of the hemisphere, but the Philippines and Haiti as well. In some of the other Christian denominations, he notes, "there's more viable community than in the Catholic Church." Few Catholic churches are as big as St. Emydius, with twenty thousand families on the rolls, but "the average size of an evangelical congregation is much smaller unless you're talking about these megachurches. But even megachurches are broken down into smaller groups."

As dioceses across the country close less viable churches and combine existing congregations, Catholic churches are getting bigger while Protestant churches are getting smaller. "Right now, the response of the Catholic Church to dealing with large numbers, is apples and oranges between Protestants and Catholics in terms of the size of congregations. Our response has been, especially here in the West, to build bigger churches." With so much emphasis on the role of ordained clergy, and smaller graduating classes from seminaries as fewer American men seek the priesthood, pastors now minister to vast congregations. Bringing in large numbers of immigrant priests, notably from Latin America and Africa, has not stopped the lopsided ratios of communicants to priests becoming even more lopsided.

The walls in the room where we spoke were covered with historic artifacts, documents and photos from Jesuit history in Asia and Southern California. For Fr. Deck, the way forward means taking the focus off ordained clergy and placing it more squarely on lay people, the millions who fill the pews every week across America. Gigantic churches, dwindling seminaries, and the twin challenges of migrations to secularism and other Christian churches can only be answered, in his view, by a church that returns to its roots in organization, and advocacy for the poor and powerless. He offers outspoken support for immigration reform as an example. "The Catholic bishops have been strong in defense of immigrants. And they've gotten pushback from some Catholics who seem to think that's not what their church should be doing.

"But that's what the Church is doing in a very direct way. Helping people with immigration issues. Advocating for reform of the immigration laws. And by helping immigrant people during COVID. The churches in Los Angeles became the center of education about how to protect oneself from the pandemic." Latinos are heavily concentrated in the kinds of work that led to heavy exposure to potentially infected people, in hospitals, restaurants, and supermarkets.

That church, according to a man who has given his life to it, is the one that will keep the thousands who solemnly headed to the communion rail at St. Emydius, with babies in arms, supporting the church for decades to come. The church will find its way, Fr. Deck insisted, and so will America. "There are signs in the heart of the American people that they're not going to accept racism and violence. Even though we suffer a lot from that in our society. That's not who we want to be. We have to look for that light in all people. And our country can serve as a light for other nations."

The future will bring new challenges to places like St. Emydius, serving large immigrant congregations. The youngsters wearing their St. Emydius School uniforms to mass will be increasingly English-dominant. The makeup of Lynwood will include more families of longer tenure in the US and new arrivals from Latin America at the same time. The Roman Catholic Church in the US has a Catholic future, but that is a truth that only gets you so far. The 2020 Census counted more than sixty million Latinos in the US. A majority of them are native-born citizens, while at the same time millions are not even supposed to live in the country by law. Their needs are different. What will keep them church attached is different.

Across America's vast and diverse religious landscape, change and adaptation are demanded as the price of staying alive. It is a story being written as you read this page.

And what became of our old friend Bhagat Singh Thind?

He waited more than a decade to try a third time to become a citizen of his adopted country. He earned a PhD in theology and English literature. After twenty years in the US, he based his renewed petition on the language of the just-passed Alien Veteran Naturalization Act. The 1935 law specifically overruled the race-based language in existing immigration law, the language that blocked Thind's struggle to become an American citizen a decade and a half earlier. The 1935 law required an honorable discharge and continued residence in the US and opened the door to the Sikh scholar and other Asian veterans of World War I. Thind lived long enough to see his adopted homeland open its doors to the people of Asia, Africa, and Latin America. A student of Emerson and Thoreau, a popular writer on religion, a widely traveled lecturer on spirituality, he died at seventy-five, more than thirty years after gaining his hard-won American citizenship.

CHAPTER FIVE

AFRICANS IN AMERICA: A 21ST-CENTURY STORY

I had no idea there were two Americas.

— Dr. Olofunmilayo "Funmi" Olopade

Let us assume you have decided to leave the country where you were born.

It is hard.

You will leave behind the familiar places and people of a lifetime.

You may have to master a new language, a challenging new climate and landscape. Your native country may now seem hostile to you for ethnic, economic, or religious reasons. You may have political beliefs that clash with the ruling powers of the day. Yet you may have found that your aspirations, your dreams of an education, your life's ambitions, simply could not be lived out in your homeland.

There is no longer any avoiding it. You have to go.

Then, you look at a map of the world. You talk to members of your extended family who've headed out to the wider world looking for a better place. One country comes up repeatedly as you talk to teachers, friends, neighbors, family members. In the long-distant past people who looked like you, people from your part of the world, were brought to that same country as *property*. They were bought and sold. They were beaten, abused, and murdered. They were forced to work the rest of their lives in captivity for no wages, and the children they produced became property, too, from the very day they emerged wet and screaming into a waiting world.

Of course, you remind yourself, that was a long time ago. Will that history have any effect on me? On my life?

The blood-soaked story of legal abuse and exploitation of Africans as property ended in the 19th century. However, what followed — while not quite as drenched in evil and cruelty — was a socially and legally tolerated form of economic marginalization and widespread abuse, with plenty of bloodshed. Many of the places where people from your homeland — now former slaves and their descendants — were living allowed only an inferior form of citizenship that resulted in lower educational attainment, shorter life expectancies, higher levels of chronic disease, and discrimination that made it hard to break the cycle of suffering.

You have heard things are better, but even in recent years the newspapers in your own capital ran stories of people who looked like you being killed by police, being confined to residential ghettoes, being consigned to a different and lower status in society.

Where would *that* country appear on your list? Would that place become the North Star, the goal for your struggle to reach to live out your dreams? Once you decide you have to leave, would you go *there,* especially if there might be other places in the world you could go?

Would an African choose to move to the United States?

Would descendants of Africans somewhere else in the world want to move to a country carrying such heavy baggage from history?

In the 21st century, the answer is increasingly yes. Thousands of Black immigrants have been arriving in the United States from Africa and Latin America voluntarily. It is a story with unexpected twists and turns, and a sign of hope that the US might be able to shake off some of its past. In this century the lamp held high by the Statue of Liberty, of "liberty enlightening the world," is not meant to speak to people from just one region of the world. It shines to every corner of the planet.

"People are still dreaming of coming to the US because of liberty, justice, and freedom, which does not exist everywhere," said Djibreel, an immigrant from Senegal.

For Solomon, who came as a teenager from Ethiopia, America's racial history did not operate as a deterrent. "I think there's more of a deterrent for someone to come from a former British colony to go to the UK than to the United States. I think the perception in sub-Saharan Africa is that it is easier to get ahead in life in the US even with its problems than it would be in the UK or France."

During the years I hosted a national radio show, cabbies — immigrants stuck behind the wheel all day — were some of my most loyal listeners. In Boston, New York, San Francisco, and Washington, DC, a driver might hear my voice giving him a destination or address, and without looking in the rearview mirror say, "Are you Ray Suarez?" On a rainy day in Washington, DC, I got to talking about a recent program on Africa. The driver was an immigrant from Somalia. After giving me his opinion of the several simmering conflicts in the Horn of Africa, his home region, he now wanted my input on another matter entirely.

"Do you have kids?" he asked. I told him I did. He followed up to see if they went to District of Columbia public schools. Yes, they did. "Ah, then you will understand my question!" He proceeded to tell me about his teenaged son, born shortly after he and his wife had arrived from Africa.

"Every year, they must fill out forms from school about various things, and they ask about your race, or your nationality. When my son fills out these forms he puts down that he is African American!" The driver checked my face in the rearview mirror. It probably didn't tell him much because I was still wondering where this story was going.

"He is not African American! I tell him not to put that down. I tell him, 'You are African!'" The cross-generational tension is a product of something very new and something very old at the same time. For much of American history, Black Americans were almost all native born. I mention to my very emotional driver that his son's high school, like most in Washington, had an overwhelmingly Black student population.

The overwhelming majority of his classmates checked, or marked, "African American" without a moment's hesitation. Since the term started to pick up traction in the 1980s it had become a virtual synonym, in everyday use, for Black. For my driver, the term was very clearly meant to denote the descendants of people brought from Africa to North America in the 17th, 18th, and 19th centuries. For him, the term was meant to describe descendants of enslaved men and women, not a Somali American son of immigrants. The driver's teenaged son, a young Black man born in America, was being challenged by his old man to choose between his friends and his life in Washington, DC, and a place he had likely never seen.

I asked the driver, "Since he was born here, and his parents are African, he has more claim to being an African American than all his classmates, doesn't he? As an African, born in America, why isn't he African American?"

He was having none of it. "You know that is not what they are trying to find out!" His agitation came from competing immigrant impulses as old as the country itself, and it was unique, derived very specifically from the Black experience in America. "Those other boys in his class are American!" His voice switched to an emphatic staccato to bang home his point. "My son! Is. An. African!"

*   *   *

In the forty years from 1980 to 2020, the number of people from sub-Saharan Africa permanently living in the United States grew an amazing sixteen-fold, from some 130,000 to more than 2.1 million.

If you read the newspapers, or watched newsreels in theaters in Nigeria, Ghana, or Senegal in the decades leading up to, and just after World War II, the US would have featured prominently. For people living in British and French colonies, the beacons of Black achievement in America would have shown brightly through the 20th century and offered glimpses of some of the best-known Black people on the planet: boxing champions Jack Johnson and Joe Louis; entertainers Paul Robeson, Josephine Baker, and Nat King Cole; barrier-breaking athletes like Jesse Owens and Jackie Robinson; trailblazing UN deputy secretary general Ralph Bunche; and, eventually, Nobel laureate Martin Luther King. Those same newsreels and newspapers would have shown you the battered body of Chicago teenager Emmett Till, lynched in Mississippi, police turning firehoses on marchers, whites torching Freedom Riders' buses, Medgar Evers's and Malcolm X's lifeless bodies, and Martin Luther King behind bars.

As the Cold War chilled, and the tug-of-war of East and West struggling over influence in the rapidly decolonizing Global South intensified, Soviet news agencies and influence campaigns in the developing world were only too happy to amplify the bad news. Moscow-sponsored information campaigns were bringing America's ongoing racial struggle to audiences in Africa, Asia, and Latin America through the 1950s and 1960s. That explains in part why the Washington-based broadcaster Voice of America rushed to announce the results of the *Brown v. Board of Education of Topeka, Kansas* ruling in more than thirty-four languages worldwide.

The 2020 Census counted just over 330 million people living in the US. After decades of wrestling with the definitions of racial origins, the Census Bureau now gives people many choices for explaining their identity to the federal government. In the instructions for the race question is this language: "The category 'Black or African-American' includes all individuals who identify with one or more nationalities or ethnic groups originating in any of the black racial groups of Africa." Thus, actress Charlize Theron or industrialist Elon Musk, while born in Africa, and making their homes in the US, would not call themselves "African American," at least not on their census form.

The instructions continue, "Examples of these groups include, but are not limited to, African American, Jamaican, Haitian, Nigerian, Ethiopian, and Somali. This category also includes groups such as Ghanaian, South African, Barbadian, Kenyan, Liberian, and Bahamian." In the last few censuses room has also been made for mixed-race people to self-define, to tell the government what they consider themselves to be.

With these provisions, just a little more than one out of every seven people living in the country identify in some way as Black, some thirty-nine million people in all.

In earlier counts, from seventy, eighty, or one hundred years ago, almost all of the people tabulated in this group would have been native-born. Today, fully one of every ten Black people living in America was born in another country.

They had no such power of self-definition in 1790, the year the first census was tabulated. People from Africa had been coming to Britain's North American colonies since the first enslaved person arrived in 1619. They were imported, brought to slave markets on the eastern seaboard until 1808, when the British Navy began widely enforcing its ban on the transatlantic slave trade. In the first census the government reckoned the total US population was just a hair under four million people. That number consisted of 1.6 million white men and women, 59,000 "free people" of unspecified race, and some 700,000 enslaved people, about 18 percent of the entire population. Almost one in five Americans was held in bondage.

In 1960, the US Census counted a little over 179 million people living in the country. Of that number, just over twenty million were deemed "non-white." Almost all of them — nearly nineteen million, a little over 10 percent of the population — was, in the language of that year's census, Negro. There had been a Great Migration of many of them from southern to northern states, but very few new arrivals from abroad. Until the Immigration and Nationality Act of 1965, which changed so much about global migrations to America.

Today there are almost five million Black immigrants living in the United States, of a total African American population of more than 41 million. Their arrival in the US is so recent they represent a sizable chunk, about a fifth, of all Black population growth of the previous forty years. Like all other immigrants, they trend younger than the population as a whole and thus are more heavily concentrated in child-rearing years. Almost one of every ten Black people in America has at least one foreign-born parent.

The top five birth countries for these immigrants are Jamaica, Haiti, Nigeria, Ethiopia, and the Dominican Republic. The three Caribbean nations were possessions of three different European empires, the United Kingdom, France, and Spain. Two of the five in Africa are the most populous countries on the continent, and geographically diverse, one on the Atlantic Ocean, one near the Red Sea. One is a former British colony, and Nigerians have moved in large numbers to Britain as well. While the other, Ethiopia, was one of the few places on that vast continent that was an independent state, relatively untouched by Europe's 19th-century scramble for Africa. Toward the end of the 20th century Ethiopia ended up in a violent tug of war between East and West in the final chapters of the Cold War, when civil war and famine sent people pouring out to the countries that would take them in.

Proximity, geography, and historic ties to established communities in the US make it natural that Caribbeans comprise the largest share of Black immigrants coming to the United States. But the 2020 Census reveals that the fifty countries of Africa are sending a faster-growing share of new residents to America. Taken together, they are nothing less than a people ready to write a new history for Black people on this continent.

* * *

Dr. Olofunmilayo "Funmi" Olopade, an oncologist at the University of Chicago Medical Centers, was finishing her medical education at the University of Ibadan in Nigeria in the late 1970s. She is the fifth of six children born to an Anglican priest. Her siblings were already living and studying in the US. Today a celebrated physician and researcher, an internationally recognized expert in the treatment of breast cancer, she remembered an optimistic time for Nigeria, and a growing sense of welcome from the US.

"Jimmy Carter actually came to Nigeria to promote trade with America and investment in education." The US was searching for steady, reliable sources of oil after cutting off purchases from Iran during the hostage crisis, and Nigeria became a new source. "Anyone who had the academic merits to go to school went to school for free. And there I was, in medical school free of charge. And there was the American Peace Corps. I remember this big guy, Chuck, who came to Nigeria and he was on a local basketball team. We were friends. I was on the badminton team, and my boyfriend, now my husband, was on the Nigerian Cricket Team.

"We traveled through Africa. Nigeria was going to be the pride of Africa because we had money. Then there was FESTAC 77, the Festival of Arts and Culture. Because of the money with oil, we wanted to bring all Africans in the diaspora back to Nigeria because they'd been oppressed. We wanted to end apartheid in South Africa. It was our responsibility as young people to do that. It was a hopeful time."

When Olopade finished medical school her parents sent her to the San Francisco Bay area to visit her brother, who had been studying at Stanford. Instead of finishing his planned PhD and returning to Nigeria, he was trying to get started in a new career in the young days of Silicon Valley. She was up for the trip, after years of listening to the Voice of America and the recent visit from the American president. She got a special, low-fare ticket that gave her the chance to visit five US states for just 200 dollars ($820 in 2022). "It became clear that America was huge and was the Land of Opportunity."

Her brother had decided he was not going home to Nigeria but into management at General Electric. He wondered how his little sister could be credentialed to practice medicine in the US. She approached San Francisco General Hospital and University of California San Francisco. "They said, 'We couldn't take you in our program because we just don't take international students.' Implying that I was not qualified to be here. Then they said, 'Well, maybe you could target county hospitals.' I asked where they could be. 'Well, there's one in Chicago.'

"I looked at where I had friends. Where the Discover America ticket would take us. At the end of the summer I landed in Chicago. It was a beautiful day. I thought, 'This is great.' And they gave me a job right there and then. It was right at the beginning of the AIDS crisis, and public hospitals could not find enough doctors.

"I was young and restless. They gave me the job, but I said I wasn't married. I'm not coming because it was so important to get married. Sola was playing cricket and was my best friend in medical school. I went back home and thought about it and by November I thought, 'Okay, I have a job in America. I'm not married. I didn't want to leave Nigeria until I was married, so how is this going to work?'

"But now we were both excited about how this is a great country and maybe we should come. My brother was really enjoying Silicon Valley. Because Cook County Hospital was short-staffed, they offered me the job and I took it. I said, 'I will come after Christmas,' because I wanted to spend Christmas with my parents.

"I was already a full-fledged doctor, and after my first visit I left knowing that I wanted to come back. My husband was going to play cricket for the Nigerian team at Lord's in London," a Mecca of the game, roughly the equivalent for an American baseball player getting a chance to play at Yankee Stadium. "I was going to go through London to Chicago, and then sit for the qualifying exam, because that was the one thing standing between me and America. And I was thinking, 'Boy, it is a hard exam.' As the bus drove through Westminster Abbey, I stopped to go pray. I thought, 'If I pass this exam, I will forever serve you, Lord.'"

Olopade passed and was certified to practice medicine in Illinois. With her qualification and new job at Cook County Hospital, she was able to get her husband, also a newly minted doctor, his green card. The young family began its American journey. Until then the two young doctors had been excited to discover a new country and to get to work. Her arrival at a public hospital on the edge of an enormous, economically challenged Black neighborhood, isolated and medically underserved, began a new phase of Olopade's education.

"The first thing was this is not Palo Alto and Silicon Valley. I had no idea there were two Americas.

"The people that I took care of every day at Cook County had nothing. And the government just packed everybody in. So from my first entry, I realized how hard it was for Black people, people of color in America. Jimmy Carter had lost the elections. Reagan started with his 'structural adjustment policies,'" (which saw the new Republican president get tough on lending to developing nations), "and it was the beginning of the end for Nigeria. The beginning of the end for everything we ever dreamed of. By the time we returned to pick up our visa to remain in the US there was a military coup in Nigeria."

When Olopade was in primary school civil war broke out in Nigeria, as the oil-rich southern region of Biafra tried to break away from the rest of the country. The north-south political tension was also a religious conflict, since Muslims dominated the north and Christians the south, and persists to this day. Olopade's father, a child of the decolonizing generation, was aggrieved to watch the country fight a civil war, and did not pressure his daughter to remain, even as an old-school patriarch saw his daughter begin a career an ocean away. She recalled him saying, "Not only are you number five of six children, you're also a woman. So if they had asked me to pick who should come to America, it would not be you!"

Back home in Nigeria, medical advisors only knew of America's reputation for trauma medicine, along with pop-culture references to Chicago's Al Capone and more recent racial strife. Cook County Hospital, serving a population drawn from some of the poorest zip codes in urban

America, provided a stunning contrast with affluent, sun-drenched Silicon Valley. Olopade said, "If I had not landed at Cook County I don't think I would have learned America and the oppression of Black people the way I learned it." It was all coming at her pretty fast, marriage and immigration, a new country and a new child, and leaving life in a country where everyone was Black to make a home in a city with many Black citizens, but few Black doctors. "We were calling around for places to live. The realtor picked up the call and said, 'Oh, you have an accent.' I said, 'We are looking for a larger place and we want to move from the city.' He said, 'Where are you from?' I said, 'Well, we're Nigerian.' And he said, 'Oh, this place ain't for you, honey,' and he hung up the phone!" She laughed, recalling the encounter, and that she had not yet learned there were places two Black doctors could, and could not live.

Both Olopades were moving ahead quickly. Funmi won, and accepted, a fellowship at the University of Chicago Medical Center, which would become her longtime academic home. At the same time her husband, Sola, was offered a similar post at the renowned Mayo Clinic in Rochester, Minnesota. They split up for the training and the opportunity, but when Mayo wanted to offer her husband a permanent position, Funmi said no. "I said, I can't raise our children in Rochester, Minnesota. We have already gone to the suburbs. This will be over my dead body."

Instead, the couple settled in Hyde Park, the South Side Chicago neighborhood where the University of Chicago and its affiliated schools sit. The enormous institutional heft of the University managed to keep Hyde Park an integrated island in a sea of rapidly resegregating neighborhoods. Using a mixture of lowered density, changed traffic patterns, and physical impediments, Hyde Park was walled off from next-door Woodlawn, a formerly white working-class neighborhood that was now entirely Black, and increasingly poor. The young doctors might not necessarily have been able to put their fingers on what they felt, but Funmi saw the ways class, education, and race shaped society in a place like Chicago, far from the genteel precincts of Hyde Park.

"Sola wasn't home. I was invited to the Black Creativity Gala, put on by the Black elites in Chicago." She was the guest of a priest from her downtown church, the Episcopal cathedral. "I thought, 'Oh my God, look at all these amazing Black people! How come I've never seen them or met them?' I was speaking to a woman who said, 'Well, you know, you're from Africa. Do you think you are better than us? That the whites accept you, and don't accept us?'"

It was then she realized, she said, that many Black Chicagoans were convinced that even having education, money, and status was not enough to force open the doors to events thrown by white peers in the city. "I realized that there were not only two Americas, Black and white, but that even elite Americans were in totally different social circles. There was nothing these people had in common [with wealthy whites]." Being active in her lifelong church home — the Anglican Church of Nigeria is part of the same global faith community as the Episcopal Church in the United States — had obscured how separated social life was in the city, even among socioeconomic peers. Hyde Park was comfortable for the Olopades, among kindred spirits, "but it's a university neighborhood that Black people see as an island, a genteel, integrated anomaly floating in a sea of poor Black neighborhoods."

During the Trump years, word leaked from the White House that the President had lamented that not enough immigrants were trying to come to the United States from countries like Norway — incidentally, one of the richest countries on the planet — and instead were seeking entry from what the chief executive called "shithole countries." Trump mused that Nigerians would not want to return to Africa after their educations because they "wouldn't want to return to their huts." Nigeria was an oil power, home to the megalopolis of Lagos, a continental cultural powerhouse, and home to millions of university students. Directly relevant to the subject of immigration, it was the birthplace of the most educationally successful of all immigrants in the US. For all this, even in the 21st century, the President of the United States could not get beyond "huts," as if nothing had changed about Africa in the generations since black-and-white Tarzan films flickered at Saturday matinees in neighborhood movie houses.

Becoming rooted in America took the Olopades some time. They had arrived in the country fired up with the idealistic dream of getting the best training the US had and bringing it back to Nigeria. To hear the doctor tell her story is to hear competing strands of recollection, of having young children, advancing in a career, and watching the news from Nigeria in dismay, as the go-go years of growth gave way to sectional, ethnic, religious strife and serial coups and alternating military and civilian governments. Dreams of relocating back to Africa faded away.

The young doctors fell into a rhythm of returning to Nigeria occasionally with their growing family but did not go home for good. Funmi noted that the first new car she and Sola bought in America was bought specially with a stick shift because they planned to take it back to Nigeria. The kids were now well into elementary school, and "we knew we could no longer take them away. Our stick shift dream was dead, so I joined the faculty [at the University of Chicago] and negotiated a trip back home because if I didn't go home, my father was now eighty-three and I would probably never see him again. So before I finished my fellowship, after ten years of never going home because we could not afford it, my signing bonus was [used] to return. We had a reunion at home, and that was the last time I saw my father alive.

"That felt victorious for me that at least I got there before he died." Nigeria's economic downfall and the new military dictatorship made their birthplace a country to which they no longer wanted to return to live. "Even if you wanted to go back, you couldn't go back. So you have to make a home of *this* place."

Around the same time Dr. Olopade was starting her American career at Cook County Hospital, Solomon Kibriye was also making the long journey across the Atlantic. He was just thirteen, and his homeland, Ethiopia, was mired in civil war. A Soviet-backed Marxist guerrilla movement, the Derg, had taken over the central government. Ethnic/regional armies rose in various corners of the vast country and just over the border in neighboring countries, and those armies were conscripting younger and younger boys to fight.

"The requirement was based on height at that point because they needed soldiers so badly. My younger brother and I were approaching that height." Instead of going by the data on your birth certificate, the standard for being ready to carry a weapon into battle resembled an amusement park ride. "I was thirteen, he was ten, and our father brought us out of Ethiopia to live with our aunt and uncle in New Jersey. That's how I ended up in the United States," Kibriye said.

Interview a Senegalese or Malian, and they may mention France, the former colonial power, as a possible destination. Talk to Ghanaians and Nigerians, and London or Birmingham may pop up, as Portugal does for Angolans. Historically, Ethiopia is an African anomaly. In the great 19th-century scramble for Africa by the European colonial powers, it went unconquered and uncolonized for generations. Italy invaded multiple times and occupied the country during the early 20th century but never created the kind of links that France and Britain forged, for better and worse, with their African colonies.

"The United States was the preeminent Western and anti-communist power at the time. And Ethiopia being an ally of the East Bloc after the 1974 revolution, the US in particular seemed to attract those who wanted to get out during the Derg regime. It wasn't easy to do, but there were also a lot of people who had connections in the US," Kibriye said. His aunt in New Jersey had married an American citizen decades earlier, clearing the way for a kid fleeing communism. Ethiopians had been coming to the US for higher education during the years Emperor Haile Selassie was on the throne. Many had stayed after completing degrees, or after marrying Americans. "The US was open to receive people fleeing Ethiopia, which was a Communist ally at the time. There was a perception of America as a land of opportunity where people could work and advance themselves, and I think Ethiopians have done pretty well."

Kibriye said America's complicated racial history was not a deterrent to moving there. It was certainly less of a deterrent, Kibriye said, than for an African from a former British colony heading to the United Kingdom. "I think there is a more direct negative experience with colonialism than there would be to the more remote history of slavery. Of course the fight for civil rights was even more recent, but there were figures who were very popular in Africa like Dr. Martin Luther King and Malcolm X. They appealed to African imaginations. There was a perception in sub-Saharan Africa that it was easier to get ahead in the US even with its problems than it would be in the UK or France."

The Ethiopian-born banker and church deacon, now an American citizen of long standing, did concede that Africans may not fully understand what they are getting into until they are here. Remember Funmi Olopade's surprise at finding there were two Americas? Kibriye notes that while there may be ethnic, linguistic, and religious rivalries inside the borders of African nations, these tensions are different, "especially in a country like Ethiopia where there has been no colonial legacy. If you haven't experienced direct racism, if you were in a dominant culture, and then you come here, it doesn't hit you right away. It takes a number of years before you realize, 'Aha, I'm being treated differently because of my skin color.' Before that, you have the knowledge that it occurs, but it doesn't really hit home until you actually experience it."

At thirteen, you are not a little child, and well short of being a grown adult. You can see a lot and miss a lot. Suddenly, here he was, product of a private school in the Ethiopian capital, Addis Ababa, run along British lines, speaking English with a British accent, living with an aunt and uncle he knew only slightly. "I knew them, but I didn't know them. They weren't people I saw every day. I knew who they were, and I knew they were loving and welcoming. And they took really good care of us. But separation from your parents is very difficult at that age. The homesickness was very difficult."

If most Americans don't really know much about Africa today, they knew even less in the Reagan years. Kibriye recounts being asked by well-meaning people if he had lived in a house back in Ethiopia. People making small talk wondered if he was now accustomed to wearing shoes.

Did you go to school outdoors? In his Catholic school in southern New Jersey, classmates were surprised to hear their new classmate had gone to school in a car back in Africa. Their expectation was of "someone from a refugee camp. Or the jungle. Or the savannah."

Kibriye was homesick. He missed his family. The conditions that forced his family to get him, and his brother, out of the country persisted for a long time, well into the 1990s. The process of letting go of the dream of returning home to make his adult life was "very gradual." Before the Marxist revolutionaries overthrew the emperor, Ethiopians came as sojourners. They came for higher education, maybe a few years of work, and many then headed home. After 1974, he said, everything changed. "That first wave of Ethiopian immigrants were either connected to the imperial government, or fleeing the emperor's government, or they were feeling the strife of the revolution. So they were mostly political refugees.

"There was always the hope, 'We will go back. Communism will fall, and we'll go back.' There was a sense of impermanence, really. People worked and bought houses and opened businesses. But what struck me was that when they opened churches, they were always churches in exile. Meaning, 'eventually we're going to take this church and go home with this church.' I think it was pretty much the same with Ethiopian mosques. There was just a sense that we're not here forever."

Kibriye went back home to Ethiopia for the first time in 1986. He was a college student. The Derg was still in power, but he was now thinking seriously about moving back. "I had to renew my student visa in order to go back to the States and finish school. So I went to the American embassy, and the immigration counselor there was like, 'I'm not really inclined to give you a visa because you have a lot of family there, relatives that have been there and settled as citizens and green card holders. I don't think you'll ever want to come back, so I'm not inclined to give you a visa.'

"And I had a visceral reaction. I kind of find it funny now. But at the time it was like, 'Oh no! No no no no no. This is home. This is home. I have to come back here!' I said, 'I can't imagine living anywhere else. This is my country. This is where I belong.' He said, 'Oh, okay,' and he gave me the visa."

The years that followed brought the gradual Americanization of Solomon Kibriye. Once he decided to stay, he began to walk the legal maze that challenges aspiring entrants from all over the world. Kibriye's mother had moved to the US as well, went to work for the United Nations, and brought his young siblings with her. The kids would qualify for a green card, the status of a lawful permanent resident, when their mother did. By that time, however, Kibriye had aged out. He was too old to be sponsored by his mother as a so-called G-4 dependent.

He could ask the United States for refugee status, but asking for political asylum would have barred him from ever going back to Ethiopia while the Derg still ran the country, and it was hard to tell if the regime of Haile Mengistu was ever going to crumble. But there was another way: Kibriye had become an ordained deacon in the Ethiopian Orthodox Church as a boy. Short of clergy in America, and needing all hands on deck for a growing network of churches, the church sponsored Kibriye for a green card.

Even now, in his fifties, having lived much more of his life in the US than in Ethiopia, Kibriye is still reminded from time to time that what America sees is not an African, not an immigrant, not a naturalized American by choice, but simply a Black man. It happens when he is followed around a retail store by a member of staff as he scans the shelves. When sitting with a white coworker in a car in Queens, New York, one of the most diverse places in the world, and he is surrounded by plainclothes cops who take him out of the vehicle and search for drugs.

Once, while working at a pickup/drop-off photo booth back in the days of film cameras, Kibriye's booth was robbed at knifepoint. Once his assailant fled, he called the police. He gave what he thought was a thorough description, and officers fanned out in search. Minutes later, they returned with a man they had detained on a nearby subway platform who did not match the description he gave at all, save one attribute. He was Black.

"They asked, 'Is this him?' And I said, 'No!' And the guy was like 'Thank you, thank you!' and they let him go. They just went in there and grabbed the first Black guy they found. And you know, that shocked me. I suddenly realized that could have been me.

"They could have grabbed me and if the person hadn't had a clear picture of the person who robbed them, they might have said, 'Yeah, that might be him.' And what's going to happen? It was scary."

One turning point in Kibriye's American journey was September 11, 2001.

"I actually watched the planes go into the buildings. And I felt assaulted." The attack against America felt personal. "And I really felt, 'Okay. This is my country. I've lived here for decades and I can't imagine living anywhere else.' That kind of prompted me to get my citizenship.

"There was a time when I said, 'I'm absolutely going back to my country. Back to Ethiopia.' It was my country. But eventually the feeling came, this is my country, too. With all its flaws, with all the problems and frustrations. I've never voted for an Ethiopian government. But I've voted in every American election since President Obama. And I vote in every little local election as well. I never miss an election because I remember living in a society where elections just didn't exist. The Derg ruled Ethiopia. Or there were elections, but there was just one candidate for every office.

"It's an important right. It's a privilege. So I take full advantage of that."

For Djibreel Diagne, Senegalese by birth, American by choice, the story is pretty simple and straightforward. "I've always been dreaming of coming to the US." He majored in English at university, and watched friends and other students plot their departures for France. Not him. After college, he worked as a teacher, saved his money, and planned. In 1999, he asked for a visa, got one almost immediately, "And once the opportunity was there, I came here, and stayed."

What emerges from a long conversation with Diagne, now in the US for decades, was a determination to choose his own path and an insistence on making it on his own. Like many of his friends growing up, he dreamed of studying abroad. Unlike many of those friends, he had no relatives, no family network capable of helping him reach that goal. He had done well in high school, but the chance of a scholarship abroad did not materialize.

"I didn't lose hope. I didn't hold a grudge toward anybody. I thought, 'I'm going to make it. I have to make it on my own. I don't have to depend on other people.' That consciousness grew in me. It was that drive that got me to finish college. It was that drive that got me through the training to become a teacher. It kept me going until opportunity presented itself."

In many African societies, someone who is perceived as "making it" — getting an advanced position in the civil service, in business, or the armed forces — is expected to provide for a family network. Many of the men and women getting ahead in African capitals are connected by blood and obligation to an array of relations, often far away in rural areas. It emerges in Diagne's telling that there were relatives who might have given him a leg up, but he was determined not to ask for help.

But why America? Did it occur to him it might be a very tough place to be a Black man? "Everybody knows that, yes, slavery is part of the history of the United States. And those slaves were taken from the African continent. We know that.

"Some of those slaves came from Senegal. We know that. Or Guinea, or Nigeria, or Cameroon, all the way down to Angola. Yes, we know that. All these Black folks who are here, no matter where they come from, they are Black people. They are from Africa." Having lived north and south, and after serving in the US Army, Diagne said racism is present everywhere. He observed, "Not anymore is it allowed in the Constitution. It's not tolerated. It's not encouraged by the laws of this country. But it's hard to kick the habit."

He mourned the fact that some American politicians are, in his view, willing to help their careers by taking the country backward in race relations. Yet Diagne understands why they might. "People still hold the firm belief that they are above everybody else because of the color of their skin. It's very entrenched in society, but it's never prevented people from coming here.

"People are still dreaming of coming to the US because of liberty and justice and freedom. They do not exist everywhere."

Diagne was living and working in Alexandria, Virginia, on September 11, 2001. The Pentagon is a major regional transit hub, home not only to the US military but to an enormous bus station above ground and several rapid transit lines below. He had already passed through when the Pentagon was attacked, switched from a bus to a train and headed for work across the river in Washington, DC, when a jumbo jet slammed into the building.

Later in that fateful decade Diagne joined the Army Reserves, stayed for eight years, and was sent overseas but never deployed to a combat zone. I asked if it was a tense time for him, since he, like the vast majority of Senegalese, is Muslim. He is proud of being a student of history and has been disappointed to find how few Americans know the long history of US encounters and interactions with Islam, from the Muslim West African slaves brought to these shores in the 17th century, to the treaty of peace and friendship signed with Morocco in the 18th century, to Abraham Lincoln's correspondence with the Ottoman sultan in Constantinople in the 19th century.

If the tone, the attitude, the welcome toward Muslims has changed in the 21st century, it has not been visited on Diagne, who as a translator and advance man has worked to further the interests of a West African Muslim movement, the Mourides, for years. "I have never in my twenty-two years here felt that sentiment of hate or unwelcomeness. I have never. I have been fortunate to never encounter that."

Today a resident of Harlem, in New York City, Diagne takes pains to tell me that he not only has to correct the historical record about Islam among white Americans but battle stereotypes about Africans among the

Black residents of Harlem, namely, that his ancestors bear a primary responsibility for selling their ancestors into bondage.

While it is true that slave traders bought captives from Black Africans, the sellers most often did not see the humans they sold as "their own," since they were prisoners of war or kidnapped from other African nations and ethnic groups. The hard men leading captives to the coast to be sold to Portuguese, Spanish, Dutch, or British middlemen were not selling "their own people" any more than Adolf Hitler was bombing "his own people" in Rotterdam, Warsaw, or Coventry, or Charles Cromwell conquered "his own people" in Ireland. Conversely, he battles stereotypes that his West African immigrant friends hold about their new African American neighbors, about criminality, and lack of education. In short, he is a bridge. Maybe even better, an interchange, shuttling knowledge between one group and another.

He is disappointed there is so little interaction between native-born and immigrant residents of Harlem. That only increases the suspicions each group holds for the other. "Some young Senegalese told me that when they arrived here their parents told them not to frequent African Americans. They don't want their kids to hang with the wrong crowd." Like generations of immigrants to the US before him, Diagne is an old hand ready to guide newcomers. He told me most immigrant parents are not resentful or afraid of their new neighbors. They are instead struggling, as many have before, to insulate their children from everything they fear about a new place with new pitfalls.

"There's violence in the street. There's drugs in the street. There's all types of things that can take you down the wrong path. But that's not what they're saying. They believe that if you mind your own business and avoid hanging with the wrong crowd, you can make it. But if you don't, it's going to be hard for you.

"That's the same feeling any parents have, be it American or African, Senegalese, whatever. You want your kid to live in a safe environment, go to school, succeed in life, and be a good citizen."

I asked Diagne the question I asked every immigrant in my

coast-to-coast travels. Are you an American? His answer distilled themes you might have heard from a Dubliner in 1880, a Sicilian in 1900, or a Pole in 1920.

"I am. One hundred percent. I was born in Senegal, but I don't have anything in Senegal anymore. I don't know how to navigate it. So how can I pretend not to be an American? I can navigate here. I can have whatever I want here that I can't have in Senegal. Senegal is my home country. I was born and raised and spent half my life there.

"Anything I have. Anything I built in my life, well, this is where I got it. So I cannot deny that I am an American. This is where I live. This is where I wake up and go to work. This is where my family is. So why deny it?"

Americans can sometimes take complicated things and flatten them. Collapse distinctions. Elide differences. It makes it simpler when trying to take in a complicated world. We easily use the term "Asian American" to describe people whose ancestry traces back to an enormous land mass that stretches across much of the earth, from Tel Aviv to Tokyo, from Mecca to Manila, and is home to most of humanity. Immigrants who come from places as different as Iran and Korea might not see each other as "fellow Asians," or fellow anything, really, but find they are "Asians" once they settle in America. In that regard, Africa is no different.

There are some fifty countries on the continent. The phrase "Dark Continent" may feel a little antiquated, but it stayed "dark" in a lot of people's minds. Unknown. Undefined. Americans couldn't name more than a few African nations even during the height of the Cold War, as East and West battled for influence there. They remained unaware of the history, the dazzling diversity, and the tremendous potential of the continent. Africans, from north to south and east to west, don't share a language, a history, a religion, or a skin color. They share little in the way of cultural markers like food, clothing, music, family traditions, or craft. That tendency might have been partly flattened by the centuries of slavery, when owners aggressively moved to blot out language, religion, and folkways that traveled with captured bodies across the Atlantic Ocean. Until genetic test kits like 23andMe, few African Americans could claim a specific part of the vast continent as part of their own history. Folk memory in today's New York, Philadelphia, or Atlanta could only take you as far back as a farm in South Carolina, Georgia, or Mississippi, where your family was forced to work for nothing.

Coming as a 21st-century immigrant carries none of that compulsion to abandon who you were in order to complete the surrender to who you are. Thus the new Americans show their ethnicity, along with their race, in a way that's new for sons and daughters of Africa on these shores. The idea of asking the descendants of Irish, Italian, Hungarian, and Dutch immigrants to simply identify as "European" as a catch-all status might seem vaguely ridiculous, but that's what America did to African Americans.

We think of Tony Soprano on a folding chair in front of a pork store in New Jersey, a Cajun accordion player putting dancers through their paces in Louisiana, a glad-handing Irish pol in South Boston, and Swedes in a church procession in a small town in Nebraska as very different. Their familiarity as American "types" makes it self-evident that these people were, and are, very different from each other.

The next America may learn the difference between a Cape Verdean restaurateur in Providence, a Gambian imam leading his Brooklyn congregants in Friday prayers in a storefront mosque, and a Nigerian engineer walking into a meeting in a Houston oil company. For now, for many of us, they might all be "African." However, migration histories, home countries, and tenure in America tell very different stories as these new Americans try to make it here.

As a group, African immigrants to the United States are better educated than the US population as a whole and have higher rates of workforce participation than other Americans. An astonishing 64 percent of Nigerians hold four-year degrees, compared to around 33 percent of Americans as a whole. The most educated Africans—Nigerians, South

Africans, Cameroonians—are heavily clustered in management, business, scientific research, and the arts. Somalis, younger, poorer, and less educated, are concentrated as drivers, movers, and other transportation-related workers.

When Africans leave their home countries they are more likely to resettle within Africa than to move to other continents. In the 21st century, when they do leave Africa, the US is the number one destination, followed by the United Kingdom, France, Italy, and Canada. When they choose the US, African-born immigrants naturalize—that is, take American citizenship—at a higher rate than other foreign-born Americans.

Just as the African-born population has soared since the turn of the century, so has the amount of money they send to family back home. Those bonds of obligation that stretched from a government ministry to a farm back home are now transcontinental, with some countries positively kept afloat by remittances from the US. Unstable and fractured Somalia derives 35 percent of its national income from US immigrant remittances. After suffering its birth pains, and long years of armed struggle to separate itself from Sudan, South Sudan gets 30 percent of its national income from immigrants in the US, despite the hugely valuable oil reserves in its national territory. Even tiny Lesotho, long dependent on migrant workers who headed to South Africa to toil in the mines, gets more than a fifth of its GDP from people in America. What happened with Italian immigrants over a century ago is happening again with Africans in America.

Supporting family back home is a way to demonstrate, to yourself and others, that you are a moral person, according to Martha Lagace, an anthropologist and researcher with African Communities Together, an immigrant support and advocacy organization based in New York. "In a way, it's subjecting oneself to hardship as a way of proving one's worth." Religion reinforces the power of obligation, Lagace said. "There's an expectation that things will be hard. But a lot of people are motivated by, and supported by, religious faith."

Legal immigrants from Africa are more likely than any in the world to use the diversity lottery to gain entry to the United States, and less likely than any others to use job-based entry, like that provided by the H1B visas that bring South Asian workers to the tech sector. We are still early in the story. Like other national groups, African immigrants have clustered in places they are likely to find other Africans: New York, Texas, California, and Minnesota are the big four. The two main metropolitan areas are New York City and the District of Columbia and its Maryland and Virginia suburbs.

Just as they have clustered geographically, they have pooled up in certain jobs as well. "You'll find them in health care, home care, elder care, transportation, as both drivers and parking lot attendants. Dangerous, low-paying jobs for the men, health care and home care for the women."

One consequence of heavy concentration in big metropolitan areas, especially New York and the District of Columbia in the pandemic era, is dealing with rising rents while also making minimum wage. The paradox of heavy concentration in health care, said Lagace, is that "many African immigrants don't have health insurance, especially women of reproductive age, as so many are."

Language problems and unfamiliarity with American laws and customs bring run-ins with the police and problems in the judicial system. If a Dominican or Mexican overstays a visa and is undocumented, getting home can be easy and relatively inexpensive. Getting to Accra, Ghana, or Nairobi, Kenya, is a different matter. People who overstay technically cannot work in the US and find it challenging to leave at the same time.

In her research, Lagace has found undocumented status to land particularly hard on women. Women in much of Africa have carved out social and economic space that values their entrepreneurial skills and drive. In the US, "their lives become very constrained in this patriarchal, hierarchical situation that they wouldn't necessarily face in their home countries."

Africans came to the United States under duress for centuries. After slavery, when American missionaries fanned out across the countries, many came from European colonies to train as ministers, engineers, and doctors, and then went home.

Now, voluntary African immigration is adding something new to America's racial and ethnic mix. Like immigrants from everywhere else in the world they go to two places: where their ambition takes them, and where they are needed in order to make a living.

Dr. Olofunmilayo Olopade has won a long list of awards for her breakthroughs in cancer research, including groundbreaking findings on the predispositions of African women and women of African descent to suffer specific breast cancers at much higher rates than their Caucasian peers and the connection of cancers to specific genes. She won an award from the John D. and Catherine T. MacArthur Foundation, given to standout innovators in their fields and often referred to as a "Genius Grant." She is a member of the National Academy of Sciences and has been given Illinois's highest award to its citizens, the Order of Lincoln.

With a tossed-off line about Nigerians not wanting "to go back to their huts," the then–most powerful man in the world showed he had no idea how successful Nigerians had been in the United States. I asked Dr. Olopade if it was exhausting to have the added job of educating people along with performing all the demanding jobs she already has.

"Absolutely. It's exhausting in the academy. It's exhausting in the press. If I don't leave my small community I'm not going to have that exhaustion. I have to leave my community to be accosted by people who only see the Black in me."

We talked about the extra effort it took to bring up American kids who were also deeply connected to Africa. Or having reached the highest rungs on the professional ladder how often she is the only Black person in the room. "Because you're the only Black faculty, people then think you have to solve all the problems of disparity. You can't! We've written papers on the minority tax. It's taxing. Everywhere you are. Now with the national talk about diversity, equity, and all, you can spend your whole day explaining yourself to everybody. Fighting for a cause that you shouldn't be fighting for anymore. And it is taxing."

For all that, this world-class oncologist remains optimistic about the future in her birthplace and her adopted country. She said she is watching "brain circulation" rather than "brain drain" from Africa, an important sign of a new evolving relationship between the US and countries like Nigeria.

But sometimes, it's the little things that matter.

"Let me tell you an instance where I thought, 'Wow, I'm living in God's own country.' I was coming home for Thanksgiving from a meeting in Nigeria and I lost my passport. Thanksgiving is very important for us. I got to the airport, and I couldn't find it. Sola left me and went back [to Chicago] after I said, 'I think you should go because the kids are coming home. But what should I do?' I called the American embassy. They told me to come by 11 a.m. the next morning to get a new passport.

"I got my passport, flew home, and we had Thanksgiving."

CHAPTER SIX

YOU SHALL LOVE HIM AS YOURSELF, FOR YOU WERE STRANGERS

And if a stranger dwells with you in your land, you shall not mistreat him. The stranger who dwells among you shall be to you as one born among you, and you shall love him as yourself, for you were strangers in the land of Egypt.

I am the LORD your God.

—Leviticus 19:33–34

In early 2017, in the first days of his presidency, Donald Trump said out loud the kind of thing many Americans might have said to themselves only in private. He equated visits by non-white and non-Christian people with a danger to the United States. By executive order, the President was pushing back against the momentum of decades of new arrivals to the United States. The new president said the executive order was meant to exclude "radical Islamic terrorists." The president's political opponents called it a "Muslim ban," and it attracted ferocious opposition.

At the public signing of the new policy, the President made it plain, "We don't want them here. We want to make sure we are not admitting into our country the very threats our soldiers were fighting overseas." With that quick rhetorical sleight of hand, not only ordinary travelers, but family members, dissidents, people trying to leave behind the barbarity of the Islamic State in western Iraq and Syria, people plagued by violence and civil war, were now turned into something very different: possible suspects.

Eventually, after the courts pushed back, the Trump White House softened the blatantly religion-based nature of the policy by adding decidedly non-Muslim Venezuela and North Korea to the list of countries from which travelers were no longer welcome. With a 5–4 vote, the high court upheld that version of the executive order. The President found vindication in the ruling, "following months of hysterical commentary from the media and Democratic politicians who refuse to do what it takes to secure our border and our country."

In its opinion, the Court recognized that the President, any president, has wide discretionary power in setting immigration policy. The lawyers who had argued against the ban noted President Trump's hostile statements against Muslims. In his opinion Chief Justice John Roberts even noted candidate Trump's statements about Muslims. However, he did so as an example of the kind of call the Supreme Court had decided it could not make in an area with a long history of presidential authority and power. Roberts wrote that "the Court must consider not only the statements of a particular President, but also the authority of the Presidency itself."

In sum, the chief executive may have been demonstrably biased against Muslim visitors to the United States, but the nation's top referee, the high court, had decided a president is within his rights to be that way, and to make policy that proceeds from that bias.

As we've seen, the Supreme Court and the Congress had been moving away from restrictions overtly based on religion for decades. The Trump administration skirted that dividing line, but only barely. New arrivals from Iraq, Syria, Iran, Sudan, Libya, Somalia, and Yemen were kept from entering the United States. And at the same time, much less remarked upon, the Trump administration suspended a long-standing path to immigration: the US Refugee Admissions Program.

Parts of the Middle East, the Horn of Africa, the Arabian Peninsula, and North Africa were in full meltdown, due to civil conflict, terrorism, and violent government crackdowns. In many countries there were widespread killings of civilians, growing numbers of political prisoners, and increasing numbers of people in refugee camps. For decades the US had granted exceptions to its immigration restrictions to anyone who was a refugee from political violence, anyone from the world's huddled masses yearning to be free. Since 1980, three million refugees had gained legal entry to the US. Suddenly, that door was nearly shut. The number of refugees allowed into the United States would eventually shrink to 18,000 per year in the Trump years, to just 15,000 in the first years of the Biden administration, down from more than 100,000 in the last year of the Obama presidency.

If anything defines the beacon that America has lifted to the world, it is the Emma Lazarus poem, written in 1883 to help raise funds for the pedestal of the Statue of Liberty. The sonnet is now enshrined on a bronze plaque inside the base. Lazarus wrote the final, famous lines in the voice of the statue:

"Give me your tired, your poor,
Your huddled masses yearning to breathe free,
The wretched refuse of your teeming shore.
Send these, the homeless, tempest-tost to me,
I lift my lamp beside the golden door!"

The State Department established an umbrella agency, the US Refugee Admissions Program, or USRAP, to coordinate the resettlement work of United Nations bodies, nongovernmental organizations, charities, the US Department of Health and Human Services, and later, the US Department of Homeland Security. USRAP takes referrals from international agencies, identifies priority areas for US refugee resettlement (such as ongoing humanitarian crises), and works to reunite family members separated by flight from a home country.

Created in the last year of the Carter White House, the State Department program captured the spirit of the century-old Lazarus poem in law, making real an American commitment to opening a door for the homeless and "tempest-tost" in a world never short on conflict and suffering.

Rays of light streaming from her crown, her torch held high above New York Harbor, "Liberty Enlightening the World" was not originally intended to be attached to America's welcome to immigrants. It was originally meant to mark the centennial of the Declaration of Independence in 1876 and honor the abolition of slavery. A surge in immigrants arriving for processing in nearby Lower Manhattan, and the Lazarus poem, fused in the popular mind to re-create Lady Liberty as an enduring symbol of welcome to the US. What would she say in a poem written today to distill America's promise, and America's welcome? This great big country is still exceptional for the number and variety of people it brings in and has allowed in for more than two centuries. Yet that welcome can run hot and cold.

Ours is a world on the move, with millions across the globe displaced—yet those taking flight are finding it increasingly impossible to enter the US. The much smaller number of refugees accepted in recent years are allocated, first of all, to reunification for refugees with family already in the country. By the final years of the Biden administration the annual refugee quota set by law stood at 125,000, up from 18,000 set in the last years of the Trump White House. The admissions are broken down by world region: Africa, Near East and South Asia, East Asia, and Latin America and the Caribbean.

Trump's executive order barred the very people you might assume refugee policy would be designed to welcome. Religious minorities in Syria, Iraq, and Iran have been under constant threat: Zoroastrians, Bahá'ís, Christians, Yazidis, Mandaeans. Since they came from countries on the list proffered by the President and blessed by the Supreme Court, they have been lumped in by law with the very people they were trying to flee. The pandemic has also slowed processing, arrivals, and resettlements. After using the Trump-era cap in its first year, the Biden administration, plagued by backlogs, rising demand, and ongoing emergency demands for admission, raised the number to its highest official level in thirty years.

The status of refugees is currently a political football, carried, passed, and kicked by both parties in different directions. I sat down with Mark Hetfield, president and CEO of HIAS, a refugee-aid organization that was once the Hebrew Immigrant Aid Society, but is now simply known by its acronym. During our long conversation on American refugee policy, Hetfield smoothly navigated between pointed questioning of the Trump policy and a "benefit of the doubt" assessment of what the US government may be up to at any given time. He knows and has worked with many of the people who stand on the front line, who fear that one slip could jeopardize the future status of unknown numbers of future applicants. Governments have the right to sift and examine all potential refugees. "It will only take one or two bad actors coming in through the refugee program to blow up the program for everybody else."

That heightened caution, perhaps completely understandable in Hetfield's telling, also has to withstand this simple fact: "In the history of the refugee program, since 1980, more than 3 million people have been resettled through it, and not a single one has committed a lethal act of terror on US soil. Yet the entire program is right now using the bulk of its resources making sure that no bad actors come in through the program."

America is experiencing a security panic. "There is so much collateral damage. So many innocent refugees who are in desperate need of resettlement won't get it because secret evidence is being held against them and the benefit of the doubt is never given to the applicant right now."

Tempest-tossed refugees who come to America for succor face extraordinary hurdles. When challenged, the evidence against them is hidden from them. It's a very different standard than the one that would apply in a trial, where the state carries the burden of proof, and is required to show all defendants the evidence against them. In an immigration proceeding, as Hetfield said, that different standard and evidence the applicant "could address and overcome" is often used to devastating effect. "None of this so-called intelligence that's used against them would ever be able to be employed for any purpose inside the United States. Nobody has the courage to look at this and actually do a cost-benefit analysis and realize this is doing a lot more harm than good."

Since the end of the Cold War, which gave us the Jackson-Vanik Amendment and a rush of Soviet Jews to the US, Jewish refugees have generally not been among the "wretched refuse" or "the homeless" fleeing persecution or oppression back home. Yet what was once called the Hebrew Immigrant Aid Society is as busy as ever. "We were able to change our focus," said Hetfield, "from helping people because *they* are Jewish, to helping others because *we* are Jewish." It was not really a change in the more than century-old mission, but a broadening of it. "By the mid-2010s we were in a very strong position that this was our identity as an agency. We're an agency that helps refugees regardless of who they are or what they believe."

When a gunman headed to the Tree of Life Synagogue in Pittsburgh and killed eleven people there, he was, in part, inflamed by the work of HIAS. The agency attracted the anger of a vicious antisemite, not for any work involving bringing Jews into the country but because, as he described it, HIAS was bringing in "hostile invaders to dwell among us." In a web post, the killer made his twin obsessions plain: "It's the filthy EVIL jews [*sic*] Bringing the Filthy EVIL Muslims into the Country." While the synagogue mass murder may have brought the agency and its name to a wider audience, HIAS was already long a target of right-wing extremists, antisemites, and subscribers to "The Great Replacement Theory." The target of the attack, the Tree of Life congregation, had joined HIAS in a special "National Refugee Shabbat" just days before the attack.

By the time I sat with Hetfield in a conference room, it was long after the killings, yet I was asked not to tell people the location of the offices and to be quiet about our meeting. Getting to HIAS headquarters inside a small suburban office building was complicated, on purpose. The antipathy of the synagogue gunman could now be twofold: the agency was still hated as a Jewish organization, and this was compounded because it helped people of many religions and nationalities to come to the US.

Hetfield sees America today, simply, as "a less welcoming place." He called events in 2015 his "wakeup call" for his agency. It was the year of the terrorist attacks on the Bataclan theater and a kosher supermarket in Paris. "The reaction in this country was against Syrian refugees, or more specifically, Syrian Muslim refugees. And you had thirty-one governors, thirty of them Republican, coming out saying they would not allow Syrian Muslims in their states." The early presidential field in the 2016 Republican primaries, packed with more than a dozen hopefuls, unanimously said the same. "It was a real eye-opener," said Hetfield. "And you had legislation passed by the House, thankfully not by the Senate, that made refugee resettlement of Syrian and Iraqi refugees virtually impossible. I never thought in my lifetime I would see people who were so openly discriminated against because of where they were born and what their religion was. But that's exactly what was happening, and there wasn't even an attempt to hide it."

We used to welcome refugees. We still do, but not so easily. Even when they are refugees because of our own decisions, policies, interventions, and wars.

The US was deeply enmeshed in Afghanistan for two decades, from the first year of the George W. Bush administration until the Biden years. In twenty years, a vast array of American projects, from the efforts to establish a national army, to dozens of civil society projects, to enormous investments in education and job training, were undertaken in order to make Afghanistan very different from the country that gave Al Qaida safe haven and a place from which to command terrorist operations around the world. Doing that work meant creating a small army of men and women who worked with and for Americans. Those projects created an enormous pool of citizens who could be targeted as collaborators if the Taliban once again took control of the country. By 2021 there were millions of Afghans who could not even remember a time before the US invasion, occupation, and long-term military mission there. With a median age around seventeen, the majority of Afghans were born after America toppled the Taliban government.

The prospect of the Taliban retaking control of Afghanistan loomed steadily larger, from the Obama years to the Trump years to the Biden years. And American public opinion steadily turned against an endless presence there. By the time Biden finally pulled the plug, very few were arguing that we should remain in the country—even if many argued that our exit was too hasty and too sloppy. America was never likely to establish a permanent military presence in Afghanistan. But our long intervention in that country meant that we had worked with a huge number of local translators and other helpers.

They were put at serious risk when we left. Did we bring them here, as refugees?

Only a relative few. The US took in a carefully controlled number of Afghans as the faraway country melted down, leaving some elected officials able to both insist on "extreme vetting" and pound away at the Biden team for leaving people behind. Only in Washington can an elected official, without fear of contradiction, cheer one administration for slamming the door shut, then excoriate the next one as it deals with the consequences of a shut door.

A man I will call Amjad Ghafari has lived with the consequences of superpower politics for most of his life. He was a boy when the Soviets came rolling into Afghanistan at the end of 1979, establishing a subordinate Marxist state on the USSR's southern border and beginning their decade-long attempt to subdue the vast country and bring it into Moscow's orbit.

Through the rest of Amjad's childhood a series of Soviet-backed leaders ran the country. In 1989, Soviet troops withdrew, leaving behind a government scrambling to stay in power by transitioning from Communism to Islamic nationalism. The gambit did not work. Once the Soviet Union collapsed, so did its client government in the capital, Kabul, replaced by an unstable series of coalitions as ethnic and regional factions vied for power. America, which had armed the mujahedeen while they were rebelling against the Soviet-backed regime, lost interest and left behind a great deal of weaponry, mostly in the hands of Islamist fighters. Into this world came Amjad, a newly trained military man who had completed university and military academy.

When the Taliban rose to power, Amjad went underground, becoming a clerk in a pharmacy. "The Taliban, they asked me, and sometimes I told them I was educated to six years, just the sixth grade. Not more than that.

"The situation was very bad in Afghanistan. The Taliban, every day they kill people." Amjad figured being publicly associated with the old armed forces and the old political order was risky. He kept his family safe, and his mouth shut. "It was better they didn't know I was an educated person. One hundred percent."

He moved his family to an area of Kabul where they were not known.

He and his wife had three young children as the Taliban ran their country, and the public visibility of women became more and more restricted. "My wife was at home like a prisoner. Like a hostage. Not go outside. Not go outside to buy something from the shops. All the time my wife and my mother were home. It was too hard for the women."

Then came the September 2001 terrorist attack against the United States, and the refusal of the Taliban government to surrender the Al Qaida members who were based in Afghanistan. America suddenly regained its interest in the country, and invaded. The Taliban, conservative Islamist fighters, many of whom came to adulthood in refugee camps in Pakistan during the Soviet domination of their homeland, were now on the run. Soon, America's allies took charge in Kabul.

Amjad remembers the early optimism that accompanied the defeat of the Taliban. "When the US came to Afghanistan, all of us, all the poor people were so happy. So happy. Because our people had a lot of work from the US Army when they were coming into my country. Because they brought peace for us in Afghanistan. They were so happy for the US Army."

Living through yet another regime change reopened opportunity for the still-young career officer. "When the US Army came to Afghanistan I went to the Air Force. I was working at the medical company, and I learned a little bit of English at that time. I told them I was a pilot ten years before. I didn't fly for almost ten years, but I want to come join and serve with you."

There were few aircraft to equip a new Afghan air force. Amjad and his fellow Afghans worked with US advisors to rehab the small compliment of working aircraft, which were eventually augmented with new equipment bought from Russia. Later, Amjad was chosen for further training in the US, and was sent to Fort Bliss near El Paso, Texas. After completing his training for night warfare, he headed home.

He said his life was on track. His children were getting educated. He was serving his country as he was trained to do and forming close friendships with his American mentors. "I find my way. I find my job. I find everything. I was happy. My family was happy. They were too happy." I knew what he meant, but that phrase "too happy" stuck in my memory.

As the Taliban reconstituted itself as a potent fighting force, and the American timeline in Afghanistan lengthened, Amjad's life became more complicated. "Because I worked with the US guys side by side, and shoulder by shoulder, and I fight with them for twenty years against the Taliban, and before the US come, some of my mentors know about that. From 2016 they start warning me. They are directly warning me and also they wanted me to go." The ill omens did not end with warnings from his American partners.

"My older son was in the university but some of the Taliban guys told my son, 'Please tell your father not to work with the US guys, because that's not good for us.' My son told them, 'I am proud of my father. My father is a pilot. He is working with the US guys in Kandahar. I am proud that my father is a professional pilot.'" They came back and warned him again. The next encounter was not just a warning, but a kidnapping attempt. "The third time they shot at him with a pistol. My son got shot in the leg. After that the police people arrive, but the kidnap people escape from that place and the police could not find them."

His American partners quickly requisitioned an aircraft and flew Amjad home to Kabul from the far south where he was part of ongoing operations against the Taliban. "I saw my son; his leg was broken. After that, I change my house. I change my house from this place to another secret place. After that, the Taliban found my own house, too. They wanted to kill me, kill my son and all my family.

"After that, some of my friends, the US guys, they tell me, 'Please be careful. Some of the enemy are trying to find your place. Please go outside. To another house. Change your house.' After that, all of my family know, all of my job know, my commanders know, the Afghan Defense Forces guys know.

"I was asleep at home at one o'clock in the middle of the night, I got a call. I thought they were calling me for a job, to go somewhere for an operation." The voice on the other end of the line said, "I am a two-star general, but for tonight I am in this place. Some of the enemy is around your house. They want to kill you. Or kill some of your family, so please be careful. Our people are around your house. Do not go outside of your house."

"After that, maybe ten minutes after that, I got another call: From the ADF. He was a general, too. He told me, 'You are Amjad Ghafari?' I told him yes; he told me, 'Brother, be careful, don't go outside from your house. If someone calls and tells you to come outside your house, do NOT come outside your house.' During that time all of them, my mother, my wife, my children, all of them wake up in my home. I told all of my family, 'Please relax, please relax.' "

I asked Amjad why, given the increasing danger, he did not spirit his family out of the country, and why he did not consider leaving himself. "That was a bad situation for me and my family but I was not running from the Taliban. I was proud to fight against them because they were terrorists. They were not good for my country. They were not good for the whole world.

"But some of my mentors, my advisors, they know about everything. In 2016, 2017, one of the majors told me, 'Please send your family to the United States.' I told him, 'United States people are in Afghanistan. That would be my shame to send my family to the United States.'" In a very long conversation that covered thirty years of his country's history, Amjad's conclusion was simple and logical. "The US Army came from far away. Far away from the United States, far from their beautiful houses. They come to my country from their situation. That would be a shame for me if I go to United States now. My family would not be good based in the US, because my US friends are coming from their homeland to Afghanistan and a bad situation, and why, if they're here, would I go to the United States?

"That's not good for me. I told them, 'No. I will stay here with you in

Afghanistan with all of my family.' So I stayed with my US friends in Afghanistan and with my family."

When I asked him, in retrospect, whether he had made the right decision during the Obama years, he wavered. "Now I think at that time I made a mistake. Why did I not send my family at that time? Once I was put on the danger list in Kabul?" Looking back, he recalled all the times his American friends had tried to alert him to the rising danger. "Because we had a good relationship, a relationship with each other like a brother. For this case, they help me, I help them. Because together we want to destroy the enemy, and terrorism."

Afghanistan fell the way Ernest Hemingway's character Mike Campbell went bankrupt in *The Sun Also Rises,* "gradually, then suddenly." All during the late 2010s, as the US approached the twentieth anniversary of its invasion, Amjad fought the Taliban with the new Afghan armed forces, alongside American forces and advisors.

He returned from a mission to an air base in the south, near the border with Pakistan, when Amjad said a US advisor told him, "The Taliban is coming to Kabul." When the Afghan pilot expressed disbelief, his American partner told him again, "They are in Kabul! They are in Kabul!"

The end had gradually been approaching for years. Now it was arriving all at once. "I got an order from my commander and from my chief of staff, please make safe those aircraft. Because if the Taliban come they will take it, because suddenly they are shooting by rocket and the aircraft will be destroyed. If they catch it here they will take all that aircraft. Please save the aircraft and make a plan.

"I told him, okay. But I didn't know that the Taliban was taking all of Afghanistan. Or that our president escaped from there. I will tell you, what I told my pilot, what I told my passengers, what I told my crew chief, what I told all of them: we have to get the aircraft out. After that I told to them we will get them out to keep safe our aircraft, our boss, our commander." He was overseeing the military crews of multiple aircraft. His family was not part of the group.

"We were talking to Uzbek guys, maybe we will go to over there. And maybe we will come back during that same night. During the night we will come back to Kabul, and then go back to Uzbekistan. But some of them said, 'After we go to Uzbekistan we will stop our flights, when we are in Uzbekistan to go there, and be out of danger.' When we left to go to Uzbekistan around nine o'clock in the night, I was the leader of all the group. I was the leader of all that operation. I brought all the aircraft to Uzbekistan. I identified our group and requested permission to land."

Amjad was surprised when the tower refused permission to land. The officers in the Uzbek control tower told the group to turn around and head for Pakistan, which would have meant crossing hundreds of miles of increasingly hostile Afghan airspace to reach the country's southern neighbor. He gave the tower his handle and flight identification number again, and again requested permission to land. He was denied again.

"I told my group not to try to land on the runway but to come alongside of me. I told them, 'We are landing on the taxiway not on the runway.' When we landed over there, we shut down the engines, then some of the Uzbek forces they come over there. But when we arrived over there we learned that our president of Afghanistan had fled before us and he went to Qatar." In fact, Ashraf Ghani, president since 2014, had also flown to Uzbekistan, and was now in the capital, Tashkent, as Taliban fighters swarmed through his presidential palace.

Amjad was now, effectively, an officer in a nonexistent air force, sworn to serve a nonexistent political order. What now? He had assumed he would secure his aircraft, gather his men, and head back to the fight. In an instant, it seemed, there really was not much of a fight anymore. He was not being given safe haven by "friendlies." He was under arrest.

"I want to talk with some of the Uzbek people, I want them to give us some place for our group, for our people. I thought they would select some site for where we would park our helicopters, our aircraft. We are talking with them at this time, when I came to talk to some of their people they told me, 'No talking, no talk English, stay over there, stay over there.' They come and they search all of us, they took our pistols, they took our body armor, they took our rocket-propelled grenades, we had a lot of our M-24 guns (sniper rifles). They took it all and did not allow us to go back to our aircraft.

"I asked them, 'What's happening?' They told me, 'Your president has escaped, and all of Afghanistan has been captured by the Taliban.' During that time, I am thinking about my wife, my children.

"I looked behind me and saw that I had no way to return to my homeland. And all of my family is now in great danger in Afghanistan. And I could not help them in any way. I was very heartbroken. You know what I am saying, brother? I cry and cry and during that time what was the worst thing, the worst thing, was what I thought before would not happen! To lose everything, including our family! We lost all of it."

There was the immediate problem of being in Uzbek custody, and the medium- and long-term problem of protecting his family as the Afghans he had fought for years were taking control of every part of the country. His wife and children were lying low in the capital. He was able to get out of Uzbekistan in fairly short order, and to the US with an asylum grant. While telling me his story, Amjad teared up, his voice grew husky. He apologized, then continued.

"They [his family] move from one house to another, two months in one house and then to another house, then two months to another. Because they are hiding. The first year my family was in the greatest threat over there. After that, the Taliban arrested my brother, and now my brother is in the Taliban jail. I couldn't find some way to bring them out."

He feared his sons were in a different kind of jeopardy, facing immediate arrest by the Taliban if caught on the streets of Kabul. Amjad sent money through channels to get his sons out of Afghanistan. After failing to get across the border into Iran or Pakistan, they headed to nearby Kazakhstan. After fewer than two weeks, his older son was in an accident that left him paralyzed from the chest down. When we spoke, Amjad's sons had just been given humanitarian parole. Now in the US, they are beginning the task of becoming permanent residents of the United States.

When Amjad heads to work in Southern California, his thoughts are eleven time zones away, in Kabul. "My wife and my daughter, they did their examination, they did their interview, they dropped their passport with the US agency in Afghanistan, but I don't know what happened. They promised for me that my family would get a flight on the eighth of July but it was delayed. I don't know why it was delayed." The women have been granted Special Immigrant Visas, under a program created by the State Department for families that worked for the civil or military operations of the US during the long sojourn in Afghanistan.

"Over there, my sons, my daughter, they don't have a place for life, they don't have money. Because we sold our house, and all our things, brother, so my family, now they don't have anything. They are at home all the time. All the time they are crying. My wife and my daughter they are crying. And I am here crying."

Amjad will not concede that he has become a victim of circumstance. Or that his old American friends should have stayed in his country longer or fought harder. Again and again he made it clear to me: He believes his countrymen, not the US, should be blamed for Afghanistan's sufferings. Especially, he said, his country's leaders. "The United States for twenty years they help me, my family, my country, my people. But we lost all of that! Who is to blame!? Our leadership people are to blame. Our free people appreciated that. Our people appreciated all the United States did for my country. If our leaders had been people who were good…the Taliban would not have been able to take over my homeland.

"When I was in Uzbekistan I realized our whole leadership was involved in bribery, in smuggling, they were not good people. All of them are now living in other places. Some of them live in Turkey, some of them live in Russia, some of them live in Germany, London, and United States. But for twenty years I was with them, I was with my US Army friends, now I know all of them were taking bribes.

"Why, when they were not businessmen, each one of them has more than five hundred million dollars? Each one! You know what I am saying? From where did they get that kind of money? They have beautiful houses in Turkey, land in Germany, they bought it. The US guys, for twenty years, fought with them. They were the generals, and they got rich!"

As he awaits his green card and the arrival of his wife and daughter from Afghanistan, Amjad plows away at whatever work he can find. At an age when many Americans are already thinking about a glide path to retirement, Amjad is thinking about how to start over. "As long as I have power in my body I work. I didn't care for what kind of work. I just want to make better. When I get my family over here, I will go back to school for more education, I will improve my language, I will get more training to make myself into some kind of maintenance technician.

"I know about electrical, I know about power, I know about water stations. I know about how to repair them. I know about how to repair the TV, I know how to repair transformers. But I don't have any documents for that. Once my family is here I will go to one of the high schools or the universities to learn more about that and get a certificate, and after that I will start my work. I want to fix up a shop for electrical, for dishwasher, for everything."

Amjad doubts he will ever be able to live in Afghanistan again. Once the ever-present distress over his family is relieved, you get the sense he will make the best of a difficult situation. "Before I had one house. One home. Now I have two houses, two homes. The United States is my Homeland Number Two.

"From the beginning, from 2001 when I saw the US Army, when they are coming...they come from far away, from their house, from their homeland, they come to help us. And it was my job to help the United States people in Afghanistan. I am proud of all my US friends.

"Now my feeling is too good. So much good. Because here, when I go outside and some of the US people see me and we talk, and I tell them I was a pilot they tell me, 'Thank you for your service.' They help me a lot. I am proud of these people.

"I am not proud of the people who did not defend Afghanistan. I am like a 'US guy.' I want to stand at the side of my US brother in every-thing. Because that's my way, that's my feeling, because some of my men-tors, in fact two or three of my mentors, their children send me gifts for welcome to the United States! But my family is still over there. That is still my concern."

America owes a lot to its Afghan allies, many of whom (and/or their fam-ilies) were left behind in the chaotic withdrawal of 2021. For most Afghans who were able to escape to the US around the fall of Kabul, parole was granted for two years.

By mid-2023, almost one hundred thousand Afghans had asked for some form of permanent residence in the US, either asylum status as ref-ugees, or status under laws written to speed the process for those who assisted the US government or military forces during two decades on the ground. Approaching two years since the last military transport loaded with servicemen and -women left Bagram, fewer than five thousand had made their way through the system and could live without fear of depor-tation or review.

This illustrates a central paradox at the heart of American law and custom: the persistent impulses toward both exclusion and generosity. It is true that the US has, over the long haul, been a welcoming and gener-ous country. At the same time, Americans have also often voiced misgiv-ings about that same generosity, fearing becoming a patsy. After passing legislation to quickly handle an influx of Hungarians after the abortive anti-Soviet revolution in 1956, to resettle large numbers of Vietnamese after the American withdrawal in 1975, and Cubans after the island's communist revolution from the early 1960s all the way into the 21st cen-tury, there is now gridlock.

Congress is closely divided. For Republicans, breakdown at the border and the fallout from the chaotic withdrawal from Afghanistan are weap-ons to use against President Biden and congressional Democrats. So there is very little interest, at least in the short term, in permanent solutions to the insecurity of thousands of Afghans. Even normally politically potent veterans' groups, who have fiercely advocated for Afghans on Capitol Hill, have managed to make little headway.

During 2022 and 2023, the new Taliban government broke promises to the international community to observe international human rights norms, particularly concerning women's rights and allowing aid agencies to use their own standards in hiring female staff. These developments racheted up political pressure on the Biden White House to protect Afghans in the US, and to continue to find ways to extract Afghan allies who were left behind during the 2021 evacuation. That means finding a way to work with a government in Kabul that American authorities find repulsive and unpredictable.

Mahsa Khanbabai is an immigration attorney in Boston who has worked with a large number of Afghans in recent years. She told me there were pinch points in the refugee pipeline that were proving difficult to fix after the spike in demand around the fall of Kabul, and the aftermath of a Trump administration that slammed on the brakes for processing refugees. There are labor shortages both on the government side, Khanbabai said, and on the not-for-profit and private voluntary agency side. "There's basically a whole group of volunteers raising money to pay Afghans who could translate documents. All of these government proclamations and websites with information on how to apply for reunification have to be translated into Dari and Pashto. Then you have the backlogs of applying for work authorization."

Dealing with multiple state and federal agencies, trying to track the fates of relatives back home, and trying to put together the resources of daily life after running out of a home country often with little more than what you can carry creates a challenge that is simple and complicated at the same time. "There's not enough resources yet to help Afghans do the things they need to do to just have a basic, functional, daily life," Khanbabai said.

In one important way, an Afghan arriving in the US in the 21st century shares something fundamental with the Irish fleeing to this country after an unsuccessful uprising against British rule in the 18th century, a refugee from 19th-century pogroms in czarist Russia, 20th-century Mexicans fleeing civil war and pouring into the Southwest, or Haitians fleeing social chaos and natural disaster a century later: If people from your country, racial, and ethnic group have already arrived and put down roots, there is a social and institutional world ready to help you resettle. If you are part of the first wave, on the other hand, it can be really hard. Khanbabai contrasted a small-town Afghan arriving alone, or in a small family group, with someone from Italy or Ireland arriving at the beginning of the 20th century. "While there is an Afghan community here in the United States, they haven't acclimated, not enough time has passed for them to be really entrenched in American society. And to have developed connections and wealth.

"They look different. They dress different. They eat differently. Americans are not really used to seeing someone like that. So there's maybe more hesitancy in wanting to welcome them into your home and into your community because they seem different. Average Americans don't feel comfortable with their Afghan neighbors yet. And the Afghan community itself does not have the resources and wealth and connections to provide everything needed.

"It's not going to be a turnaround in one week or one month or maybe even one year. But we need to spend the time and the resources to invest in the Afghans to be able to have them be productive members of society. There's no easy solution. It's time and resources."

Khanbabai had been taking on many of the Afghan cases pro bono, without fee, or at a severely reduced fee, which she calls "low bono." She told me there was a limit to how much work she could do that way, but that she was seeing burnout and strain throughout the network of attorneys with Afghan clients. "Lawyers don't get trauma training like physicians do. There are wellness issues for the immigration lawyer community. And there's this expectation, 'Oh, you're an immigration lawyer? You should take on this case for free.' Doctors take on humanitarian cases, but nobody expects a doctor to just take on all these cases." Khanbabai said the need for help always outstrips the supply. She wishes the private bar would pick up some of the slack.

Afghan families still finding their feet in the US have been reluctant to talk to me for publication, even with assumed names and the reassurance that I would strip their interviews of any identifying characteristics. They are still very skittish about the US immigration process and the possibilities of Taliban retribution against relatives back at home. Khanbabai, the daughter of Iranians who came to the US as refugees, said too little attention has been paid to the mental strain of fleeing a country, struggling to make a new home, while worrying about those left behind. "Iranian and Afghan culture are very similar. In these cultures you don't talk about mental health issues. It's not as acceptable as it is in American culture. It's kind of taboo. I do fear, for young people, that they're going to feel a sense of isolation. Women as well. A sense of isolation, fear, worry. We need to provide the resources for them to deal with that."

Time can heal, or at least obscure, the memory of struggle and trauma. Especially if you are lucky enough and work hard and long enough to settle down in the end. Given how hard many immigrants work, there are plenty of inspiring stories to be found.

The air in a factory in Hayward, California, south of San Francisco, is warm and dry and loud with the noise of conveyor belts, robots, and packaging machines. That same air is redolent with the aroma of butter and sugar. As Andrew Ly shows me around Sugar Bowl Bakeries he is eager for me to see how mechanization has relieved the drudgery of some jobs, while still leaving plenty to do for his cherished workforce.

Ly, and his brothers and sister, came to the US after the Vietnam War. His family, part of Vietnam's sizable Chinese minority, had lived in South Vietnam during the long civil war, with America fighting on one side and China assisting on the other. His father had fled China for Vietnam during the long period of Japanese occupation and civil war in the late 1930s. War and instability followed the family to Indochina. Ly called the long conflict between North and South Vietnam "horrific" and "unforgiving." When America finally tired of the Vietnam War and decided to declare "Peace with Honor," withdrawing and leaving the country vulnerable to a complete takeover by the communist North Vietnamese government, the family concluded it was time to move again. "I tried to escape three times, and I failed three times, but I was lucky enough not to get caught. The third time I partnered with a friend to flee with a small boat from a different city, just so the locals didn't know that we intended to leave Vietnam." That would have brought punishment and closer surveillance, Ly said. By the end of 1978, the new Communist government allowed people to leave if they surrendered their property, even if no country agreed to receive them as refugees. The path was open to try to leave again. "So we partially escape, and we were partially legal with them. We left Vietnam in October 1978." Ly was twenty-three years old.

"The idea was to go to Singapore or Malaysia. We knew that the earlier boat escapers had been robbed by Thai pirates. So I intended to go thirteen hours straight to the east, and then turn toward Singapore. It was intended to stay out of the pirates' route. But after six hours, seven hours, people on the boat were impatient. So we made a turn. And that's how we got caught by pirates. Twice."

Ly estimates there were thirty people in the small, open boat. In return for passage for his own family, an experienced captain joined them for the trip across the open ocean. Their pilot, Ly said, was indecisive. Though he had agreed with the original plan to try to sail past the pirate-infested waters before making for Singapore, he eventually gave in to the people who urged the more direct route. When pirates pulled alongside, the young men aboard the refugee boat considered trying to overpower their assailants. Some argued, "We could easily overpower them, tie them up. Push them into the ocean. Kill them. Take their boats away." Instead, as Ly counseled, rather than take a chance with an attack, they offered no resistance. They agreed they would resort to violence only if the pirates began to assault the women aboard. After carefully selling all they had in order to get permission to leave the country, they were at sea with nothing but the clothes on their backs. They were out of food and water. They avoided another run-in with pirates, but as they approached the Malaysian coastline they were intercepted by the coast guard. They were allowed to dock but not disembark. Malaysian authorities insisted the boat keep moving.

By the time Ly's boat was towed back out to sea, conditions had changed for the worse. "We were so scared. We went toward Singapore again, but the ocean had become so unfriendly." The overloaded boat was rocked by larger and larger waves, and the refugees agreed they had no choice but to head to shore again. The boat headed for the Malaysian coast once more. Again, there was no welcome for the increasingly desperate Vietnamese. "They shot at us. So we moved along the coast and saw a small village and steered our boat to it, and when we hit the sand we destroyed the boat."

That's what it took for Ly and his family to escape Vietnam. In the late 1970s thousands of desperate people were heading out into the South China Sea from Vietnam's long, snaking coastline. The government in Hanoi, now master of the entire country, was settling scores, seizing private property, and sending hundreds of thousands to reeducation camps. Regional neighbors like Thailand and Malaysia were overwhelmed, and those governments were not friendly toward the large numbers of refugees, popularly called "boat people," desperately taking to the ocean waters.

On the Malaysian coast, civilians were not happy to see Ly and his fellow passengers. "The villagers came with their sticks and stones. They tried to stone us away and rob us again. Luckily for us, a delegation of reporters from the *Far Eastern Economic Review* was passing by. They were hunting for news. They protected us, and they went to the International Red Cross to tell them to come pick us up. They stayed with us until somebody came for us, to take us first to a station, then to a permanent refugee camp.

"That night they gave us instant noodles to make. That instant noodle was named Maki. It is always in my memory because that was the best dinner in my lifetime. I was so hungry."

Like so many of the people who have talked to me about coming to the United States, Ly's story is an agglomeration of accidents, hurdles, and sheer grit. Walking around his thrumming bakery, now almost seventy, he relates a story full of happenstance. This happened. Not that. Then this happened. Not that other thing. Had impatience not led frightened people to change course early, pirates may not have boarded their boat. They might have reached Singapore. Malaysia has a large and thriving ethnic Chinese community. If they had landed and received a different welcome, Ly and his siblings might have made new lives in Malaysia. Had journalists not witnessed the hostile reception as they came ashore, they might not have quickly ended up in a refugee camp with food, shelter, and the opportunity to make multiple asylum requests. More than forty years later, there's a framed copy of the cover of the *Far Eastern Economic Review* on the office walls of the Sugar Bowl Bakery with a photo snapped by a reporter who just happened to be standing there when Ly and his brothers waded ashore.

"We actually applied to five countries to go to; America, of course, number one. Switzerland, number two. Australia, number three. Canada, number four. France, number five. The next morning, the Switzerland delegates then accepted us, and we accepted them."

Ly was relieved by the prospect of going to Switzerland. His mother's eyesight was failing. He believed his mother would get proper treatment for her condition. Yet fate intervened again. "That evening the US delegates came and called our name, and when we went over, they accepted us, too. So we went back to the Switzerland people to say, 'You know what? We are going to America.'"

Ly had grown up in South Vietnam, coming of age during the height of the American presence in the country, and then watching as the US withdrew and North Vietnam took complete control. The American record was, to be charitable, decidedly mixed: more than a million Vietnamese had died. Much of the north was in ruins from bombing.

Defoliants had destroyed forests and created an environmental disaster. The sustained American presence, more than a decade long, had brought drugs, prostitution, and cruelty along with an attempt to stand up an independent, anti-communist Vietnam in the midst of the Cold War.

Ly's view was far more understanding. "Americans, and people from all cultures, get angry. Some of them get angry because people were shooting at them and they couldn't always shoot back. Angry things happen during the fighting, during war, during battles.

"But the majority of Americans, if you look at the GIs, they have very good hearts. They help our children. They give meals. When I was growing up, I would look at a GI, and they would give me a cigarette.

"But let's say the Agent Orange. That was not their decision. That was a high-up decision. So you can't blame them. There was killing on both sides. And the people who made people pregnant? It's not only Americans. They are human. These things are human things. The unreasonable beating and killing happened on both sides.

"One of my neighbors was a few years older than me. The Viet Cong [guerrillas fighting in South Vietnam on the side of the communist north] wanted him to join them and he didn't want to. He was stabbed twenty-three times and left to die. The son of my mom's best friend, they [local supporters of the South Vietnamese government] thought he was Viet Cong, and they killed him, even though he's not. This happened on both sides. Two doctors from the big city came to our village to see their patients. My mom was one of their patients. One day we were walking home from school and saw their bodies hung on a tree. People thought they were spies for the republic [South Vietnam]."

Some of the Ly siblings were already in the US. Sending family members ahead to secure a foothold in the whole family's eventual destination is a tradition as old as immigration. Ly's oldest brother was in San Francisco, his youngest in Texas. The youngest brother sponsored the family members in the refugee camp, who landed at Travis Air Force Base in Fairfield, California. "I didn't have a dime to make a phone call to my brothers. Luckily, there was a lady who saw me standing by the pay phone, and she came over to offer to make a phone call for me."

The family united in San Francisco, under the sponsorship of Catholic Charities. Ly attended English classes for a year, and then went on to City College of San Francisco and earned a degree in accounting. "I worked as a newspaper carrier, as a janitor, some of my brothers worked as dishwashers, and my sisters-in-law worked as seamstresses. We pooled our money together and bought a coffee shop with a bakery in San Francisco. The coffee shop had been struggling. The owners didn't know how to manage. We thought, okay, if we get there, and all the family members work there, we can make some kind of Chinese pastries because back in Vietnam, one of my brothers knew how to make Chinese pastries."

Ly and his partners did not know much of anything about what Americans wanted to buy in a coffee shop. Cookies? Muffins? Donuts? It was all new, but the brothers worked around the clock, teaching themselves what they needed to know to make things work, and discarding the things that did not work. Ly started making the rounds, trying to broaden the market for the goods coming from the brothers' ovens. He sold baked goods to Asian markets, and American-style convenience stores and groceries. Other suppliers "sold the donuts for thirty cents per piece. So we sold our donuts at twenty cents per piece because of the advantage with all family labor.

"I credit our success not only to hard work, but our willingness to sacrifice. To work hard. To work seven days a week. And we save all the monies. We didn't take any kind of vacation. I didn't take a vacation for ten years. I bought my clothes at the Goodwill — until I knew my fiancée, and then she decided to change those clothes for me." Ly stuck to the business side of the operation, he said, while his brothers concentrated on the baked goods. "I tried to stay focused on building customer relationships, hiring people, accounting systems and finance. I am a risk taker, but a reasonable risk taker."

It was Ly's "reasonable" appetite for risk that allowed the family to kick the business up into a newer, higher gear. For years, the family members had pooled their money and opened new Sugar Bowl outlets. The coffee shop business had grown to seven stores, and the baked-goods supply business was all from one small commercial bakery. Ly knew these two businesses, while outwardly similar — donuts are donuts — really involved two entirely different business models. His family members were each managing one Sugar Bowl coffee shop, while Ly expanded manufacturing to supply hotels, restaurants, and retailers. The Great Recession of 2008 and 2009 finally brought a reckoning.

Hotels were suffering. The coffee shops were suffering. Ly brought in a nephew for product analysis. After running the numbers, they realized just three products produced 80 percent of sales, and the rest of the extensive range of offerings all combined for just 20 percent. Practical and unsentimental to a fault, Ly knew what he had to do. Donuts and Danish may have gotten the family to this comfortable plateau, but the road ahead was going to mean going all in on the things that sold the best and getting rid of everything else. Long-standing relationships and honest dealing, Ly said, lowered the risk. "When we reached out to banks and to machinery manufacturers, they trust us. That's how we set up the lines to make just three products."

If all America's history of immigrant success stories comes flooding back to you in an instant, you may have just bitten into one of Sugar Bowl's madeleines. They became one of the three pillars of the new business. Ly convinced his relatives to sell all the coffee shops and pool their money to buy an enormous commercial bakery on the outskirts of the Bay Area. Palmiers, the crunchy, buttery, hand-shaped cookie was product number two, and a small chocolate cake, the "Brownie Bite," was the third. "We keep on making these three simple things, and that's how we scale it up. When we focus on simplicity, our quality's better. Our productivity's better. So actually we do less for more instead of do more for less."

Today, you can find Sugar Bowl's palmiers, madeleines, and tiny cakes across the country in big box retailers like Costco, Walmart, and Safeway. When the Ly family propelled its operation into the big time, it took many of its suppliers with them. The company buys a lot of flour, sugar, and butter. When Sugar Bowl more than doubled its production by opening a new bakery near Atlanta, one of his original vendors came east with the company. "He opened up a manufacturing plant there just to serve us." After beginning as a middleman who did not even have his own company, his partner has shared in the brothers' success. "He sells us plastic containers. At first, he made them in China." When Sugar Bowl grew its monthly order twenty-fold, it made sense to the supplier to make his containers in Georgia instead of buying them overseas.

His company is worth somewhere between $100 million and $200 million. Ly is semiretired now, but still a familiar face on the bakery floor, where he greets his workers, many immigrants from Asia and Latin America, as they mix, bake, sort, package, and pack up pallets full of snacks for shipment throughout the American West. He described the automation of different lines and reported proudly that the increases in productivity from the robots, for instance, rapidly boxing up uniform numbers of freshly wrapped madeleines, did not result in staff reductions. Instead, he said, efficiencies brought by the robots have increased productivity, strengthened pricing power, and increased sales.

Back in his office, with the bustle and noise of the factory muffled to a distant hum, Ly is exultant when he talks about America. For him, proof of what the US offers comes from a look at the country's competitors. "I think America is always progressing. This is still the best country on earth. Of course some things can be better, but look at our system. We always change, every two years, or four years, or six years, and eventually it changes, slowly gearing to the future." Ly said he did not want to name any particular country, but the US has only one rival in the size of its economy: China. "Yes, maybe they can do things faster. They can do anything in the snap of a finger or change policies. America's not going to be the biggest economy in the world. But it doesn't mean the biggest economy is going to dictate the whole financial system of the world.

"They don't have an immigration system! When their populations get older, or the kids don't want to get married early, their populations will be decreasing, and their economy's going to be going down. In America, same thing; our kids don't want to get married too young. Some of them don't get married, and our population got older.

"But we have an immigration system! You can pick a hundred thousand from Europe, fifty thousand from Asia, ten thousand from Africa. You can pick executives, high tech, farmworkers, dishwashers. And all of these will be growing the economy for America."

Ly believes only a minority of Americans are hostile to immigrants. "The majority of Americans are still open-minded. Very open-minded." He worries about the resentment toward illegal immigrants and hopes the problems at the border can be addressed and a working system developed for the good of the country and the people who "jeopardize their safety, their life, and may walk thousands of miles to get here." Now a citizen for more than forty years, Ly has no doubts about American values, and how his hard work combined with the openness of the country to create an unquestionable success.

He is right about people wanting to be here. In recent years few people have wanted to move to Russia. More people might want to go to China because of its rapidly growing economy, but China makes it difficult even for Chinese nationals to move to big metropolitan areas to work.

In response to people fleeing here from places that have become difficult to live, like Haiti, Venezuela, Syria, or Myanmar, there is a common complaint: "If we let in everyone who wants to come, we would be overrun. We would be swamped." It is a plea for rationality, buried inside a boast, embedded in an illusion.

The rational observation is that the United States is still considered a desirable destination by refugees in many places. The implicit boast is that everyone wants what the rest of us have, a legal and established place in the US. The illusion is that this country is so desirable, everyone from everywhere wants to come. Talk to immigrants, even refugees running for their lives, and you will find that all things being equal, most people would prefer to stay right where they are. They want to be surrounded by the familiar people and things they grew up with, speaking their language, in safety and in comfort.

Americans are not, in the main, familiar with daily life as lived in other places in the world. Just a little over a third of Americans even have passports, even decades into the post–9/11 era, when the blue booklet with the seal of the United States is required to enter Canada, Mexico, and nearby Caribbean islands that never required them before. It may be fortifying to believe that given the chance, everybody on earth would move here. Growing, record numbers of increasingly desperate people have been heading for the southern border in 2021, 2022, and 2023. Having talked to people on four other continents about the way they see America, I can tell you it simply is not true.

The country is admired yet feared. The country is regarded with envy and also resentment. The country fascinates and lures even people who head to American embassies around the world to shout their displeasure at a foreign policy decision or to protest military action. When I covered one of the largest anti-American demonstrations in European history — against the installation of medium-range nuclear missiles pointed at the Soviet Union in the last decade of the Cold War — people who were intimately familiar with US culture and politics brimmed with anger over the way the country uses its power. Yet they also expressed their love for the culture and their desire to visit. An emotional grab bag of sentiments came spilling out of people who both lived protected by American military might and wished it were not necessary.

> At a neighborhood bar in Harare, Zimbabwe...
> Waiting for a TV crew to break down equipment from a
>   shoot in Peru...
> Hanging out with students after giving a lecture in China...

What emerges from the guts of people who watch the US from far away is a powerful mix of fascination, attraction, and revulsion. I have been asked about the homeless on the country's streets, about the access to and cost of health care, about music and movies, about conditions in the American cities where relatives who have emigrated now live, about why America "wants to run the world." I've even received a detailed argument that because the competence of the American president is so vital to the peace and security of the rest of the world, foreigners should get a vote!

We are living through an era of intractable war, ethnic cleansing, and disastrously incompetent governments. Untold millions simply cannot squeeze a decent living from the place they live. There is human-driven climate change, and human-driven state failure, along with an inability to have a rational international conversation about how to respond.

The masses of suffering people at our borders are a symptom of that worldwide system breakdown. A young man who cannot find work in his Guatemalan town after a year of bizarre torrential rain and farm destruction did not bring the rain. He did not create the conditions for international coffee markets. He did not create the danger and dysfunction of his country's legal system. He did not contribute to the creation of an economic system that leaves him few alternatives, either in his hometown in coffee country or in the capital, Guatemala City. He has to make a living. If you were he, you would not simply sit down and die. Neither will he.

Just over the border in Honduras and El Salvador lie some of the most dangerous cities and towns in the world. The gang grip on life in some Central American cities has put entire families in danger — not only the teenage boys recruited as street soldiers but their parents and their sisters, if they refuse. Threatened with death by gangsters, a young man may try to make a case he has "a well-founded fear of persecution" if he can make the treacherous journey to the US-Mexico border. Yet all too often, the farm boy from Guatemala is dismissed as merely "an economic migrant" and denied entry to the United States.

The rancor toward people trying to save their lives, or to give their children better lives, has increased even among evangelical Christians. Elected officials in the US, especially at the state level, are competing to see how much biblical teaching they can slide into public school classrooms, hoping to begin test cases on prayer and Bible study up the appellate ladder to the Supreme Court. At the same time, they ignore the values deeply enmeshed in the stories and teachings contained in that Bible.

In the Bible, they are called strangers, sojourners, or merely foreigners. The Hebrew Bible makes repeated references to people from other lands, how they are to be treated, and whether or not they should become part of your own people if they live among you. In the Gospels, Jesus holds up love and welcome as among the highest values of His followers.

The Secretary of Homeland Security, Alejandro Mayorkas, a naturalized American and a refugee from post-revolution Cuba, insists the US did not create the global human surge tide that faces dozens of countries. But that does not give this country the luxury of ignoring it. "The world is dealing with the greatest displacement of people since World War II in the western hemisphere. Our entire hemisphere is gripped with a migration challenge."

The way we, as a people, see refugees may be nothing more complicated than an alternate way of answering the question "Who are we?" Americans who cast a skeptical eye at a flood of asylum requests suspect desperate people just want to tap into American bounty, nothing more. Those people are right when they say this country cannot simply throw open the gates and take in every poor person in the world. Often enough, it seems, that exaggeration, calling the long lines of people trying to come in an "invasion," or a "flood," betrays two mistaken conclusions: First, that "everybody," if given the chance, wants to leave their own home and come to America. Second, that "that was then, this is now"; this country could once be the place that could offer refuge to the world's tempest-tossed but not anymore.

Is everyone who turns up at the border anxiously requesting admission someone who is "owed" consideration like Amjad Ghafari, or possessed of the nerve and luck to become an enormous success like Andrew Ly? It would be foolish to suggest it. It would be just as foolish to deny it. We are asked, by thousands of strangers, to sit in judgment of their claims of danger. Our decisions — ours not because we all make them, but because we all own their results — say something about the hopeful refugees themselves and their often desperate need for a new start.

Just as important, these individual decisions and their accumulated results also say something about us. A mute green giantess in New York harbor once silently said, "Send them to me." What is it we want to say now?

CHAPTER SEVEN

AN ASIAN IMMIGRANT? WHAT'S THAT?

Looking forward, arrivals from Asia are projected to comprise a greater share of all immigrants, becoming the largest foreign-born group by 2055.

— Pew Research Center

It sounds pretty important, and it is. After decades of Spanish-speaking immigrants from elsewhere in the western hemisphere being the largest single group of arrivals in the US, people from Asia will outnumber them at midcentury. Remarkable. But what does it mean?

What's an Asian? Who's an Asian? Can a term become so big, so all-encompassing, that it obscures as much as it reveals? When the Census Bureau, academics, and experts are quoted in an article, or sit in a television studio and confidently say, "Asians are changing American demographics," what do they mean?

Are they talking about Hamdi Ulukaya, the Kurdish immigrant entrepreneur and the creator of Chobani yogurt, the burgeoning dairy products empire? Are they talking about the workers speeding under the East River in New York, crowding the 7 train heading into Manhattan jobs from the vast Chinese immigrant communities in Queens? Are they talking about former governor and presidential candidate Nikki Haley? A Jew who left Soviet Central Asia looking for greener pastures in the United States? California-born Korean American standup comedian Margaret Cho? All of them? Only some of them?

Even the authoritative Migration Policy Institute says simply, in a research publication, "As of 2019 there were 14.1 million immigrants from Asia residing in the United States, representing a 29-fold increase from 1960. Today, people born on the continent of Asia account for 31 percent of the 44.9 million immigrants in the United States. *The number refers to national origin, not race or ethnicity; while most immigrants from Asian countries identify as Asian, others describe themselves as White or as members of other racial groups*" [emphasis mine]. "Latino" is a confusing blanket that covers people from a vast range of countries, but at least they speak a common language. "Asian" is an even bigger and more confusing blanket.

A later report from Pew Research, one of the country's outstanding sources of research and data on American demographics and identity, grasped the nettle. In Pew's "What It Means to Be Asian in America," the research organization notes that Asian Americans come from twenty different countries and face the "challenges of navigating their own iden-tity" because of the expectations and assumptions that come with the label "Asian."

China and India have replaced Mexico as the leading countries of ori-gin for new immigrants, representing both an increase from those Asian giants and the many recent years when immigration from Mexico was either at net zero, or in negative growth. Better times in Mexico and a tougher economic environment in the US saw Mexican-born US residents heading home in bigger numbers than new arrivals. Similar to Asians today, Latinos in earlier decades have similarly insisted they are not one thing, "Hispanic," or "Latino," and noted cultural, national, and regional differences in their countries of origin. However, their shared history of Spanish colonization, legacy of the Spanish language, and widely shared Christian beliefs provided Latinos with cultural throughlines that are much harder to find among people who come from the world's largest land mass, from countries comprising more than half the planet's population.

Coming up the stairs from underground into the pedestrian crush on Main Street in Flushing, it is possible for a moment to believe that all the millions of recent arrivals have come to stand with me at this very inter-section. Settled almost four hundred years ago, the old Dutch settlement of Vlissingen, which morphed over time into "Flushing," is tucked up on one side against the site of the 1964 World's Fair, the home ground of tennis's US Open Championship, and the New York Mets' home of Citi-Field. On the other side lies an enormous new settlement of Koreans and Korean Americans. Jets overhead are finding their approach to LaGuardia and Kennedy airports, peddlers are squatting on the sidewalk calling out their wares, and Asian pop is pouring out of speakers mounted to storefronts heading in all four directions from the corner.

The New York borough of Queens, the largest of the five counties that make up America's largest city, has been transformed from the place where Archie Bunker sat in his easy chair and loudly opined on what was bugging him in that day's newspaper to become the most dazzlingly diverse county in the country. It is home to an enormous Chinatown, Koreatown, and South Asians from India, Pakistan, and Bangladesh. It also hosts large populations of Colombians, Peruvians, Central Americans, Mexicans, and other Latinos; Central Asians from the former Soviet Union; and some of the newest kids on the blocks, Nepalese, Bhutanese, and Cambodians.

Today on Main Street ambulances struggle to thread their way through choked traffic, school holiday crowds pile into Chinese regional grocery stores, travel agencies, and the surprising food hall at the New World Mall. It could have easily been plucked out of a Southeast Asian capital and dropped intact into Queens. I homed in on a dumpling joint, with four masked women tucking fillings into dough, as a fifth slipped her food service gloves on and off to take orders and make change in between preparing piles of dumplings. The menu was similar to the joint around the block from my apartment in Shanghai. I ordered, took a seat, and waited for a hand signal to retrieve my steaming bowl of black-peppery broth, crammed with cabbage and pork dumplings in their silky wrappers.

Fortified, it was time for me to head back into the scrum. Multigenerational families came in and out of stores, passersby dickered over the price of crabs, greengrocers tended the astonishing bounty on offer, keeping pyramids of mangoes, squash, and peppers ready for sale. Harried UPS and FedEx drivers vied for double-parking space with delivery trucks bringing stock to and from stores. The trick is parking your truck close enough to the line of parked cars to allow traffic to move around you, while still leaving just enough space to slide a handcart piled with packages up to the tiny front lobby of a small office building.

Amid the hectic hollering of buying, selling, car horns, and herding kids, one man is trying to sell himself to the passing parade. Dany Chen came to Queens twenty years ago from Guangdong Province, after graduating from one of China's few government-permitted Christian seminaries. Now a pastor in Queens, the fifty-year-old cheerily buttonholes acquaintances and introduces himself to strangers. He has launched a campaign for Flushing's seat in the New York City Council. Pastor Chen is cheerful, charismatic, and authoritative. He has spent years encouraging his fellow immigrants to naturalize, and vote.

His number one issue? Crime. It is a much bigger problem, he said, since the pandemic. "Robbing on the street, store robbing. Home invading. It makes me so sick and tired. How come this community should be in this kind of chaotic situation? People are panicked, frustrated, and people are so sad. We demand change."

The political novice talked with me about what he saw as an inadequate number of Chinese speakers at police emergency call centers and the local precinct house. About his desire, in the pulpit and in the Council, to speak up for values apart from money. "I know life is a gift from God. So every moment is a gift from God. Every day could be my last day. So I use all my heart and soul to serve the Lord, and serve my people. Some people don't know English. I help them with translation. And help them read the latest news. Help men filling out forms. Such a simple act, but they are afraid to do it!"

I mentioned the distrust and caution about interacting with the government that can be commonplace among many immigrants. Chen spoke up for the desire of his neighbors to hold on to their Chinese selves and, at the same time, commit fully to their new home. At the same time, Chen is a deeply American "type," going back to the earliest immigrant waves and the embrace of his new home. His message is red, white, and blue. "We are American. I commend American citizens. We love this country because of the freedoms. Because of the rights. Because of the free expression. Because every day people can do what they want. That's why this is the homeland of the brave. The homeland of heroes."

From time to time he would break away, greet a voter, press a flyer into a waiting hand, and return to our conversation. Would he tell a young man in a Chinese city today to come to America, after his homeland has become much wealthier, and is now able to offer a better life to its hundreds of millions of striving young people? "If you want this American lifestyle, free expression, to be able to chase your dream, to live out your values, I would highly recommend people come to this country.

"The Mayflower brought all those people. Looking for a place to worship God....What I fight for is Him." Chen points a finger heavenward. "One day I'll get paid by Him, not paid by this world. Even lawmakers, even the city councilmen, even those in the Congress and Senate, we are all public servants. We love our people. We serve their needs."

We part with a selfie, and Chen returns to pressing the flesh.

In another part of my life I spent a lot of time in northern Queens. I baked bagels in the early hours of the morning on the main drag in the Rego Park neighborhood. After the morning baking, I moved to the front of the house, nervously practicing a skill I somehow never picked up at home, slicing lox thin enough to meet the exacting standards of my Eastern European Jewish customers, descendants of a much earlier immigrant wave.

That old Rego Park has long been consigned to history. The bakery is now a Central Asian delicatessen, offering goods from Uzbekistan and Kazakhstan. Ladies' shops offer modest attire that might attract both the large number of Asian Jews who call this area home, or Muslims from Western China. There are men in *shalwar kameez,* the traditional ensemble of narrow cropped trousers and long overshirt. There are women in headscarves, and women in jeans so tight you could count the change in their pockets. They are now all at home here in Queens.

Bukharan Jews are now more at home in Rego Park than in Bukhara, or Bokhara, a legendary Silk Road city now in Uzbekistan. An ancient Jewish community, more than a thousand years old, saw the Jackson-Vanik Amendment (which opened the door for Alexander Vindman in Chapter 2) and decided it wanted out, too. Like the Russian, Baltic, and Belarussian Jews who took advantage of the Cold War opportunity, Bukharans began to decamp for Israel and New York. When the Soviet Union dissolved, another big wave headed for the exits again.

I met Imanuel Rybakov in his Rego Park apartment. He is one of the chroniclers, one of the memory-keepers hoping to preserve Bukharan identity in the crowded new world of Queens. For decades, more than a century, boosters have bragged about how many people from a particular place had made their way to America. Chicago often bragged it was home to more Poles than any city outside Warsaw. New York State gushed that it had more Greeks than anyplace but Athens.

In the modern era, colonization and decolonization, as well as Cold War and cool peace, have created something quite different: a world where racial, ethnic, and religious minorities simply pick up and go someplace new, leaving their origin point, their homeland, behind for good.

Garifuna—descendants of people captured in West Africa and transported to the New World—created a culture, a language, a new way of life for themselves on the Caribbean coast of Central America and in some of the island nations, particularly St. Vincent and the Grenadines. Today, the largest center of Garifuna life is the United States, but more particularly New York. People from the Caribbean islands of Barbados, St. Vincent, and Montserrat have dispersed as well, in search of opportunity. Arabic-speaking Christians have dwindled to tiny populations in their ancient homelands of Lebanon, Syria, modern Israel, and Iraq. This exodus made Dearborn, Michigan, a more promising home for the ministry of the young priest Halim Shukair than his home in Lebanon.

America has become an ark. America becomes a place that offers the freedom to be what you are, a version of what your ancestors have been for centuries. Yet at the same time, America offers a powerful cultural challenge. As a thousand years of Bukharan life in Asia dwindles, a large and prosperous community has taken root in Queens. Can you come to the US to preserve what you were, while not allowing the powerful, seductive culture of your new home to make your children forget the old one?

For Rybakov, the long journey that preceded chatting with me at a dinette table in Queens started with his parents visiting New York in the early 1980s. "They saw America, they saw New York, and their cousin explained to them that there is opportunity to come here for a living. He can fill out affidavit for them. They had an idea about coming to America, but they have parents, senior parents in Soviet Union. So they came back. I was a child, and I heard my grandparents talking about the idea to move to the United States. Some of my relatives did not support this idea since we had a good life living there.

"But Soviet Union collapsed. And economy changed. Inflation started, and Bukharan Jews started to move." With the collapse of the USSR,

Rybakov and his family became part of a Russian-speaking minority inside the newly created Republic of Uzbekistan, a Muslim-majority state. As Jews, they became an even smaller minority inside a minority. "The majority of Bukharan Jews moved from Uzbekistan in 1993. We received refugee status at the time and came here with the status."

Rybakov was no longer the little child who overheard tales about America. He was finishing high school. I asked if coming at that age, leaving everything behind to come to New York, was particularly difficult. As a seventeen-year-old getting off the plane at Kennedy Airport, just a few miles from what would become his new home in Queens, was it tough?

"The majority of my family lived in New York, and I was happy to join them. I was happy to see my close relatives, who I didn't see for several years." He saw greater opportunity for himself in New York than in a changing Uzbekistan. There was the matter of English. He had learned the language in school, but "it was a little bit tough, a little bit difficult to pass the ESL (English as a Second Language exam) since I was not so little. I had to catch up English as a first language. It took me for several years to be able to pass the ESL test on the reading and the writing."

If Rybakov had any second thoughts, he would not have had long to indulge them. His letter of invitation granting refugee status was good for 90 days. He had to quickly decide whether he was in or out. He was in. He worked part-time as a waiter during the school year, and in a Russian deli during the summers.

Looking back, Rybakov said two things smoothed his adjustment in particular: moving to a part of Queens where large numbers of Bukharans had already settled, and the range of social services for refugees from both the government and immigrant aid organizations. "For several years while they learned English, they could take English courses at NYONA, the New York Organization for New Americans. They received food stamps as low-income people. Medicaid, and also welfare. When I came and had interview in NYONA, they said that my English is good enough to go to school. I don't need public assistance. So I went to school. I didn't have food stamps. I wasn't on welfare. I was a student."

Through twenty years in the country, Rybakov has maintained close ties to the Bukharans of New York and Israel. His wife came to New York from the Bukharan community in Tel Aviv. He contributes to the Queens newspaper for Bukharan Jews and is active in his Bukharan synagogue. As the wider world of American Jewry looks sometimes with dismay at data on intermarriage (rising sharply), synagogue affiliation and attendance (falling), and even belief in God (ditto), Rybakov seems completely serene. "I follow the concept of the community which says that we came here not to assimilate, but we came here to integrate into American Jewish life while preserving our culture and identity."

I asked how he could be confident about that preservation when other American Jews were so worried. Over the long haul, would Bukharans, could Bukharans, remain a distinct group inside American Jewry? Would his son, motoring around the apartment with his toys, marry an American Ashkenazi Jew, a descendant of generations of Eastern European immigrants? A Sephardi, from Jewish communities who came to New York from Greece, Turkey, Italy, and the Middle East? A non-Jew?

"I would say that the majority of our community marry each other from the community. But of course, there was some percentage of community members who marry people outside the community. From other Jewish ethnic groups. Even non-Jews." Rybakov was insistent, Bukharan life in New York will continue. He is working to make sure it does.

He finished a degree in business administration and went to work at the United Jewish Appeal of New York. During the years working at that revered social service organization he nursed the idea of a college course on Bukharan Jewish history. His alma mater, Queens College, had established departments of Russian Languages and Jewish Studies. The department chair liked the idea. The director of Jewish Studies suggested Rybakov himself should teach the new course, since he had already written part of several published histories of the Bukharan diaspora. In a

2023 report *The Economist* estimated the remaining Jewish community in Uzbekistan numbers no more than a few hundred. It makes the act of remembering even more vital.

The Bukharans have created a dense, busy, hybrid life for themselves in Queens, complete with a network of businesses and synagogues and publications. We talked about language, in a version of a conversation that goes on all over Queens, concerning Spanish, Korean, Bengali and Gujurati, and a host of Chinese dialects. Would his children speak Bukharan Russian? Would his grandchildren?

"We mostly talk Russian at home with kids. And we want them to know the language. Maybe as second language, but to know that language. As a father, I'll do my best to make sure they know it. And if their spouse will be able to communicate in that language, they might talk that language at home as well as with the kids. But probably it will not be their first language. But they will be able to have some knowledge. And I hope that my grandchildren will have knowledge of that language."

Rybakov looks back in gratitude. He is proud of what he has been able to accomplish in America, and optimistic about the future. He said, without hesitation, "I am an American. I am a proud American," and later, "God bless America." He noted that preserving the culture of a small people inside a large population was something Bukharans did for centuries, as Russia, and then the Soviet Union, ignored the history of the people in its midst. He noted that in just a few decades in the US, more books, scholarly papers, and monographs on Bukharan history, culture, and language had been published than in the centuries of Bukharan life in Central Asia. His message to other strivers who are thinking of coming to America: "Welcome. Try it."

Much larger than the other boroughs of New York, Queens has grown in population to just over 2.4 million people, making it the twelfth largest county in the US. In recent decades it has become one of the most diverse places in America. The latest census counts more than half a million Asians alone.

As I ride the subway past churches, synagogues, mosques, and packed neighborhoods, the people watching is pretty great. A cricket team of young South Asians piled on to my train car, dressed in matching black uniforms and caps, lugging their equipment bag, with flat bats peeking out of the drawstring top. About a dozen boys in all, their excited chatter was a delight to eavesdrop on, as some spoke with the distinctive music and lilt of South Asian varieties of English, while others sounded like native New Yorkers. As CitiField slowly came into view, the boys did agree on one thing, after comparing their varying levels of experience and knowledge of "America's pastime," their conversation peppered with "dude" and "bro": baseball, came the conclusion, was just a more boring version of cricket.

Two Latina high school girls boarded the train, accompanied by a mutual friend, a tall and skinny Chinese boy. The trio stood in the crush, laughing and joking, making small talk. The girls both spoke English to the boy, one sounding like Queens, and the other with a Spanish accent. During a lull in the ride the girls spoke to each other in Spanish about a mutual friend, then one turned to the boy and translated, and all three had a laugh. As we rocked and rumbled above the crowded landscape, it was a 21st-century moment, created by massive forces of history, law, economics, and world trade. It was also a tiny, human-sized Queens encounter.

The Dutch colonial governor of New Amsterdam, Peter Stuyvesant, allowed Jews and French Protestants to settle in what later became New York. Black captives from Africa were brought to Manhattan to work. Native people came from their nearby villages to trade. New York has been a mixed place since day one. That banal truth, however, touches an endless human drama of comings and goings, of potato famine, poor Italians seeking work, Jewish refugees from Eastern Europe; of the Great Migration from the South, of white flight and Cold War.

In an old city like New York, ethnic succession, neighborhoods rising and falling in status and desirability and image, is a constant. You cannot tell the story of New York without it. The legendary Little Italy of *The Godfather* is not really the home of an Italian community as much as an ethnic consumption zone for tourists as Manhattan's historic Chinatown pushes north and Greenwich Village pushes south. A collection of Brooklyn neighborhoods, the second stop on American family journeys from teeming tenements and port-of-entry neighborhoods, once resegregated after the migration north of African Americans fleeing the Jim Crow South. Then, a few decades later, thanks to the pressures of proximity to Manhattan, educated, high-income white people pushed priced-out Black renters out of those same neighborhoods.

Similarly, in Queens, the ethnic turnover has been faster, with some neighborhoods flipping from non-Hispanic white to all those Asian and Latino groups that I found in Flushing. After spending several days in Jackson Heights, mingling with shoppers in the jammed commercial district along Roosevelt Avenue, savoring the quiet on a street closed to traffic during daytime hours since the pandemic, watching women get their faces massaged and their eyebrows shaped in a busy salon, watching a woman sell tamales from a cooler while rocking her sleeping infant in a stroller, and catching a glimpse of the Manhattan skyline looming over Northern Boulevard, I wondered: Can it last?

Can this "peaceable kingdom" of Colombians, Indians, Bangladeshis, Pakistanis, Ecuadorans, Nepalese, and on and on and on, really last? Or would the weight of history push this frantic, busy place to become something else, as it has over time in every other neighborhood in New York? At this moment in time, a snapshot of a neighborhood has been created by thousands of tiny decisions made very close by, across the river in city hall, up in the state capital, Albany, and in faraway Washington, DC. Those decisions created the street with a tall, dignified man with hair dyed a shocking bright orange in the style of Bangladesh solemnly walking his grandchild past a knot of women chatting in Spanish right after school pickup, as kids scramble around their feet. People hustle cell phone subscription plans, religious tracts, and costume jewelry meeting the needs of very different national aesthetics. Somehow it all works.

New York, like many other places in pandemic America, lived through a living space crisis, and is far from done with its aftermath. Tens of thousands of families suddenly couldn't make rent. Later, interest rates and rents both shot up, and families wondered whether they could stay in New York at all. Rhoda Dunn, a real estate agent who has been selling in Jackson Heights for fifteen years, asked the obvious question. "I don't know where people are going to go. Where in New York City are you going? I don't even know."

As a reporter I have covered gentrification for decades. Across the country, from Boston to Los Angeles, there are accelerators and there are brakes for neighborhood change. Demand can be an accelerator. Supply is a brake. The mix of housing types, single-family detached, multifamily, apartment houses, and the supply of developable land can flip a neighborhood or slow change to a crawl. Are large numbers of units in apartment buildings rent-stabilized, that is, forbidding landlords to impose large rent increases from one lease to the next? I asked Dunn if that encourages people to stay put. "Jackson Heights is not a developers' paradise. They can't get the land. Or they do get the land, and they're not going to be able to do anything with it, because so much of the neighborhood is landmarked. That landmark designation is going to protect the core, the basic integrity. The only real development that can happen is sort of on the outskirts, like along Northern Boulevard and Roosevelt. And that's kind of crazy because that's where the number 7 Train is," the elevated train thundering over the main commercial street. "Who wants to be by the number 7 Train?"

Of course, chief among the variables there are the immigrants themselves. When they find their feet, get a little American traction, can pool enough money with a brother or cousin or aunt to put a down payment on a two-family home in their next stop, off they go. For more space. For better schools. For a driveway to replace a parking space you have to circle the block for twenty minutes to find. Then someone else comes in, and the human drama continues.

Dunn reminded me of an aspect of neighborhood marketplaces I had not considered. Jackson Heights, built in the 1950s as a planned community, had an unusually large number of cooperative apartment houses, co-ops for short. Unlike a condominium, where a buyer makes a bid for apartment 312, and then secures a mortgage to finance the purchase of that unit, a co-op buyer becomes a shareholder in the corporation that is the building. A buyer has to secure a mortgage loan; she also has to be approved by the co-op's board. Many boards are tougher than the banks. They might require the buyer to possess eighteen months', even two years' worth of mortgage payments. It acts as a fearsome barrier to entry and gives boards the unique and perhaps exclusionary ability to be gate-keepers. For immigrant families this aspect of the market creates an incentive to buy houses rather than apartments. The down payments and reporting requirements are less burdensome, and you can choose the number of extended family who can join you in the house without a nosy co-op board reviewing your life choices.

Dunn is African American and a big booster for Jackson Heights. Being both politically engaged, and working in a business that has often contributed to the detriment of her people over a long history, she is very sensitive about displacement, gentrification, and the social interplay between longtime residents of a neighborhood and newcomers. Selling homes and apartments for more than a decade in Jackson Heights has given her a good feel for who is coming and who is going, in a community she is now sure will not go the way of so many urban neighborhoods in America. "It's not class based. It's not even race based. There's a strange thing that goes on with the South Asian community, for instance. You have people who used to come here as children with their parents who were from India. To buy all their groceries and foods and everything. Maybe their parents even started out originally living there. And then they all moved out to Connecticut or

New Jersey. Well, guess who's moving back into the neighborhood? Their children!"

While just over a third of American households live in rented homes, almost two-thirds of New Yorkers do, the highest percentage of any big city. The pandemic brought an initial drop, but supply and demand had the last word. A severe housing shortage has created upward pressure on already eye-watering rents: By the end of 2022, the average New York rent was over $3,700 per month, among the highest in the nation.

I was already thinking about renting and gentrification as I hustled down a long street lined with massive apartment buildings before crossing one of Jackson Heights's major arteries, Northern Boulevard. On this unseasonably hot spring day, with the weatherman forecasting dangerously high ozone levels, there was the huge, hazy Manhattan skyline. Right there. A row of skyscrapers loomed, like the Emerald City, at what looked like the end of the boulevard. I had forgotten just how close we were, both as the crow flies and the subway rider lurches, to New York's hub of employment and business activity.

Chock-full of restaurants, close to Manhattan, close to two major American airports and a major-league ballpark, Jackson Heights might seem to be right in the crosshairs of gentrifiers, people who find themselves priced out of Manhattan and Brooklyn. Younger, educated couples looking for a place to live come to Dunn, and tell her things she said she finds encouraging. "The people who are moving to the neighborhood now, they really want to send their kids, they'll do everything they can to send their kids to public schools. There are people who are trying to make sure non–English speakers are not being talked down to. I feel like they want to be inclusive. They don't want to come down from the mountain and start telling these Latino parents, these Asian parents, what to do." Public schools have often become the place where the battle for resources has played out in changing urban neighborhoods around the country. So far, said Dunn, this particular drama has not unfolded in Jackson Heights.

I have covered wrestling matches over local schools in neighborhoods across the country. Hearing Dunn describe new people ready to use the local public schools, I wondered how much had to do with the assumption their own children would be both safe and academically challenged in schools where a large portion of the students are of East Asian and South Asian ancestry. Stereotyped as it may be, it seems reasonable to wonder about whether the "new people" would be as evenhanded about majority Black or Puerto Rican schools. As Dunn noted, "There are very few Black people in Jackson Heights," and the US Census backs up the perception with data: the area is roughly half Latino (mostly Colombian and Mexican, with sizable Ecuadoran and Central American populations), about a quarter Asian, and 2 percent Black.

The neighborhood of just over one hundred thousand residents is stable, densely populated (62,800 people per square mile versus 2,430 per square mile in Los Angeles County), has low crime rates, and is over half foreign-born. That is an immigrant population higher than New York City as a whole (around 40 percent) and more than three times higher than the US as a whole, as of the 2020 Census (14 percent). There is no sign of the kind of blockbusting or panic-peddling that transformed New York City neighborhoods in earlier decades. Has Jackson Heights caught lightning in a bottle? Is it an immigrant district that will change, as so many do, but organically, in a humane time frame?

"I think our city policy, housing policy, planning policy, needs to be centered around a simple concept: Keeping people in their homes and their communities." Shekhar Krishnan is Jackson Heights's member on the New York City Council. He's the first Indian American elected to the body, and one of two South Asians who came to the chamber after the 2021 elections. The other, Shahana Hanif, of Bangladeshi descent and the first Muslim woman elected to the council, is from Brooklyn. In a stunning reflection of how the city is changing, two Korean Americans and a Cambodian American joined the council after that same election.

Councilman Krishnan was a housing attorney working in Brooklyn before deciding to jump into politics. Still in his thirties, tall and slim, he speaks rapidly and with intensity about the problems and prospects of his district. He understands the interplay of high demand, rising rents, and wanting to remain near extended family. He concedes that the history of New York is a story of what urban sociologists call ethnic succession, as groups in different stages of their American journey come and go. "The issue in Jackson Heights isn't communities that decide to leave. It's the many immigrant communities and communities of color that want to stay but are priced out.

"I can't tell you the number of South Asian and Latino families I talk to who tell me they can't afford the rising rents. We need to find affordable housing, but it's so difficult with our long waiting lists and our lottery systems to qualify for it. If you decide to leave because you can't afford to pay your rent here, it's going to be very difficult to find another place right around here."

For all that, when people from new countries with little history of movement to the United States find their way here, they are still often coming to Jackson Heights. "The biggest, fastest-growing communities right now, in addition to our Bangladeshi community, are Nepali communities, are Tibetan communities. And they come here as many other immigrant communities do from South Asia or Latin America. They need to feel welcomed here, too, and feel like they can stay."

One solution, if you can call it that, was to build out and finish basement spaces as rentable apartments. Some complied with building codes requiring access to the outside, minimum ceiling heights, and specified sizes and numbers of windows. Many did not. The rents are affordable for low-wage workers, and in neighborhoods like Jackson Heights, families wrestling with enormous mortgages get help with making their monthly nut. The councilman knows there is a dark side, too. The added units do not appear on city records because the owners do not want their real estate taxes and water bills raised. "So many immigrant families who live here live in basement apartments. But they're not legalized. They're not protected. They're very susceptible to danger. In Queens eleven people died in basement apartments during Hurricane Ida." The number of basement deaths in Queens matched the death toll from the 2021 storm for the entire state of Louisiana.

Krishnan cosponsored a resolution calling on the state to legalize those apartments, because in a tight market "that's a form of affordable housing readily available, to protect tenants in their homes, and give small homeowners a steady stream of income and rent. And it's a way to keep people here. For so long there's been this assumption that you can keep these neighborhoods affordable by bringing in market rate housing"—the politician showed a flash of housing attorney past once again—"but you can't rely on the private market to generate truly affordable housing. It's never worked."

The talk around "maintaining neighborhoods" is one that is always risky. When Jimmy Carter campaigned in South Bend, Indiana, during the hotly contested Democratic primaries of 1976, he talked about the use of federal power to shape where taxpayer-supported housing is built, and what form it takes. Even after two decades of rapid white flight and resegregation, this was a tricky topic. Carter promised he would not "use the Federal Government's authority deliberately to circumvent the natural inclination of people to live in ethnically homogeneous neighborhoods."

The remarks, coming as they did just after he said he would not oppose any group trying to maintain the "ethnic purity" of their neighborhoods, brought a firestorm. The headline in the next day's *New York Times,* page 1, above the fold, blared "CARTER DEFENDS ALL-WHITE AREAS." Democrats running to his left gleefully pounced, while his allies glumly said he had to move quickly if his campaign had any chance of recovery. After scolding reporters about their interest in the statements, he apologized.

Almost half a century later I sat in an amazing immigrant neighborhood, in the shadow of the Manhattan skyline, and listened as a young, former housing lawyer and history-making councilman walked some of the same territory, fearlessly and confidently. "There's never been an Indian American elected to the city council before, and for it to be from Jackson Heights, where the immigrant community really started in this country, is so historic. And so I understand the context of how these neighborhoods remind people of home so much, and the importance of fighting against their erasure."

Krishnan excitedly told me of two honorary street renamings in the district, adding Bangladesh Street to a stretch of 73rd Street, and Little Thailand Way to a section of Woodside Avenue. "Hundreds turned out for it in the heart of the Thai community." It was during Thai new year, and a short time later, he said, "We had a freedom fighter from Bangladesh at 73rd Street's renaming. He was crying to see the Bangladesh sign there. They carried me on their shoulders as they celebrated.

"I was thinking with the street namings you're permanently changing the landscape of New York City to recognize histories and stories of communities that are often untold or forgotten in the pages of New York history. It's far more than just naming a street. It can connote so much more about remembering home, why you came here, the power and presence of a community here."

In the midst of a long conversation about the finer points of zoning and land use laws, market forces, multilingual applications for city programs, and access to green space in a seriously under-parked neighborhood, I kidded the councilman, asking if even with all his success and reputation, his parents were disappointed that he was not a doctor. He smiled, briefly, talked about breaking the mold, then got serious. "I think they're more, as any immigrant parents would be, utterly nervous and always have been about politics. And very understandably so."

It is deeply embedded in my hundreds of conversations with immigrant families over the years that the best course for them is to keep their heads down and call as little attention to themselves as possible. Many carry with them from the old country, wherever it is, a distrust of politics as a device for making one's life better. Krishnan added that his parents' chief concern was "making sure we're okay as a family; that's the most important priority," and concerning their son, a worry whether "you can navigate a system that fundamentally seems structured and set up against you. That's probably their concern more than anything else, but many immigrant parents and families feel that way about politics, especially here in this country because they've been hurting for so long."

As a councilman in New York frets about immigrant Queens residents being able to afford a house, politicians elsewhere are not so sure they want Chinese immigrants to buy houses at all. A bill circulated in the Texas legislature in 2023 that would make it illegal to sell land or homes to Chinese citizens, even green card–holding, permanent legal residents of the United States. Texas SB147, or "an act relating to the purchase of, or acquisition of title to real property by certain aliens or foreign entities," would amend the state's property code, and would also bar "citizens of China, Iran, North Korea, or Russia." At several places in the language of the bill it refers to "entities," like companies or governments, but then adds "any individual," and makes no distinction for condition of residence in the US.

There was a ripple of speculation and concern in right-wing media about Chinese ownership of US farmland. Defeated Arizona gubernatorial candidate Kari Lake tweeted that this country should "take every square inch of US Farmland [sic] back from China immediately. Do not leave them with a single blade of grass."

The impression purposely created by the legislation and rhetoric is that China is buying large amounts of American land. The US Department of Agriculture estimates there are roughly 1.1 billion acres of farmland in the country. The best estimates of how much of that land is owned by Chinese government–related enterprises? Roughly thirty-five thousand acres, or about one-twenty-sixth of 1 percent.

Nancy Qian is an economist, a professor at Northwestern University in

Illinois, and was born in China, and raised in Texas. She told me she was not surprised by the increased speculation about China. "In the United States right now there's a rising fear of political competition with China. And that's well-founded in some sense. A lot of fears were heightened when a Chinese balloon was downed over the US. China and the US have really been increasing the tension. It's really attractive to voters to think that by shutting the Chinese out, that we Americans can do more. Unfortunately, it's not true, and it's not going to work."

The professor noted that China is nowhere near the top of the list among foreign owners of American farmland or other properties. While she stressed her own affection for Texas as her first American home, she saw the proposals as a reaction to the rapid changes in the state's demographics. About a quarter of Texans are now foreign-born, much higher than the national average of 14 percent. "Texas is a very diverse state. They're immigrants from everywhere. The Chinese make up a very small group.

"You can say this is a puzzle. Maybe this is actually reasonable. With the increasing diversity it makes it harder for people in Texas to find a unifying issue for them to agree on. And one of the easiest things to agree on is pointing out and highlighting the negative influence of a very small but prominent and notable minority that doesn't have a lot of voting power." The number of racially "Chinese" people counted by the 2020 Census who would be blocked from buying real estate numbered about sixty thousand. In the same census, it was reckoned thirty million people live in Texas.

The bill's sponsor, Republican state representative Lois Kolkhorst, said when she introduced the measure, "The growing ownership of Texas land by some foreign entities is highly disturbing and raises red flags for many Texans. By comparison, as an American go try to buy land near a Chinese military base and see how it works out for you. It would never happen there and it shouldn't happen here. Passing this law delivers some basic safeguards to ensure Texans remain in control of Texas land."

The economist likened the scapegoating to what the US saw during the 1870s. At a time of economic distress, Congress drafted and passed the Chinese Exclusion Act. "US policymakers came up with a quick political solution by blaming the whole thing on the Yellow Peril, on Chinese immigrants stealing American jobs."

In her network of immigrant friends and colleagues across many universities, Qian said she saw a rise in anxiety first with rumors about intellectual property theft and espionage, then with the rising anti-Asian hate crimes that arrived with the COVID-19 pandemic. "People would say things to them like 'We're going to have to nuke China.' It was emotionally stressful because they have family and friends in China. Hopefully it won't ever come to that. But I do think the space around Asian Americans is closing a little bit in terms of how free people can feel. How free, and safe."

Looking at the problem as an economist again, Qian said the best move for Chinese companies, with or without participation from the Chinese state, would be not to invest in any assets in the United States. "That includes land. It also includes mines and timber because ultimately the US government controls the land and controls the ports. It can control where coal goes. It can control where timber goes. These investments are really bad for the Chinese." Ultimately, she said, this is really more about politics than the real size of purchases and their economic impacts. "And it's simplistic politics. It's politicians assuming that the American voter can't really think things through."

There were marches. Petitions were delivered to the state legislature in Austin. Activists kicked the resistance into high gear and went on television to help the story go national. Some of the ugliest episodes in the long history of Chinese migration to North America, like various states' Alien Land Laws and the Chinese Exclusion Act of 1882, were invoked to push back against the Texas measure.

In the face of backlash, and legislative and legal scholars speculating that the proposed law was unconstitutional, the original language was eventually withdrawn. Rep. Kolkhorst altered the bill to apply the restrictions more narrowly to the purchase of farmland, energy extraction, and timber harvesting land by companies and organizations recognized as posing a risk to the "national security of the United States" based on threat assessments from the director of national intelligence. Kolkhorst defended the original and amended versions, and insisted it was never "picking out someone of a certain origin." By the spring, the senator had withdrawn the section seeking to regulate homebuying entirely. A Florida bill seeking to limit Chinese nationals who wanted to buy a home included similar but less burdensome restrictions on potential buyers from Syria, Venezuela, North Korea, Iran, and Russia. All these nations have seen an increase in new arrivals in Florida, but many are fleeing their homelands, not seeking to create a foothold in the Sunshine State for hostile nations. In Florida's case, a governor with national political aspirations, Ron DeSantis, has already signed the bill, which will face legal challenges. Other states are in various stages of following suit.

Rep. Gene Wu of Texas said he had never seen Chinese Texans so politically motivated before this controversy erupted. His parents bought their first house in Texas when they were still living in the state as legal residents, not citizens. "My question is, what does my childhood home, this dinky little house that my parents bought for $60,000, have to do with national security? I've not gotten an answer." Then Wu raised the issue that irks many immigrant-descended populations in the US, but particularly Asians. "There's this idea of perpetual alienness, this idea that Asian Americans can never truly be American, they can never truly be loyal, they can never truly be one of us. And this is something that our community has struggled with since there was such a thing as an 'Asian American.'"

More than forty years ago, a Chinese immigrant named Vincent Chin was at a strip bar in Highland Park, Michigan, with friends for his bachelor party. The early 1980s were a time of resentment of Japanese economic success, especially felt in Michigan, where fuel-efficient Japanese cars had been eroding the dominance of American automobiles as gas prices rose.

A Chrysler plant supervisor, Ronald Ebens, and his laid-off autoworker son-in-law, Michael Nitz, accosted Chin, using racial slurs and blaming him for the Japanese success of Japan's auto industry. The men got into a fight and were ejected from the club. Unwilling to let the matter go, Ebens and Nitz went looking for Chin, and forty-five minutes later found him outside a fast-food restaurant elsewhere in Highland Park. There the two men beat Chin severely, inflicting injuries that led to his death days later.

Vincent Chin was buried on what was supposed to be his wedding day. Ebens and Nitz would go on to plead down to manslaughter from the original second-degree murder charge, and the pair was sentenced in a Michigan courtroom to probation and a modest fine of $3,000. Later they would be tried on federal charges of violating Chin's civil rights. In that case Nitz was acquitted and Ebens found guilty on one of the two counts. The verdicts were overturned on procedural grounds, and because of pre-trial publicity in Michigan, the retrial was held in a federal court in Cincinnati, Ohio. This time, Ebens was found not guilty of all charges.

Writing in 2012, historian, and now president of Queens College of the City University of New York, Frank Wu said the Chin case created the identity and label of "Asian American" from what had been disparate groups with complex and varied migration histories. At the time, Asians represented only an estimated 1.5 percent of the US population, a share that has quadrupled in the decades since. Writing in the *New York Times,* Wu said "no single episode involving an individual Asian American had ever had such an effect before. And none has since."

Activist, teacher, and filmmaker Renee Tajima-Peña told me there is a long history of looking at Asian-descended people as compliant and non-threatening, which accompanies the long history of anti-Asian violence and hate crimes in this country, going back to rampages through the first Chinese neighborhoods in California in the late 19th century. During this latest rise in violence against Asian Americans, Tajima-Peña said, according to the FBI and various university studies, "the hate incidents involve predominantly white" attackers, especially white men, with Asian women as the most common targets.

Activist Helen Zia, one of the leaders of the backlash to the original verdicts in the Vincent Chin case, finds even Asian success can be weaponized. Asian success is leveraged to unfavorably compare the struggles of Black and brown people in America with the relative success of Asians. White hostility to efforts to address past discrimination in hiring and higher education is leavened by finding Asian allies to join in cases against affirmative action. Zia said the pandemic stripped away the comfort and cocoon of achievement in America, "realizing that they're not safe, and neither are their children, if they want to walk the streets, or their elderly parents can't take the garbage out."

The way the pandemic spurred violence against Asian Americans was a reminder of the way America can oversimplify, flatten out, erase the boundaries that a people may see in each other, that others looking in from outside can miss. Wen Ho Lee, a Taiwanese scientist working at the Los Alamos National Laboratory near Santa Fe, New Mexico, was charged with stealing US nuclear secrets and handing them on to the People's Republic of China. Though subjected to some of the worst treatment the US justice system could dish out to a suspect, he was eventually charged with only one count of improperly handling data at the lab.

In much the same way as "Chinese" are reduced to, and conflated with, "China" for an immigrant homebuyer in Texas, Lee, born in Taiwan when it was still a Japanese colony, was merely "Chinese" and thus a possible spy. Eventually, the trial judge in his case apologized to Lee for his treatment in custody and harshly scolded the US government for its handling of the case.

The label "Asian" can define. It can also confine. It is at once rising in common speech, becoming more frequently used to describe a fast-growing group of Americans, and becoming less useful. Today, a majority of self-defined Asian Americans are immigrants. Time and subsequent generations will force a big, complicated country to get its adjectives straight. Pew Research is right when it notes the label "Asian American" is "US-created." In their focus groups, Pew found a "disconnect" in their focus group participants between how they see themselves and how they are seen by others, creating a "complicated relationship" with the pan-ethnic label. One participant, who describes herself as Taiwanese American, told Pew, "I feel like I just kind of check off 'Asian' on an application or the test forms. That's the only time I would identify as Asian. But Asian is too broad. Asia is a big continent. Yeah, I feel like it's just too broad."

As people from dozens of nations in Asia continue to head toward the US, becoming the newest kids on a lot of American blocks, they will supercharge the journey toward the country's midcentury demographic tipping point. Just as Latinos have transitioned to becoming even more heavily native-born, the immigrant majority among the new Americans from Korea, the Philippines, Pakistan, India, and elsewhere will have children here, who before too long will also bear the next American-born generation.

We have talked a lot about the recent past. Let us now look ahead to what waits for us in the coming years. The good, the bad, and the imponderable.

INTERLUDE

Shri Thanedar

"I want to be in no other place"

In February 2023, like millions of other Americans, I sat down to watch the President deliver the State of the Union address. Unlike millions of other Americans, I continued to watch long after the speech was over. Call it "professional habit."

For people who have covered Washington politics, the scrum that accompanies the president's entry into the House of Representatives, and the back-slapping departure, is a "Who's Who in Washington" moment. It gives the viewer a chance to check who particularly wants to press the flesh and get a little face time. That night, as Biden left the dais to shake hands on the House floor, one of the newest members of Congress politely waited his turn, grabbed his quick conversation with the Most Powerful Man on Earth, and then continued to watch Biden work the room, smiling from ear to ear. On television, it looked one part an "I've got to pinch myself" moment, and one part (in a way that would gladden the heart of congressional staff) a chance for the freshman to stay "in the shot" for a long time.

He was Rep. Shri Thanedar, on the job for about five weeks, a long way from his boyhood home on the Indian Ocean in Karnataka state in southwest India. At that moment I realized I had to talk to him, about his life and his long, circuitous journey to a seat in the national legislature.

"I was extremely happy." Thanedar, from a respectful distance and still smiling ear-to-ear, followed the President after his bit of face time, as Biden continued to greet members of the House. "I had a long conversation with the President. We talked about Detroit. We talked about cars. And we talked about him coming to my district in Detroit." Rep. Thanedar called the President "a car guy." Relishing the moment anew, he called it "unbelievable." I put it to him that growing up in India, he would have thought it extremely unlikely to meet, much less know, the President of the United States.

"That's absolutely fair."

Shri Thanedar is one of eight children, six girls and two boys. His father was a low-level clerk in the Indian court system. "When he worked, the family was doing okay," he recalled, but explained that two events would push the family toward economic crisis. The customary payment of a dowry for each of the six daughters, and the assumption that the bride's family would bear the costs of elaborate weddings, depleted the family's savings. Then his father was forced to retire and given a lump sum pension.

At fourteen, and one of the youngest of the eight, Shri began advising his father about how to manage the family's dwindling resources. His father, who had lived in a rented home all his life, had his eye on a nice house in town, which would have used up much of the government payment. "And I said to him, 'Hey, you want to buy. Give me some time. Let me go around and look for you before you finalize on this beautiful home you like.' I went around and looked and found two homes for the same price, but these homes needed a lot of work. I came back to him and said, 'What if you buy these two homes, we'll fix it, live in one and rent the other one.' Kind of my first business venture.

"I helped him fix those houses. I helped him find a renter. It helped the family a little bit. At least the family had some income. The education of the children and the marriages had started taking their toll. There came a time when my mother said she had nothing to feed us. Everything was empty. She would go to the neighbor's home, borrowed a cup of rice flour and made a paste. Then she threw it into boiling water and that was our only meal in twenty-four hours."

While the rental and purchase plan might have, in the short term, saved the family from financial ruin, destitution was never far away. "Our house was the size of a one-bedroom apartment. We slept on the floor most of the time. We ate on the floor. There was no running water in the home. That is what life became for us."

Thanedar was from a Brahmin family in India's caste system, "so we were not supposed to do menial work. But I realized the family needed help, and I got a job as a janitor cleaning offices." While holding down a job, Thanedar was determined to stay in school. He was also in a hurry. He qualified for an Indian government subsidy for low-income students, which made his education essentially free. "I would go out and work, but not tell my family because they would have been heartbroken if they knew their son was working as a janitor." He surreptitiously supplemented the family income, quietly folding his income into family purchases. "My mother would give me a little bit of money to buy groceries, and I would buy her a whole lot of groceries. She always thought I was just a good bargainer."

Thanedar graduated from high school at fourteen and from college at eighteen. He took a job as a bank cashier and was now openly supporting his family. "A bank job was the best job a low-income person could hope for. Because you get a steady income. It's a good, safe job." He had excelled in science and wanted to continue his education. His small-town family was worried about his intention to go to graduate school in Mumbai. He continued to send the family money from the giant city, living frugally and working as a scientific assistant, checking the levels of radiation exposure of the workers in an atomic research center.

It took a bit of subterfuge to make it all work. He could only begin work on a master's with permission from a top supervisor in his department. Permission was denied. "He said, 'You are a government servant, a government employee, you are supposed to do your job and not do anything else.' I said, 'Sir I will do my job and in my spare time do this. I don't see a problem.' He said, 'You can go now. We're done with this meeting.' So I went straight from his office to the university and took admission for the master's program."

Think of it as an educational "Don't ask. Don't tell." The subject was closed for Thanedar's bosses, and the new grad student quietly continued to compartmentalize his life. He graduated with top honors, won a gold medal. With a freshly completed degree in hand, he asked his supervisor for a promotion to the next rank up the ladder. "And he said, 'Absolutely not.' And I said, 'Why? I've done well!' And he said, 'But you did it unauthorized.'"

It was a textbook case of the bureaucratic mind at work. Many people in Thanedar's situation might have simply started to look for other job opportunities in India, powered by his strong academic credentials. Instead, he began to plan for a move to America. It was 1978. India had not yet undergone its own modern economic and technological revolution, and the US had not yet become the beacon it would later be for bright and ambitious graduates.

"Now, almost every major city household has a person, or knows a person who has gone to America. But back then, it was rare to go to America." He began applying for PhD programs in the US and was accepted at the University of Akron in Ohio. His tuition would be paid, and he was promised $300 per month for teaching undergraduates. He could not head for the airport quite yet. Thanedar did not have a passport and was told that as a civil servant he needed approval from his supervisor to have his application approved. "He said, 'On only one condition. If you resign your job right now I will sign your form.' So I resigned my job, and he signed."

The next task was securing a visa to enter the United States. Back then, Thanedar explained, there were no appointments. That was the case in a lot of countries, where long lines snaked from the entrance to American consular offices in capitals around the world. "You just had to go there early in the morning and stay in the line. And they will take a certain number of people, then close for the day.

"So I went and stood in the line at 5 a.m. Even at 5 a.m. I am like the fortieth person in line. People slept there all night. You cannot go to the bathroom or go anywhere because you'd lose your spot in line." He recalled his number was finally called at 11 a.m. "I was taken to a window where there is a middle-aged white woman named Virginia. Even though I knew English, I didn't know how to speak well. I had studied English as a language but was not very conversant in it.

"She asked me some questions, some that I understood, some that I did not. And then she pushed the papers out and she had stamped 'Rejected.' When I saw that, that she had rejected my visa, I lost consciousness. I had never lost consciousness in my life before then. I had not eaten anything all morning, and I fell to the ground. I just collapsed on the ground.

"When I opened my eyes, there was a security guard standing next to me, and Miss Virginia was standing there with a glass of water. She gave me the water, but not a visa. So now what do I do? I've lost my job. I still have to send money home. I'm doing odd jobs to supplement my income.

"I was told if you supply more things, supplement your application, you can resubmit for reconsideration. So I submit it again with more information." The outcome was the same. His officer, Virginia, had asked, as is customary with student visas, if the applicant planned to return to his or her home country. Thanedar had said he would be returning to India, and she simply didn't believe him. "She asked me, 'Why would you come back?' I then tried to show her that we have a little bit of property. My father owns a little land. That's what I did the second time. The third time I said, 'Someone here has offered me a job when I come back.' That wasn't good enough." He finally placed a call to the University of Akron, a complicated thing at the time, and had the supervisor who invited him write a letter saying, "We need this kid because we're working on some very important projects for America." It was early work on rechargeable batteries. "I thought with that letter she would be convinced." Yet even with an invitation in hand to take up research at an American university, he was rejected for a fourth time.

Now unemployed, Thanedar was struggling. There were days he had little or nothing to eat. The days were marching forward toward the day he was supposed to report for work in Akron. He decided to try one more time. "I take that whole stack of papers that she had rejected with nothing new to give. I go up to the window, and they tell me to come back at 4 p.m. At four they said, 'Give me your passport.' I said, 'Why do you need a passport?' They said, 'If you don't give me your passport I can't give you a visa.'"

He wondered why Virginia had finally changed her mind. It turned out she had not. "They said, 'She's gone to America for a vacation. Her assistant is now looking through her cases, saw your papers, we liked them, and approved them.'" At the time of his visa interviews, Thanedar said, he was being completely sincere and truthful about his intention to return to India, to his family and all that was familiar. The US offered more opportunity, but the pursuit of a PhD was more of a means toward an end that saw him making his career in India with an admired American credential in hand.

Yet once he arrived, he said, "I started getting interested in American life." The young doctoral student liked what he saw in Ohio, and concluded his fellow Indian students were making a crucial mistake. "Lots of times the Indian kids come here, and they try to make a little India here. They eat Indian food. They listen to Indian music. They almost try to do all the things they would have done back in India. I was a little different.

"I was fascinated by the American dating system. Unlike the arranged marriages over there, the life here was different. I was fascinated that a person can choose another, a partner that he or she really loves and likes as opposed to being told who to marry.

"And I fell in love with an American girl. I fell in love with the American life and by the time I graduated in 1982, she and I were in a relationship. I was fascinated by this country. And at that point, I felt that I'm not going back." Though still insecure about his English, he was given an award for outstanding teaching assistants. Living on just $300 a month, and still sending money home, he could not afford to return to India when school was out of session.

"I'm stuck here. My father's aging. I know his health is bad. I want to see him badly. I can't go back. And in summer, I can't keep my rooming house. I was living in a small rooming house, paying like seventy dollars a month." During the summer there was no stipend, so keeping the room was out of the question.

"I had bought a car for $200. An old Oldsmobile car. That, I would sleep in. In the summer it got too hot to sleep in the car. Because I was a graduate student I had a key to the chemistry building. So I started sleeping in the seminar room." He worked on experiments in the evenings and spent the night in the building. "I always got up around 7 a.m. But one day I could not, and at eight o'clock, my professor and a few other professors walk into that seminar room and see me sleeping on the floor with my sleeping bag. I was really very embarrassed, picked up my things, and ran out of the room. I was really worried they would throw me out of school because of what I did." Wary about repeating his mistake, Thanedar began spending the night in homeless shelters when it was too hot to sleep in the car. It was only at the awards ceremony at the conclusion of his studies that Thanedar realized his professor's flattering mistake. "He said, 'Shri is so dedicated that many times he's been known to sleep in the department.' He did not realize I had no place to go. He thought it was because I was so hardworking."

Once again, Thanedar had to scramble, to improvise his next move and try to satisfy a long list of conflicting impulses. "I was in love with America. I didn't want to go back to India for good. I wanted to go back to India to visit my family, and I wanted to stay in America.

"I can't get a job because the economy is horrible, and being in the US on a student visa made it particularly hard to get a job, because the employer would have to justify why a foreign national should be given a permanent visa so he can work in the US.

"I applied to 150 different places after my PhD and got 149 rejection letters. I finally found a professor at the University of Michigan who would hire me as a postdoctoral scholar and then would help me get a green card." Lawful permanent residence would make it possible for Thanedar to both stay in the US and go back home for a visit. First, he had to report to Ann Arbor. His summertime "apartment" on wheels now had to make it from Ohio to Michigan, which was not a sure thing.

"I put all my worldly belongings, which was only one suitcase, into the same car I had been sleeping in, and I came to Ann Arbor, Michigan. The car did make it, but I parked in the wrong place, and I got a parking ticket that wiped out half my net worth."

He completed his work in Michigan. Then he found a job at a small lab in St. Louis. When the owner decided she wanted to retire, Thanedar put $3,000 on a credit card, padded out the purchase price with a bank loan, and became a business owner in the United States. "And I grew that business to an America-wide network of research labs. At one time I had over five hundred employees. That business at one time was worth over $200 million.

"I looked at this little business, and this woman, she's a scientist. She's sixty-five and had this little business for the past forty years and her revenues are flat at $150,000 a year. She drew a small salary. It was a break-even company. I think I can do better. And it was worth the risk. She solved very tough problems, but she had no marketing skills. She had no business skills. If I can marry the technology with the business and the marketing, I felt this business could grow and be very successful." Thanedar worked for the owner for nearly a year at fifteen dollars an hour. He was confident, by the time the sale was completed, that the risk "was minimal because I fully understood and had studied the business."

Meanwhile, success in his business life was not being matched by success in his personal life. While charmed by the American way of dating and mating, "I found after two failed relationships I was heartbroken. Those breakups were very hard on me. After the second breakup I said, maybe this thing about falling in love and finding a partner is not for me.

"I decided to go back to the Indian system and decided to get married in an arranged marriage. Because I now have a green card, I'm able to travel safely because I know I can come back. I went home and got married, saw my family, and came back. She was a doctor, a neurologist, and her research took a number of years. We got married in 1984, and she came to the US in 1985.

"Now life was good. I was making $28,000 a year [some $80,000 in today's dollars]. We had a good life. We had a nice apartment. Two children were born, my two sons. But in 1996, after ten or twelve years, she committed suicide." His boys were four and eight years old. He found a lot of his Indian friends melted away, quietly assuming he was in some way to blame for his wife's death, even as he struggled to hold himself up for his children. Luckily, he said, the business was solid and sustainable, because between his grief and the need to care for his sons, "I didn't really focus a lot on the business."

Once again, he looked to his homeland. "I went back to India and found my current wife. I had lost my first wife. She had lost her husband in an accident. We didn't know each other, but we were on a similar road. She didn't have any children. We got married in 1999, and she came over and helped me raise the children."

Thanedar once again focused on his business, as it once again grew substantially. "I bought a lot of businesses all across America, about eight different businesses in Florida and Michigan, in New Jersey, in Colorado, and in St. Louis. The combined revenue was in the $65 million to $75 million range. But 90 percent of the business was focused on drug development, on new pharmaceuticals." That was the mistake, he said. Too much of the business was concentrated on the development of new medicines, and in the recession of 2008 and 2009, that business dried up.

Revenue, and profit quickly disappeared, along with his ability to service the $24 million loan he had taken to finance the expansion. "I kept telling the bank, 'Give me some time and I will turn this around.'" He certainly tried. "I was working fourteen and eighteen hours a day on the business, just frantically, frantically working and pleading to the bank, 'give me time.'" Eventually, the bank concluded it could sell Thanedar's assets to satisfy the debt. He had one more shot: a private equity firm offered him $135 million, which would allow him to maintain a going concern, satisfy his creditors, and wait out the recession. A letter of intent was agreed to a week before the calamitous collapse of the global financial services giant Lehman Brothers.

That sale never happened. "And so they foreclosed on my home. They foreclosed on my business. As they were foreclosing they gave me a cardboard box and said, 'Take your personal things with you.' As I was leaving the office for the last time I saw in the lobby two awards I had won. They were Entrepreneur of the Year Awards from Ernst and Young. As I was putting them in my box I said, 'I'm going to win a third one someday.'"

He was fifty-five years old and starting all over again after hustling his way to a wildly successful fulfillment of the American Dream. The bank notified him it would arrive to take possession of his home in a week. "The home I had designed and built is now going to be foreclosed by the bank. The bank owned everything. So my wife and I put together all of our belongings in a rental truck." He had found a small laboratory in Ann Arbor the landlord was willing to rent for a reasonable rate. The bank was still liquidating his assets to satisfy loans. He was not even sure, he said, that he could hold on to the little money he had in savings without the bank coming for that, too.

In 2011, Thanedar was fifty-eight years old. The bank was finally satisfied. At an age when many business owners are strategizing about retirement, Thanedar did not feel like he had a lot of time to turn things around. He started growing his start-up's business, and in six years posted $11 million in annual revenue. "And in July 2016, I won that award again, Entrepreneur of the Year from Ernst and Young."

By this time, Shri Thanedar had seen more highs and lows than most people on the planet. Hunger and privation. Academic success. Homelessness. Love and loss. Career gambles that paid off, and career gambles that left him close to penniless. He drove his Rolls Royce Phantom back to the leasing company and drove back home in a rental truck.

Repeating the trick of growing a successful company was satisfying, and yet not enough, at the same time. He began to look ahead, look back, and take stock. "I have achieved my American Dream. And what is my life supposed to mean? Am I going to keep accumulating wealth now for the rest of my life? Is that what my life's supposed to be?

"I'm looking around and seeing that people are hurting. People are suffering. And so I said, 'I'm going to sell this business.' So I get an offer for somewhere around $35 million. And I said, 'That's good enough. That's fine.' So I take one and a half million of that, gave it to my employees, and I sell 60 percent of the business, retain 40 percent of the ownership, and I'm not running the business anymore."

After a life filled with nerve, risk-taking, and self-belief, Thanedar was going to change direction. He decided he would next go into public service, and he set his sights on a surprisingly ambitious position. He planned to begin his new career as a public servant as governor of Michigan.

"At the Thanksgiving table I shocked my family when I announced that I am considering a run for governor. My wife said, 'Politics is dirty. You don't want to do that.' My younger son said, 'Dad, do you realize what they will do to you, and all the attacks? Why would you want to do that?' My older son said, 'That's a great idea, Dad. Do it.'"

Michigan politics was a tough home field for a rookie season. There were vicious regional rivalries, complex and daunting racial politics, cities large and small in decay and decline. The Democratic primary race would pit Thanedar against experienced politicians with high name recognition and established constituencies. He decided to enter the race a little late in the season, and to lean in to the unlikely nature of his candidacy: his name and accent.

Looking back, it sure sounded like he understood what a long shot this all was. "I'm the most unlikely person. A person with an accent. A person who didn't 'look like us' and didn't 'speak like us.' Nobody's going to support that person! It's okay for him to be a computer guy. It's okay for him to be a scientist. But an immigrant that speaks with an accent to be a governor of our state?"

Michigan had two previous foreign-born governors, Jennifer Granholm until 2011, and John Swainson from 1961 to 1963. Both were born in Canada, however, a far cry from Karnataka on the Indian Ocean coast. The Democratic primary would pit Thanedar against Gretchen Whitmer, a former Minority Leader of the State Senate, and Abdul el-Sayed, a physician and former executive director of Detroit's Department of Health.

The immigrant entrepreneur-turned-politician tried to address his lack of name recognition by putting paid ads on television early in the race. If you are lucky, this boosts recognition in a way that starts to bring in new money before you run out of the money you raised to get started. As Thanedar retells it now, Whitmer's skills as a politician were underestimated, most importantly by him. She remained above the fray, while el-Sayed trained his fire on his fellow first-time politician, using Thanedar's wealth to doubt his progressive credentials. His campaign was initially self-funded, and the costs began to mount. He tried to keep up with Whitmer as his polling began to decline. He ended up spending more than $10 million of his own money on the way to a distant third-place finish. "In the white areas, I lost big. I lost big, especially in the northern areas. One, I ran a bad campaign. Two, the state was not ready for another businessperson as governor. And three, the state was not ready for an immigrant to be governor."

At the same time he was losing, badly, he was now committed to public service and set his eyes on a more winnable race. He moved from Ann Arbor to Detroit and ran a focused, door-to-door campaign for a state representative's seat. Aided by a field split seven ways and the lack of an incumbent, he won, and headed to Lansing. "I did good work. I brought a lot of money to the district for education, for mental health. And I never missed a vote in committee and never missed a vote in the house. I had a 100 percent voting record. My work ethic, and the money that I brought in — more than any state representative in twenty years — ended up with people liking what I did."

Michigan was losing a congressional seat after the 2020 Census, setting off a scramble among the state's members of the US House. Incumbents and aspirants waited to see what new political realities would be created by the new state map. Thanedar had his eyes on a congressional race now. His family home was in the district of nationally known "Squad" member Democrat Rashida Tlaib. "I have nothing against her. I am running here because this is my district. This is where I live. This is the place I represented in the State House." But the map had changed. Rep. Brenda Lawrence, a US veteran, was facing a difficult new constituency and decided to retire after four terms in Washington rather than seek reelection. Tlaib would also now be running in a newly mapped district, and not against Thanedar.

The seat he aspired to now included much of Detroit, and once again, his race was largely self-financed. Historically, this district was home to a large Black majority and sent John Conyers to Congress for fifty-two years, one of the longest tenures in history. With the retirement of Brenda Lawrence, the region would have no African American member of Congress. Various Black candidates stepped forward and succeeding in splitting the vote so many ways that Thanedar was able to win the Democratic primary and faced token Republican opposition in the fall of 2022 in this overwhelmingly Democratic district.

He was sworn in at the beginning of 2023. He currently ranks 430th in seniority out of the 435 members of the US House of Representatives. In a country where some congressional freshmen have been aspiring to the office for much of their lives, and having that goal shape choice of school, profession, and home, Shri Thanedar took the oath of office just a few weeks shy of his sixty-eighth birthday and just a few years after he'd decided for the first time to run for elected office.

Does he like the job?

"I love it. You saw the joy on my face on the State of the Union Day. But that's how I feel every day. The person who got rejected for a visa, who fell down to the ground, now sits on the Homeland Security Committee. I am ranking member on one of the Homeland Security subcommittees that protects America's borders, the borders I could not get in some forty-three years ago. Only in America could such a miracle happen.

"Maybe in the third year after I came to this country I felt I want to be in no other place than America. What attracted me was the freedom. The freedom to live your life the way you want to live. The principles this country is based on are unlike any other country. In 1981, in '82, I was very convinced that this is where I want to spend the rest of my life."

CHAPTER EIGHT

LOOKING AHEAD TO THE NEXT AMERICA...

...who do we mean when we say "us"?

Gail was from Poland. Zoltan was from Hungary. Nancy was from Israel. Raminder was from India. New arrivals to the US would be placed in my elementary school classrooms in Brooklyn in the mid-1960s. We were a couple of grades younger, a small and unthreatening welcoming committee to give immigrant kids the hang of English, and school, in a low-risk environment. I would love to ask them, now that they are approaching seventy, what they made of the wide-eyed bunch of us. We had no idea what life was like in another place: not in communist Hungary, developing India, or still new and idealistic Israel, for that matter.

Along with the new arrivals were the kids we sat with in class and played with on the streets, whose parents came just before they were born, people whom earlier censuses would call "immigrant stock." Angel and Manuel's parents were from Cuba. Paul's parents were from Germany.

Lily, Sammy, and Mickey's parents were from China. Domenico's parents came from Italy, as did Cesare and Vito's, Anthony and Lucy's, and Sebastian and Maria's. The day after Open School Night, we kids gossiped about who among our schoolmates had to endure a trip with their own parents to face the music on how they were doing in school. They were dragged along so they could translate their own achievements, or shortcomings, from English to whichever language, to their own parents.

I could not remember a time when I did not hear other languages spoken in my house, on the street, and in the stores. At the corner store the grocer would stop an animated conversation with another customer in Yiddish to take the list written by my mother from my balled fist, wrapped around the money to pay for the groceries. At the *salumeria,* a butcher in blood-specked whites barked orders in Italian to his workers and took orders in English at the crowded display case, bursting with pig trotters, sheep heads, fat sausages, and expertly tied *brasciole.*

It was not a big deal, and it was not *not* a big deal, either. It was just the deal. The way things were. In the decades that followed, I watched as America, and Americans, ran hot and cold on immigration, and elected officials were always ready to descend into demagoguery if they thought it would work.

In Brooklyn, your world could get bigger and wider as you got older, able to roam farther and farther from the front door of your apartment building, by bus or subway or bike. It wasn't until I was a young reporter, traveling to more and more of my own country, that I began to realize that I had grown up in a way that would not be familiar to most of my countrymen and -women. Time, assimilation, and geography had made millions of Americans strangers to their own histories. The dip in foreign-born Americans in the 1960 Census, before things changed yet again, meant much of the country was pretty uniformly native-born. Who came from the Old Country? Old people!

The kind of immigrant memory that gets passed along with language began to wither. In plenty of houses, parents spoke foreign languages not to encourage their children to be bilingual but to have a conversation in front of their children that could not be deciphered by them. Native-born adult children of parents who learned English as a second language, when asked about their own language proficiency, would reduce their fluency to a few categories: food, prayers, and dirty words. Driving in New Jersey, I was inching along in slow-moving traffic when I saw it: a silver SUV with a big New York Yankees logo slapped on the side, and just above it, another sticker, with this slogan, "Your [sic] in America. Speak English." Let that speak for itself.

The foreign-born people I saw in the streets of my childhood were part of the last trickle before the flood. They were those who managed to get into the US before the 1965 law changed everything. As I think back, the only Black immigrant I knew was Sylvester, the superintendent, or super, of the apartment building across the street. He was West Indian and, for the time, an anomaly. Why an anomaly? Because in our little universe, as in most of the United States, Black people and immigrants were two entirely different groups of people.

As we trundled ahead in a group exercise in acculturation in one part of Brooklyn, a member of Congress from another part of Brooklyn was drafting the new formulas that would end up transforming the math. Rep. Emanuel Celler, whom we met in the first chapter of this book, looked back to the fears motivating the US Congress in the 1920s, when the doors to immigrants were mostly shut. "Forty years of testing have proven that the rigid pattern of discrimination has not only produced imbalances that have irritated many nations, but Congress itself, through a long series of enactments forced by the realities of a changing world saw fit to modify this unworkable formula so that today it remains on the books primarily as an expression of gratuitous condescension."

The America of 1964 is gone, a place both remote and transformed. The Immigration and Nationality Act of 1965 is now as remote from us historically as it is from Woodrow Wilson screening *Birth of a Nation* at the White House.

And as for transformed, the 1960 Census noted that foreign-born Americans were much older than native-born people, and that the foreign-born population stood at the lowest percentage in a century. Today's immigrants are collectively younger than native-born Americans and their proportion is among the highest it has ever been.

The act is history. There are no do-overs. What we should be figuring out now is how to play the hand we have been dealt by that history. It could break us. At the same time, there is no reason it has to. As the US moves toward its more diverse future, the world is moving toward a gray one. A tidal wave of aging is breaking over the world, and the midcentury planet will be a place where people over sixty-five will be at new and bizarre levels never seen in human history.

As South Korea, China, Italy, and Japan will wrestle with enormous numbers of retirees, supported by shrinking numbers of workers, the situation we experience in the US will be different. Oh, we will still be a pretty old society, all right. But we could be a lot older if it weren't for immigration. As demographer Bill Frey at the Brookings Institution reminded me, there will be a modest but steady population growth in coming generations because of the high levels of immigration and the higher levels of childbirth in immigrant families. "If we had not had immigrants in the late 1990s and in the early 2000s, really the late 1980s as well, we would have a much older population than we have right now. And that puts us ahead of countries like Germany and Italy and Japan and several countries in Eastern Europe. The reason we have this kind of demographic growth, and it's not a big growth anymore, but an advantage over a lot of those countries, is we were open to immigrants."

Fertility in the United States has not been at "replacement level," that is, a rate of childbirth that would keep the country at level population, since 2007. The twin shocks of the Great Recession and the coronavirus pandemic has now pushed fertility down to well below replacement level (1.64 births per woman of childbearing age, whereas the replacement level is about 2.1 children per woman). In 1960, in the midst of the baby boom, the rate was 3.65. By 1970, the rate was still above replacement, at 2.48. In 1980, and in all the years thereafter, a decline in fertility meant the average woman of childbearing age would never again have enough children to replace herself and an adult partner.

Having more mouths to feed or educate alone is of limited utility. But having a stable or growing population of working adults to help care for the expanding, aging cohort of retirees is essential. It is the relationship in the size of birth cohorts that is crucial. The median age of residents of the United States continues to rise, and now stands at thirty-eight years. Though the median age of all foreign-born residents of the US is even older, forty-six, the age of new arrivals — legal and illegal — is just thirty-one. That number, too, has been rising.

The pandemic spurred many older workers "on the bubble" to move up the date of their retirements, cash in their chips, and begin the more heavily consumption-based, and less production-based, portion of life. By 2035, the number of Americans over sixty-five will have jumped from less than sixty million today to close to eighty million. If the working-age cohorts behind them are not both numerous and productive, there will be no way to finance the support and care for that aged population.

People who come here to live from other places in the world lower the median age upon arrival, and then do it again when they bear children. In recent decades, they come from places in the world where women expect to rear more children than US-born women. Americans who fear high levels of immigration transforming the essential nature of the country need only look at the lived experience of the people who are coming here and especially at their children.

Pitting those "good immigrants" who "followed the rules" of earlier generations against their shadier and more suspicious equivalents of today is a commonly used framing for nostalgia, self-aggrandizement, and drawing distinctions. It becomes the foundation stone for a strained argument that sees the descendants of immigrants from earlier waves find ways to simultaneously revere their own forebears and question the fitness of more recent arrivals. That flex can take people to some strange places and allow some remarkable juxtapositions.

Without fear of contradiction and no sense of irony, people will proudly recount their ancestor's work as a ditchdigger, maid, rag and bone picker, field hand, or dishwasher as a prelude to this country's boundless opportunity for affluence and comfort. The broader the socio-economic gap between a desperately poor immigrant forebear and their comfortable descendant, the better the story. Yet that same proud great-great-grandson or -granddaughter may also, just a moment later, cast doubt on the ability of this country to take new people in. They negate the hard, dirty work done by many immigrants today, the 21st-century equivalents of rag-and-bone picking or ditchdigging and doubt the same transformations that took place in their own family's history can ever happen again. A portion of the country's voters are prepared to make the work that lies ahead—whether we like it or not—simply more difficult.

Over the decades, the newspaper rack at the candy store near my childhood apartment saw fewer, and thinner, editions of immigrant newspapers selling to fewer and fewer customers. Some moved from being dailies to weeklies. All, from *The Jewish Daily Forward* to *Il Progresso Italo-Americano* to *Nordisk Tidende,* carried more and more stories in English and fewer and fewer stories in Yiddish, Italian, and Norwegian. When I went home to visit my parents in the 2000s and 2010s, those old stalwarts started to disappear entirely, replaced by *V Novom Svete* ("In the New World") in Russian and *The World Journal* and *Sing Tao* in Chinese.

That languages rise and fall as living tongues on the streets, in the stores, and over the radio is not an earthshaking development. It has happened in the US for a century and a half. The problematic part comes when the descendants of long-ago immigrants proclaim that their own family's choices—to set aside and forget the old country language—must be the only legitimate choice for everyone else. Of course, English-language acquisition *is* coming just as quickly for today's immigrants as it did for previous generations. Yet for the most easily triggered, hearing another language spoken "in the wild" is taken as evidence that today's immigrants are not learning English, are not acculturating, will never "be like us."

During one of the cyclical tussles over bilingual education, Mario, a Mexican immigrant, asked me, in English, why America would demand "that I become less than I am. Less than I was the day I arrived, by forgetting Spanish? Why not encourage me to be more by adding English?" I did not have a good answer for him then, and I do not have one now. The Census Bureau's American Community Survey reported that a little more than one in five people living in America speak a language other than English at home. About one in twelve report they do not speak English well. One of every eight residents of the US speaks Spanish at home. All it takes is a difficult transaction at a store counter to get too many native speakers of English steamed. Talking it out, you may find that the person complaining about service employees with insufficient English has no idea whether the person they encountered arrived ten years ago or the day before yesterday. For them, the people of today "never" learn.

I know better. I know some of my friends' parents were never more than barely functional in the language of their new home after long years in the country, in part because they arrived as adults. The romanticized memories of the linguistic abilities of long-dead ancestors become another switch used to swat, denounce, and demean people trying to keep their chins above water as they learn a new way of life.

One aspect of automated American life that appears to particularly bug volunteer members of the language police is the robotic prompt from the other end of the telephone to "Press 2 for Spanish." I have talked to people who see it as the sign of an erosion of the primacy of English in American life. They fume about Quebec, about an American future where they'll "have to learn" Spanish, and so on. They usually run into this offered option when conducting business. You need to dispute a credit card charge. You have a question about your utility bill. You need to report that an ordered item never arrived. I try to offer a modest set of suggestions: "Don't press 2. Take care of your business. And don't worry so much!"

The very idea that once settled, people from other places start to become part of "us" is under assault. It is one of the reasons I talked to so many Americans by choice. It is one of the reasons this book exists. When

Ronald Reagan stood at the foot of the Statue of Liberty on the 210th anniversary of the Declaration of Independence, he reminded his countrymen of the threat of disunion, a crackup, that always loomed in a dark corner of the national self. "All through our history, our presidents and leaders have spoken of national unity, and warned us that the real obstacle to moving forward the boundaries of freedom, the only permanent danger to the hope that is America, come from within."

Much of the rest of the speech touched on the commonplaces of patriotic oration on the national birthday, the meeting in Philadelphia, the patriots who died in our wars, the fundamental differences between the United States and other nations. Along with the boilerplate Reagan delivered a bedrock message in a way that seems dated across the decades but still resonates. "Tonight we reaffirm that Jew and Gentile, we are one nation under God. That black and white, we are one nation indivisible. That Republican and Democrat, we are all Americans. Tonight, with heart and hand, through whatever trial and travail, we pledge ourselves to each other and to the cause of human freedom. The cause that has given light to this land, and hope to the world."

I never thought I would live to see a day when there would be so much open disdain for the ideas that were once accepted in our public discourse, without question, as American guideposts: That the US should not seriously discuss breaking apart, after the bloodletting of the Civil War. That the genius of the system was to allow people from everywhere to take a shot at becoming American. That what held us together was more substantial than what kept us apart.

Granted, some of these principles were just heartwarming frabbajabba. Some were just soy filler in speeches on national holidays. Some were more ideals and aspirations than they were established facts. They were continually reiterated because our notions of who we think we are, and who we hope to be, needed repeating even in the face of decades of failure to realize their full meaning. There has been massive pushback against immigrants before, and there will be again.

I am neither soft-hearted nor soft-headed enough to believe that our failures to honor principles of inclusion, acculturation, and acceptance represent a complete break with our past, a permanent estrangement of ourselves from ourselves. We have not moved to some new place that violates who we are and who we have been. Instead, we have been backsliding. We unlocked the door and let our crazy cousin out of the attic. This latest era is not a betrayal of who we are but a reminder that our worst selves are always there, lurking, an opportunistic infection waiting for the chance to burst into full flower.

For better, and worse, the US has been heavily involved in the rest of the world, an expression of our overwhelming military might, economic power, and cultural influence. There are countries in the world where both benign and malign US intervention, overt and covert, has sent ripples through their histories that demand constant reckoning. Like a giant who cannot see what he is crushing underfoot, the US has sometimes paid little attention to the aftermath of its actions and given little credence to historical memory.

When the Sandinistas finally routed the last remnants of the Somoza-era armed forces and the US-funded "Contra" army, Daniel Ortega spoke to an enormous crowd in Managua. Draped across the plaza was a giant banner bearing the familiar silhouette of Augusto Cesar Sandino, the man who led the rebellion against US occupation of his country from the late 1920s into the 1930s. When Ortega spurned American overtures and embraced the decaying Eastern Bloc, Americans wondered, once again, "Why do they hate us?" Nicaraguans of all political stripes might have come up with a theory.

When the Guatemalan Revolution ushered in the first democratically elected government in that country's history, the new president, Juan Jacobo Arbenz, enacted sweeping land reform. Arbenz also expanded the franchise and allowed opposition political parties to organize. Land redistribution was anathema to powerful American agricultural interests, and rising Cold War tensions had American policymakers portraying Arbenz as being on the wrong side of the line between East and West. The Central Intelligence Agency backed a military overthrow of the Arbenz government in 1954. Guatemala did not have stable, freely elected governments again for thirty years. I would not suggest an awareness of what our government's desires and muscle have meant to the rest of the planet must result in no border, no requirements, no rules, and no standards. What I am suggesting is a greater modesty about what American history has meant to the world: for a teenager escaping violence and dysfunction in El Salvador, for an Iraqi English teacher who ended up as a translator for American forces, or for a Filipino contemplating a move from a former US colony to the US itself.

Americans who want a functional immigration system are right. Every country on earth has the right to control its borders and make rules for itself about who gets to visit and who gets to stay. The US is no different in that regard. What is different is the accompanying assumption of rights, obligations, and the ability to effect change around the planet that comes when you assign yourself the status of Great Power. As the United Kingdom learned when its colonial empire disintegrated, you may not simply get to walk away and indulge in active forgetting. Nicaraguans know the Marines chased Sandino through the mountains. Dominicans know the Marines splashed ashore in an invasion in 1965. Iranians know the US was involved in the overthrow of the closest thing that country had to a democratically elected government in 1953. Mexicans know about how the US obtained Texas, New Mexico, Arizona, and California. Guatemalans know the power of United Fruit was greater than that of its voters.

When Donald Trump advised the four members of the so-called Squad in the House of Representatives to "go back where they came from" it was not a violation but a reminder. Three of the four, Reps. Alexandria Ocasio-Cortez, Ayanna Presley, and Rashida Tlaib, are US-born. The fourth, Rep. Ilhan Omar, is a naturalized citizen who arrived in the US as a thirteen-year-old from Somalia. All four are every bit as much US citizens as the then-president of the US, whose mother was a naturalized immigrant, and whose father was the son of naturalized immigrants.

Ocasio-Cortez and Presley have forebears who were "American" longer than the former president. As someone who has had people over the years suggest I "return" to other places in the world, I heard what he said and immediately knew what he meant. And so did you.

Other American presidents might have thought something similar in private moments, even joked to that effect with intimates. What was different now was the willingness to say out loud what might have previously been an ugly sentiment expressed in private. Being a national leader might have, at another time, been thought to require that suggesting fellow Americans go someplace else is something that could not be said out loud. *USA Today,* in a content analysis of Trump speeches, found the candidate and president used such terms as "alien," "criminal," "killer," and "animal" more than five hundred times to describe people trying to enter the US. These terms may just operate as applause lines at a rally. They may fire the imaginations of an unstable fringe as well. The gunman who drove hundreds of miles to an El Paso shopping center to commit mass murder said he wanted to repel the "Hispanic invasion of Texas." The irony of doing it in a city that takes its name from a nearly 350-year-old settlement called *El Paso del Norte* was probably lost on him.

On September 5, 2016 *The Claremont Review,* a publication of the conservative think tank the Claremont Institute, ran an influential essay from an author who took the nom de plume "Publius Decius Mus," Latin for "The More Public the Better." It was called "The Flight 93 Election," and we now know it was the work of Michael Anton, a conservative speechwriter who worked for the National Security Council in the Trump administration.

The dramatic title of the essay is meant to remind the reader of the morning of September 11, 2001. One of the four jetliners commandeered by terrorists did not reach its target, but instead crashed in a Pennsylvania field after passengers banded together to attack the hijackers. Anton's pseudonymous advice to voters was simple: "Charge the cockpit or you die."

The hyperbole seems ludicrous. "A Hillary Clinton presidency is Russian roulette with a semiauto. With Trump, at least you can spin the cylinder and take your chances." In short, for Anton, under a Clinton presidency a bullet to the brain was guaranteed. With Donald Trump, you only had a pretty good chance.

What followed in the essay was an unsurprising litany of just how bad things were in America as the country approached the end of the second Obama term. Anton lamented the influence of his political enemies on universities and the media, the tendency of the American Right to "self-censor," a notion that by 2024 seems positively quaint. What caught me up short, then and now, is this passage: "Third and most important, the ceaseless importation of Third World foreigners with no tradition of, taste for, or experience in liberty means that the electorate grows more left, more Democratic, less Republican, less republican, and less traditionally American with every cycle.

"As does, of course, the US population, which only serves to reinforce the two other causes outlined above. This is the core reason why the Left, the Democrats, and the bipartisan junta (categories distinct but very much overlapping) think they are on the cusp of a permanent victory that will forever obviate the need to pretend to respect democratic and constitutional niceties. Because they are."

There are little verbal traps and snares scattered throughout, hot words like "importation," "traditionally American"—what is that, exactly?—and "junta." Anton's own Lebanese and Italian ancestors were, presumably, "imported" to the US, and over time became "traditionally American," perhaps with Mediterranean and Levantine cultural residues that made the family, and Anton, who they were. His own family's transformation was, in his telling, not going to be part of the American experience for new arrivals. "Junta" is another attempt at delegitimization, long meant to describe governing cliques that rule without the consent of the governed.

Previous generations of European immigrants came to this country from absolute monarchies, governments run by strongmen, and from countries not noted for their contributions to the history of democratic self-rule. In the 19th century, nativists speculated that the desperately poor and powerless Irish fleeing famine and British oppression in Ireland would never get the hang of democracy. Later, they would say the same of the people coming down the gangplank onto Ellis Island from the czarist empire, the recently minted Kingdom of Italy, and the thousands fleeing the chaos of Mexico at the end of Porfirio Diaz's decades of dictatorship.

Harvard historian Samuel Huntington said much the same in a 2004 cover story for *Foreign Policy* magazine, "Jose, Can You See?," taken from his book *Who Are We? The Challenges to America's National Identity,* in which he overstates the political impact of high levels of Latino immigration, especially in the southwestern US, and speculates on the future unity of the country, judging Latinos to be a threat to future "cultural and political integrity." In the book, he quotes one Texan who lists traits that hold Latinos back: "lack of initiative, self-reliance and ambition, [and] low priority for education."

A dozen years after Huntington, for many, it has become an article of faith: not only that the essential character of the country is being transformed before our eyes by unsustainable levels of immigration from "the Third World" but that this is being engineered as policy to create a permanent population of new citizens who will keep Democrats in power.

Hazleton, Pennsylvania, was elevated by the anti-immigrant right as a cautionary tale about immigration. A small industrial town in northeast Pennsylvania, it had been in decline for decades, its aging population, descendants of German and Irish immigrants, supplemented by Poles, Slovaks, Russians, Lithuanians, and others. As the veins of coal in the nearby hills petered out, other industries rose, and the city quintupled between the Civil War and World War II.

The postwar decades saw gradual decline as Hazleton's population descended from 38,000 in 1940 to 23,000 in 2000. But then the population began to rise as Dominican immigrants began moving west from the New York metropolitan area. Hazleton is 115 miles from Paterson, New Jersey, and 135 miles from the Bronx. Rapidly rising real estate prices in the New York region pushed Dominicans to make the next step in their American journeys. They bought homes that the children and grandchildren of aging residents did not want. They brought new commercial vitality to the sagging main drag, Wyoming Street. And they unhappily became a cause célèbre among Republican politicians and in right-wing media. Mayor Lou Barletta rallied his city council to pass something called the Illegal Immigration Relief Act Ordinance. It became a template for other municipalities, and one hundred others eventually passed look-alike laws. The act required anyone in Hazleton hiring anyone to do any job to first check their immigration status. It had similar requirements for any landlord renting apartments or storefronts. The act set small fines for failures to comply, and significantly, the loss of permits issued by the city to operate various businesses. In short, it turned Hazletonians into an arm of Immigration and Customs Enforcement. In addition, the council passed a law making English the city's official language.

A city in steady decline, with an ambitious politician at the helm, thus turned its recently arrived Latino population into suspects. The mayor appeared on Fox News and was in demand as a fearless warrior against the tide of illegal immigration. Yet Dominicans, whose numbers in the US had surged in the half century from 1960 to 2010, did not make very good scapegoats. Family unification rules in existing immigration law had long made the vast majority of Dominicans in the US legal permanent residents. The new people in Hazleton were routinely and relentlessly spoken of as possible "illegal aliens," but for the most part, they weren't. The Migration Policy Institute, in a 2021 study, estimated that Dominicans make up just 3 percent of the foreign-born population, about 2 percent of the undocumented population nationwide, and are more likely than the immigrant population as a whole to be naturalized US citizens.

Tragically, the words "illegal" and "alien" had been joined together at the hip, applicable or not, for anyone willing to demonize a new population—no matter that they may be reviving a sagging town. Lawsuits were filed immediately by immigrant rights, civil liberties, and business groups. Lou Barletta nonetheless parlayed his new reputation as the scourge of immigrants into a seat in the US Congress, though later attempts to move up to the US Senate, and to become Pennsylvania's governor, were turned back. The Dominicans, meanwhile, just kept on coming. Tucker Carlson, on his nightly Fox News Channel program, conceded that "most immigrants are nice" but called the changes in Hazleton "bewilderingly fast" and added that the influx of new residents constituted "more change than people are designed to digest."

Try explaining that indigestion to an aging couple or a new widow trying to sell the family home to a willing buyer. Whether or not they were designed to digest their newly assigned roles as immigration officers, the Illegal Immigration Relief Act, like other local immigration laws, did not survive judicial scrutiny. It was found unconstitutional because it assigned to local government authority over immigration regulation. Today, Hazleton has an "Anglo" mayor, a rapidly revitalizing downtown with dozens of Latino-owned start-ups, and, once again, a growing population. In the last census, 63 percent of Hazleton's residents were Latino.

Mayor Jeff Cusat, a Republican, took a five-day trip to the Dominican Republic to meet with elected officials and Dominicans in the Caribbean with links to Pennsylvania. "I thought it would be a good way to see how people who are moving here live and socialize in their homelands and see if there's anything that could help bridge the gap that there is between the people who have lived here a long time and the people moving here now." In recent years, as the city has become majority Latino, Cusat has stressed "kitchen table" rather than "culture war" issues, extolling the start-up culture among Latino entrepreneurs and avoiding the provocations of his predecessors in city hall.

The anxiety so many observers attach to places like Hazleton is cultural and is in many respects no different from what 19th-century commentators had to say about the people with cardboard suitcases heading to ferries and railroad stations from Ellis Island. The cultural anxiety is leveraged for political gain as well. Yet in some ways, Republicans fearing a permanent Democratic majority are on to something. The near term does not look good for Republicans: 48 percent of immigrants in California, 46 percent of immigrants in Florida, 60 percent of immigrants in New York, and 44 percent of immigrants in Texas identify as Democrats or lean to the Democratic Party. That does not mean that every other immigrant leans the other way, far from it. In Texas and Florida, states that are home to enormous immigrant populations and where Republicans dominate the legislature and the governor's office, just 18 percent and 26 percent, respectively, identify or lean Republican.

As the US becomes increasingly religiously unaffiliated, almost a third of Democrats have no religious identity, while just 12 percent of Republicans do. Both proportions reflect marked decreases in religious activity among voters for both parties, but the Democratic Party share of Hispanic Catholic, Hispanic Protestant, Black Protestant, and "Other World Religions" voters shows at least a demographic orientation for Democrats more in line with where the country is already and where it is headed. Remember this the next time a Fox commentator implies only one party centers family, religious, and patriotic values. What they may really be saying is that only one party is "the White Christian Party" at a time when white Christians are a shrinking part of the American people as a whole.

The road ahead is not entirely clear. The Biden administration has talked a lot about the treatment of asylum seekers, the backlog in immigration courts, and the large numbers of people heading for the US border. The Biden team has been slow to end or cut back on the Trump-era restrictions that sought not only to reduce the flow of people trying to enter the country illegally but reduce the number of legal immigrants to the US as well. The nearly evenly divided Congress has been unwilling to stick its neck out on bipartisan immigration legislation, especially as the issue remains exploitable, with desperate people from a long list of countries trying to make their way in.

There are also demographic and political realities that give us some things to think about when trying to contemplate 2030, 2040, and beyond:

—One in four children in the US has at least one immigrant parent.

—An overwhelming majority of the children with one immigrant parent, 88 percent, are American citizens themselves.

—Six million people defined as immigrants are students, kindergarten through college.

—Three-quarters of the adult immigrants in the US hold high school diplomas or their equivalents from other school systems.

—Of the more than 44 million foreign-born people living in the US, roughly 80 percent, 36 million in all, have lived in the country for more than ten years.

The shifting of the post-1965 demographic tides came gradually over the decades. Today's schoolchildren are growing up in a country where racial and ethnic diversity is unremarkable. Of the 18 million children in the US with at least one immigrant parent, a majority can trace their ancestry to Africa, Asia, or Latin America, rather than to Europe.

It was different on the front end of the change. Even for the native-born. They have watched in wonder as the country that misunderstood them, saw them as "odd men out" when they were growing up, has become a very different place.

Apurva Desai jokes about "A-B-C-Ds," American-Born Confused Desis. "Desi" is the commonly used in-group term for people of South Asian birth or descent living abroad. Desai, a Boston-born and Ohio-raised son of Indian immigrant parents, is walking me through the definitions as he tells me about growing up first-generation from a new(-ish) group on the American scene.

"We would be called A-B-C-Ds, or call ourselves that. Then there were also Indian immigrants who would be called F-O-Bs, for 'Fresh off the Boat,' right? We were born here but kind of living in an environment where our parents came here in the '70s. In the '80s and '90s India became much more Western. But our parents were raising us in the way the country was before they left. Much less Western. Much more conservative. Indian peers of ours who were growing up in the '80s in India were much more exposed to Western concepts than my parents were when they left India."

Add to that generational anomaly the desire among many immigrants to circle the cultural wagons, hold America at bay (especially when being part of a tiny community of "outsiders"), and you get an idea of Desai's world. America was just outside the front door. When he stepped back over the threshold after school he was back in India.

Maintaining "Indianness" in the diaspora is not some new trick managed only for the US. Many Indians are part of multiple migrations across the world, many that eventually led to yet another journey, to the US. The British empire transported Indian workers to southern and eastern Africa, the Caribbean, and Southeast Asia. It is only when you scratch the surface, talk about family history, that you begin to hear about grandparents not from Mumbai or Gujarat but from imperial way stations in Trinidad, Singapore, Uganda, and South Africa. Desai's mother was born in Rhodesia, now Zimbabwe, and then moved back to India, while a part of the family stayed behind in Africa.

When he looks back at growing up in Dayton, Desai recalls his parents gradually letting America in. "They tried to learn the music of America. My dad had these albums. Jim Croce. The Bee Gees. I was only five or six at the time but I remember them wearing bell bottoms, trying to get immersed into some of the cultural elements of the country. But at the same time, their friends were primarily all Indian immigrants. They were trying to collectively understand how to navigate this country. How do you fit in and raise your children at the same time? You learn how the system works, and they had strong friendships with some of the other immigrants in Dayton, Ohio."

The sense that you are not like all the others is something that first-generation kids learn gradually. Desai places his own mother and father on the more "open" side of the pendulum swing about opening up to America. At the same time, "There's no concept of 'dating' for an Indian when you are a high school or middle school student. There was no concept of going to parties. There was no concept of joining organized baseball teams or soccer teams. They weren't necessarily exposed to those types of things. It wasn't a case necessarily of them saying, 'I'm going to prevent you doing that.' They didn't know about these things. And if they didn't know about it, I didn't know about it.

"When I was growing up I thought, 'I'm trying to be a little less different from all my classmates. I am trying to push away some of the Indianness. I don't want to eat Indian food all the time at home. I'm going to try to push to eat hot dogs and pizza.' It is because we're trying to be less Indian compared to all our friends. You bring friends to your home and your grandmother might be there or your mother's siblings are visiting. They're wearing saris and you're embarrassed by that, right?

"It's like, 'I don't want my friends to see this Indian clothing and my relatives looking so Indian.' You're worried about that as a child. Even the language part. My parents would speak to me in Gujarati but I never became super fluent in it. I would answer in English. I understand it but I never got in the habit of speaking it." Desai told me that even when he saw relatives from far-flung corners of the world, they all knew English much better than he knew Gujarati. English became the lingua franca. "And I didn't want to speak Gujarati in front of other people, in front of my other friends." For all that quiet struggle to fit in, Desai said he knew he was never going to completely fit in.

"In my high school class of 625 there were, I think, five Indians. Not zero. Maybe five other Asian Americans from China or Korea, and maybe three or four African Americans.

"I kind of inherently knew I was not going to be popular, just because I was Indian. We knew that. So I didn't have the same peer pressure that maybe others feel about saying [things like] 'I'm not included in some parties, or the right people aren't inviting me to the right things' that kids typically feel in school in America around popularity. I didn't necessarily feel like there was overt racism or anything. But you just kind of knew that, just because we were different or my parents didn't know about dances.

"Most Indian parents won't let their kids date. So I never even thought that was an option. But I never felt bad that I didn't go to dances or parties because I never had that expectation. But today, Indian kids will have a different feeling. Even in a school with only ten Asians, they will have that expectation." Desai said he and his small group of non-white peers had to become adept at "code-switching," that is, changing language and style of communication depending on the circumstances, depending on the group.

"We were able to interact and behave in a certain way with our Indian community and our parents and their friends, and uncles and aunties, then more Western when we were at school, and interacting with classmates." Desai found navigating a hometown with very few Indian peers required the flexibility needed to fit in and left a teen and young adult open to hints of selling out. "If you're talking to Indian relatives who are growing up in a more diverse city like New York or Los Angeles, where there are more Indians and more Indian culture, they'll be like 'You're not Indian. You're not exposed to the same Indian stuff we are.' Or 'You seem more American' than our children are in some of these bigger cities. You did feel at times you were living more like a white American than some of your peers."

For many Asians, this framework runs smack into a paradox created by this country's long binary — black and white — view of race and racial identity. Learning that means solving the riddle of "where do I fit?" on the fly, with no guidebooks, and no hard-and-fast rules. "You talk about white privilege, especially more recently in context of African Americans.

We are always going to be lumped into a similar white privilege in terms of having the police in front of us. We're not considered threatening to them, the same way whites are not viewed as threatening. So we have 'Asian privilege' in that context. I don't know if anyone's called it Asian privilege or Indian privilege, but we have some of those benefits.

"Indians are generally on the higher end of economic achievement in the country. Of course there are taxi drivers and others, but in general they have reached a level of economic achievement in the country. That is perhaps a big part of the reason why we're not viewed as threatening compared to other ethnic minorities in the country. This is particularly true for me where I grew up compared to an Indian who grew up in Los Angeles, or Jackson Heights, or in Edison, New Jersey. We'll be viewed as a little bit more American than other Indians who grew up in the bigger cities of America."

Indian peers may accuse you of whitening up, and white sources of authority may confer unwanted privilege, but there are invisible lines stretching all across the landscape. In high school, Desai would be asked whether (or it would be assumed that) he had a girlfriend back in India because he certainly did not have one in Ohio. People who encountered him on the ball field would ask if he was Cuban, since athleticism was not assumed to be in the Indian skill set. "I would explain that I am not Cuban. Sometimes you get extra accolades because they didn't expect anything of you. So when I scored a goal they'd say 'That Indian kid, he's athletic! How did he do that?' These are extra accolades that you might not get if you were just another white kid that scored a goal."

Once Desai was out from under parental oversight, a student at the Miami University of Ohio, he found there was something he wanted to be: more Indian. "Now I no longer had my parents and their social life and so weekends were usually not naturally defined for me. We didn't have that driving us so I had to go make Indian friends. I had to seek that out." He joined the student group. He eventually became an officer in that group.

In the late 19th century, American vaudeville was full of comedians portraying Dutch and German greenhorns, with routines relying heavily on ethnic accents and "fish out of water" themes. A genre of slapstick even took on the name "Dutch comedy." Americans of other origins would portray Irish immigrant characters lampooning greenhorns who were part of urban life across America. Infamously, generations of white performers portrayed Black characters onstage. White men, Freeman Gosden and Charles Correll, portrayed "Amos 'n' Andy" on the long-running radio comedy series centered on the title characters, Black men in Chicago, and later Harlem. Later, a first-gen son of Hungarian immigrants, Bill Dana, would play "Jose Jimenez," a genial but simple-minded Bolivian immigrant known for his fractured English.

Apu, manager of the Kwik-E-Mart in the *Simpsons* animated sitcom, is a hardworking, earnest, highly educated, naturalized Indian immigrant from West Bengal. Over the decades of his character arc he experiences many of the highs and lows of immigrant life, including life as an undocumented worker, getting naturalized, and bachelor life in Springfield, ending with an arranged marriage. Did the cartoon Apu bother the real-life Apurva Desai? "I never had a problem with it. I mean, I viewed it as comedy. I viewed it as a stereotype of stereotypes. If people asked me about it, created a new conversation for me, it would mostly be about the humor of the character and the show." First-gen comedian Hari Kondabolu, born in Queens to immigrants from southern India, created the documentary *The Problem with Apu,* chronicling the comic's increasing disenchantment with the cartoon character, and added the voices of Asian American performers to make the case. Desai said of his namesake, "It seemed to be such a caricature that I don't think people ever came to me and said, 'Oh you must have lots of relatives who are just like this guy,' or 'Your extended family must be living in this manner.' That didn't happen."

We are in new territory. I am scolded for pessimism from time to time. Believe me when I tell you I held on to the belief that the open declaration of invitations to national disunion were a passing aberration, like Rep. Marjorie Taylor Greene's speculation about a possible "national divorce." Our crazy cousin did not slip out of the attic unnoticed. The old, creaky door was swung open, and he was invited down to the parlor floor to mingle with the guests. A few years after he advised people to return to countries they were not from, President Trump speculated about the constitutional qualification of Kamala Harris to run for president. Because both her parents were immigrants, Trump said, "I heard today that she doesn't meet the requirements," though Harris's birthplace of Oakland is unquestionably part of the United States.

The candidate for reelection was channeling an article in *Newsweek* by law professor John Eastman, a fellow at the conservative research center the Claremont Institute, and later a codefendant in the Georgia election fraud case against the former president. Eastman made the claim, widely derided and debunked by other legal scholars, that because neither of Harris's parents, natives of Jamaica and India, were citizens at the time of her birth in 1964, she was not a "natural-born citizen" under the meaning of the Constitution's requirements to hold the presidency, or the 12th Amendment, which laid out the requirements for holding the office of vice president.

I assume Donald Trump knew full well the Democratic Party was not going to drop Harris from the ticket. I assume he had no interest in the intricacies of the 14th Amendment, which granted full citizenship to formerly enslaved persons and their descendants, or could name the landmark decision *United States v. Wong Kim Ark*. The case enshrined birthright citizenship, or *jus soli,* the idea that anyone born on American soil is a citizen. It was, once again, the country's legally chosen leader throwing a lit match onto a pile of oily rags and then casually walking away. Long before he became a candidate for president in 2015, the New York real estate mogul and reality television star did much the same with the assertion that then-president Barack Obama was not born in the United States.

He set the fire. He said investigators he had sent to Hawaii "couldn't believe what they were finding." On April, 7, 2011, live on NBC's *Today* program, the future candidate told Americans, "I would like to have him show his birth certificate, and to be honest with you, I hope he can. Because if he can't, if he wasn't born in this country, which is a real possibility, then he has pulled one of the greatest con jobs in the history of politics." A lit match is tossed into a flammable public, and the arsonist simply moves on.

Five years later, at a news conference in his Washington hotel, candidate Trump said, "President Barack Obama was born in the United States. Period." He refused to talk any further about the idea he had cultivated for years for two reasons: it had done its work, and now he wanted to be taken seriously. He declared the matter closed. Even later, it emerged he never even sent investigators to Hawaii in the first place.

By 2020 it seemed we had become inured to the casual foolishness involved in his saying, as Trump did on Laura Ingraham's program in 2011, "He doesn't have a birth certificate, or if he does, there's something on that certificate that is very bad for him. Now, somebody told me, and I have no idea if this is bad for him or not, but perhaps it would be, that where it says 'religion,' it might have 'Muslim.' And if you're a Muslim, you don't change your religion, by the way."

Method, and madness. Tell a highly self-selected audience of Americans that the President of the United States is a liar, a foreigner, and that not only is he a member of a hated religion but must remain a member of that religion. Birth certificate? Fake. US citizenship? Fake. Even his adult baptism and the joining of a church in Chicago? All fake.

As a national figure, the Queens native had long since figured something out, perhaps not even consciously: By the 21st century, portraying a fellow citizen as a foreigner was a way of discrediting them. He knew it when he questioned the citizenship of the President of the United States. He knew it when he dismissed the Indiana-born federal judge overseeing the fraud case over his phony school, Trump University, as a "Mexican judge." And he knew it when he suggested four members of the US Congress go "back" to other countries.

If you think that kind of deliberate "othering" of American citizens, the casual creation of a racial hierarchy, has little impact, or accomplishes nothing significant, think again. Before the announcement of Biden's running mate choice of Kamala Harris, her Illinois colleague Tammy Duckworth was also under consideration. The *New York Times* reported the Biden political team worried about the attention her overseas birth to a Thai mother would get and steered clear of Duckworth, a disabled vet who lost her right leg and most of her left as an army helicopter pilot in the Iraq War and retired from the US Army Reserves as a lieutenant colonel.

Duckworth was born in Thailand. Her father was a US citizen who made a career in aid and development work for nongovernment organizations. She had the same claim to US citizenship by birth as Texas senator Ted Cruz, born in Canada to a Cuban-born father and US citizen mother. Being a multilingual combat veteran, and the only senator in American history to give birth while in office, was not enough to distract from her birth in Bangkok.

If you have put together anything from the stories in this book, it may be these two conflicting—yet complementary—strands of America's historical DNA: We have mistreated, exploited, and regarded immigrants with suspicion throughout our history, and at the same time, some of the anxiety accompanying modern immigration to the US is connected to the fact that the people who come here now to begin new lives are not perceived as white. The historical throughline of "hazing the new kids" is real. So are the men chanting "You will not replace us!" around a statue of Robert E. Lee. While in tension, these two strands are not contradictory.

The first idea, the sufferings and trials of past generations of immigrants, allows us to dismiss the needless suffering and exclusion of today, by allowing us to say, "Hey! My ancestors had it rough, too!" and to add, for good measure, "AND they learned English!"

A Pakistani working at a muffler shop in Brooklyn, Salvadoran office cleaners coming back to work after the pandemic sent everyone home in the District of Columbia, Mexicans turning pigs into pork chops in Iowa, a Chinese realtor in Texas, an Indian math instructor in a Texas community college, a Syrian selling cell phone plans in Michigan, a Venezuelan keeping his fingers crossed while waiting for the renewal of temporary protected status, a host of immigrants from Mexico and Central America operating rug looms in Georgia, a bilingual ed teacher in Massachusetts, an Iranian librarian in Southern California, a Haitian city councilman in South Florida, a Nigerian oncologist checking the results of a genetic screen in Chicago...they all, individually and separately, create gut check moments for us as a people.

We who by happenstance were born here, who did not choose it but benefit from it every day, have a choice to make. We can make room, as room was made for our forebears, or we can...fair is fair, right?...hold people who have come from everywhere to put their shoulders to the wheel at arm's length. Right now, it is impossible to know how hard we are going to make it. The next twenty years will have a lot to say about the next eighty years.

The Great Replacement lurks in dark corners of the national head, and occasionally bursts into the light. In floor debate in the state legislature, Nebraska senator Steve Erdman noted slow US population growth over the past half century and managed to entwine two wedge issues: immigration and abortion. "Our state population has not grown except by those foreigners who have moved here, or refugees who have been placed here. Why is that? It's because we've killed two hundred thousand people. These are people we've killed." Erdman added that Nebraska job vacancies would be filled if abortion had not been legal in the state.

Steve Bannon, former publisher of Breitbart and a close campaign and policy advisor to Donald Trump, repeatedly exhorted audiences and readers to get their hands on the French novel *Camp of the Saints*. The once-obscure dystopian fantasy by Jean Raspail tells the story of a coordinated invasion of France by non-white hordes, hundreds of thousands of excrement-eating Indians are headed for Europe, and modern liberal bureaucrats, politicians, and religious leaders dither over what to do about their arrival. Millions more lie in wait in their own home countries scattered across the globe, waiting for the Indians' arrival as a signal to pour into other countries to overwhelm Western civilization.

The French eventually make the decision to kill the Indian invaders, but by the time they do, the feckless, demoralized, decadent armed forces are no longer able to pull it off. The grotesqueries of the storyline are only exceeded by Raspail's lurid accounts of the subhuman armies of sexually deviant, undifferentiated dark people as "like an anthill slashed open."

The novel's plot points incorporate many of the obsessions of Great Replacement: the masses of the Global South destroy everything in their path and yet demand to be treated to a developed world standard of living; symbolic, high-profile actors are coerced into surrender (the British Queen is forced to marry off her son to a Pakistani, the mayor of New York is forced to bring Black families from Harlem to live in his official residence, Gracie Mansion); race is essential, as melanated millions become nothing more than types, unable to assimilate, unwilling to acculturate, contributing nothing while taking everything. Raspail's story, cited and repeated by Bannon, hammers home the idea that "they" can never become "us." The world's non-white masses will use Western liberal institutions, humanity, and rule of law and turn their power against the engine of productivity and affluence in the world, pulling humankind down to their desperate level.

John Tanton, who founded Federation for American Immigration Reform, USEnglish, and NumbersUSA—research organizations and think tanks devoted to arguing against the postwar US approach to immigration and acculturation—acquired the rights to publishing *Camp of the Saints* in the US. Like intermittent fever it drops from sight, then returns to bestseller lists. Trump's immigration adviser Steven Miller has compared its plot to recent waves of immigrants heading for the southern border. Former Iowa congressman Steve King, who reminded Americans they could not rebuild a civilization using "other people's children," said the *Camp of the Saints* "narrative should be imprinted into everyone's brain."

For years, versions of The Great Replacement circulated in corners of the internet like 4Chan and 8Chan, sites where like-minded people around the world could pool up and trade pictures and ideas. It was very easy to find the manifesto written by the young Australian Brenton Tarrant, who murdered fifty-one people in two New Zealand mosques.

In the long document explaining some of the thinking behind the worst mass shooting in New Zealand history, Tarrant looked at birth rates, immigration flows, and the fates of the so-called white nations like Australia, Canada, and the United States and said it all amounted to "WHITE GENOCIDE." Looking across the Pacific to the US, Tarrant hoped for conflict over the ownership of firearms "in order to further the social, cultural, political, and racial divide within the United States." He predicted the US would eventually "balkanize" over racial lines, "ensuring the future of the White race on the North American continent, but also ensuring the death of the 'melting pot' pipe dream."

Tarrant dated his radicalization to a long trip through Europe in the 2010s. He was particularly enflamed by the immigrant presence in France, and what he saw in small cities and towns where French-born whites were childish or old, while "immigrants were young, energized, and with large families and many children." Forty years after the publication of *Camp of the Saints,* a young man saw France as the battlefront in the battle for the survival of white civilization.

The man who would go on to shoot some ninety people on one horrific morning told of sitting in a parking lot in a small French shopping center watching "a stream of invaders walk through the shopping center's front doors. For every French man or woman there was double the number of invaders. I had seen enough." Just a few paragraphs later, Tarrant asked, "Why won't somebody do something?" And shortly thereafter, "If not me, then who?"

Considering the way information, and ideas, and obsessions move around the world at light speed, it was inevitable Tarrant's declaration would become widely read, and this killer, now serving a life sentence, would be made a hero. Just days after the New Zealand attack was watched all over the world as a livestream, nineteen-year-old John Earnest set a mosque on fire in Escondido, California, north of San Diego. A month later, Earnest opened fire during a Passover service at a synagogue in Poway, California, killing one worshipper and injuring three others.

After the mosque attack, Earnest had texted with a friend about his regret at missing the livestream posted by Tarrant, and of the manifesto said, "I've only read a little but so far he's spot on with everything," and later, "I think it's important that everyone should read it."

Tragedy is layered on top of tragedy. At the core of it all is a deep, central belief that a Salvadoran attorney in Los Angeles, a young priest from Lebanon in Michigan, an EMT from Mexico saving lives in Houston, a Vietnamese baking entrepreneur in the Bay Area, an Indian-born member of Congress, a Nigerian breast cancer specialist in Chicago, and a Kenyan military veteran in Maryland have all missed something essential about America. The conclusion of the Bannons, the Millers, the Tantons, the Tarrants, the Earnests, the Carlsons is a fundamentally pessimistic one. It is soaked in pessimism about the abiding and astonishing transformative power of America. They show themselves unable to conceive of a country where just like the Europeans who came down the gangplanks and first set foot on Ellis Island, the modern migrants who walk down jetways, and roll the dice with their lives will change this place. And be changed by it, enlivening, enriching, exciting their country and the people they share it with.

Idealism and patriotism are in healthy supply among the immigrants I have been interviewing for the last three years. Rep. Rajah Krishnamoorthi, a Democrat representing Illinois, came to the US when he was just three months old, in 1973. His father was already here, studying engineering at the University at Buffalo, a branch of the State University of New York. "Things were going great until they didn't go so great. And my father lost his income." The congressman is frank about his family's early struggles in America. "Thanks to the generosity and goodwill of the people of the US I spent half my childhood on food stamps and living in public housing." His father was finally able to finish his education and got a job teaching at Bradley University in Peoria. "We unfurled the map, loaded up the U-Haul, and headed to Illinois."

Looking back, Krishnamoorthi describes his parents as both "devout Hindus" and "devout Americans." He told me, "The assignment they gave me from the time I was a little boy was to make sure this country is here for the next families who need it." For the congressman, that means looking for ways to protect minorities, of every kind, racial, ethnic, sexual, "any minority of any stripe." Over the course of his life he has watched as the world continued to come to America, and he has gone from a childhood where he was the only South Asian kid until the third grade, to adulthood, witnessing massive celebrations in big cities for Indian Independence Day, filled with pride in significant accomplishment and optimism about America's future. As both an immigrant and an elected official, he calls recent years "painful," as he watched a tone shift in the debates over immigration, with "latent feelings that came to the surface, and expressed themselves in some very ugly ways," including the January 6, 2021, riot at the US Capitol, which he describes as a "violent culmination" of the trend.

"Look, I'm an immigrant with twenty-nine letters in my name. I check all the boxes of the kind of people these folks despise." His answer? Education, and growth. He said as a Chicago Cubs fan, optimism is in his DNA. "There's a lot of hard work that has to be done very quickly.

"Perhaps this is naive. But if you put a little more money in people's pockets, even with all the changes in the global economy that alienate them, they're broader. They're more welcoming, more open. If you don't figure out a way to get them on the up escalator, convince them their economic horizons are broadening, all of a sudden you have a large community of people the Donald Trumps of the world can convince they're in danger. It's a race against time. We've got to get people better prepared. That's the key to unlocking this puzzle."

If the economy is growing, and the gains are widely distributed, that constant undertow of America as a zero-sum game pitting immigrants against the native-born becomes a fire that just cannot get enough oxygen to spread.

The lives of the people you met in the pages of this book push back against the implicit notion that the US will be worse off, taken advantage of, if it continues to be an ingatherer of nations. Most Americans tell pollsters they are ready to take a chance on the people who have come here from everywhere to take a chance on this country.

In 2050, eighty-five years after LBJ and Teddy Kennedy promised the law would not bring big change, the America created by the Immigration and Nationality Act of 1965 will look a little different. It will taste and sound a little different, too. Graduates throwing their mortarboards in the air, newly sworn officers marching past their proud parents at West Point, the President pronouncing the State of the Union to be "sound," may all be a little different from what we have been accustomed to up until this very moment.

For all that difference, we will still be "us." What the road to 2050 looks like, smooth or rocky, is up to "us," too.

Epilogue

"ESPECIALLY THE PEOPLE"

What is America to me?
A name.
A map.
The flag I see.
A certain word: Democracy.

> —from "The House I Live In," by
> Abel Meeropol and Earl Robinson

I was born at the peak of the postwar baby boom. Now, a little while later, eligible for Medicare and Social Security, I feel more than ever like a person who can look into the arc of today's conflicts and see the generosity, anger, love, suspicion, and sentiment running like electric current through my people. Yes. You are my people. Even if you were grinding your molars and feeling your blood pressure rise earlier in the book. The point of this book is that we are *all* part of we, the people.

Through decades as a reporter my assignment was always to hold the controversies of the day at arm's length, to turn them in my hand, examine them with the detachment of a pathologist examining a tissue sample. There was a good reason for that habit of mind: to keep myself out of the story. Approaching fifty years of work in the news business I have awarded myself the luxury of being a bit more personal and sentimental. Dry-eyed and hard-headed, yet perhaps a bit more "reachable" than I have ever been in a life of examining the facts.

I now land somewhere between that objective detachment and being a blubbering old fool. When George Bailey's friends fill a basket with money in the final moments of *It's a Wonderful Life,* I can barely keep my eyes on the TV set. Sunday mornings, by the third verse of certain hymns, my voice breaks. I can feel my throat suddenly tightening. It is why they call it "choked up."

It can happen a lot when you meet new Americans. A few years ago I was in a garage in one of the dozens of small cities at the south end of Los Angeles County. Earlier in the day, I had visited a metal stamping shop, a parts factory in an industrial zone. I met a young man who had sneaked into the country from Mexico with his family years before, and the boss who was willing to stick his neck out by vouching for the young man's employment.

Fernando Fuentes arrived in the country as a teenager. The work I watched him perform at the shop — using a multiton turret press to fashion sheet metal into components for commercial lighting fixtures — showed he was good with his hands. He was grateful that his boss, who might have suspected he was not in the country legally, was willing to complete the paperwork that allowed Fuentes to stay in the country. That, however, is not what got the young man beaming, got him talking with rising enthusiasm and pleasure about his *other* work. That is what got us to the garage.

Fuentes took ordinary used automobiles and turned them into tricked-out works of art. He taught himself customization while working at the stamping plant, and now he did it all: neon lights, audio systems, upholstery, paint. He had just finished his latest creation, and in that

California garage Fuentes cranked up the audio and showed me how the colored lights pulsed and changed hues in time with the music. The open trunk showed off his skills with both sewing black leather and nestling speakers in custom carpeting. This is where Fuentes saw his future. He grinned as he showed me his recently issued driver's license, his Social Security registration, both obtained through DACA. He explained with relief that he was not living in the shadows anymore. "I'm not going to be hiding from anywhere. And I'm going to keep on doing the right thing."

Keep on doing the right thing? When you cover public policy for a living, you have to think through an encounter like this one. Did Fuentes break the law when he came to the United States years earlier? Yes. Without a doubt. Did he receive services from the State of California, like public schooling, that imposed a cost on taxpayers they did not explicitly agree to take on? Yes. Surely he did.

Then how should a society respond? What's the best play for a country that's looking at a proud, smiling Fernando Fuentes in an LA County garage, flipping switches to show a visitor the light show he created? Now that he is paying taxes, working at a local business and starting one of his own, if we were to make our decisions strictly on legal grounds and send him home, who would benefit? The question is not entirely about making judgments on the infractions of the past. The boy who was spirited over the border is now a man. What now?

Our country has nothing to gain, and a lot to lose, by sending Fuentes packing. We did not ask for, or authorize, his presence among us. He took something he was not allowed to take. But he is here. He works sixty hours a week, doing one of the tens of millions of jobs most of us do not know about consciously, do not picture, do not think of, if we are asked to describe the work of a society.

A future president might be given the green light for mass deportations by omission, by Congress's inability to draft or debate, much less pass, comprehensive immigration reform. Even childhood arrivals, like the recipients of DACA, have not been given the benefit of a predictable and secure future by the national legislature. Police cars could show up outside Fuentes's house and arrest him in preparation for kicking him out of the country entirely. The local news audience might catch a glimpse of a business owner, a worker, led from his house in handcuffs, an officer protecting the top of his head as he slides into the back seat. By now he may have a citizen wife, or native-born US citizen children, but that will not matter if the desire to "send a message" is strong enough.

If you are already on your way, trying to make your way up Central America through Mexico to the border, or already here, quietly at work in a Chicago luncheonette where you will remain when your visa expires, or if you are a fourteen-year-old appearing before an immigration magistrate, answering questions through an interpreter, sending Fuentes home will not matter. People do make decisions about themselves, their families, and their futures in response to information taken from the real world. Yes, they try to weigh the up- and downsides of personal actions. Yet decision-making can be clouded as well as clarified by life in the real world. If where you are is bad enough, you are likely to conclude your decision by saying, "Anything is better than this."

We are a worried people these days. We are worried about a sometimes-hard-to-understand present. Millions of us look at our kids and see an even harder-to-understand future for them. You might figure the last thing we need in the midst of all that confusion and concern is a lot more company. I wondered aloud during a broadcast whether the sudden spotlighting of the hard, and normally hidden, work of so many immigrants would earn them a little sympathy, if higher wages and more respect seemed like too much to hope for as the pandemic restrictions sent Americans indoors and out of each other's faces.

Immigrant cleaners disinfecting buses and trains sickened and died. Immigrants killing and packaging pigs and chickens died in large enough numbers to reshape the COVID statistics in the small towns that are home to meat processing plants. The enormous number of immigrants who care for the elderly and infirm, long before the widespread availability of vaccines, got dressed, commuted, and spent their days with their charges, some unwittingly bringing COVID into the houses where they worked, some unwittingly taking it home to their families. (While just under 14 percent of the residents of this country were born somewhere else, that number rises to 40 percent for home health care workers.)

A disproportionate share of the people dubbed "essential workers" were immigrants. They got some attention, and at a moment when public-facing jobs could mean serious illness, many got raises, too. Yet low-paid immigrant cashiers and stock clerks were no match for suddenly surging unemployment and later rising inflation and the politics that became social conflict by other means.

Temporary protected status, or TPS, has been offered to people from some two dozen countries around the world, from nearby Haiti to far-away South Sudan. It allows an individual from a country that is dangerous, in tumult or civil war, a respite in the US. TPS recipients are able to work in the US, even travel out of the country and return on temporary travel documents. The national emergencies or civil strife that opened up the US to people from Venezuela, Lebanon, or Nicaragua may be transitory, however. Those troubles may subside and make it possible to return to a specific hometown or work. What's the best outcome then?

If a person given temporary refuge wants to go home, great. Yet if, in years working in the US, the TPS holder makes a life for themselves here, is there a national interest in compelling them to return home? In 2017 and 2018, Donald Trump terminated the TPS status of refugees from El Salvador, Honduras, Nepal, Haiti, Sudan, and Nicaragua, which added up to hundreds of thousands of people. President Biden rescinded those terminations, but it amply illustrated the precariousness of the asylum.

There are fewer than 400,000 TPS recipients in a country of more than 330 million people. Even in places where they are numerous, like

Florida, Texas, California, and New York, their presence or absence amounts to a rounding error. The legal advocacy group Forward US estimated TPS holders contribute some $22 billion in wages to the country's GDP. Yet the obvious objection arises: If *temporary* protected status never requires them to go home, even after ten and twenty years, it doesn't seem very temporary.

Sure. That is right.

Again, it is a question not only of the black-and-white text of the law but what we want the law to accomplish. The numbers involved are small. The countries in the program — including Syria, Sudan, and Lebanon — are so dysfunctional that even when they return to an earlier state of functionality, sending people home hardly counts as humane. Of course, it is possible to argue over the list. Surely the crises in Liberia and Honduras are over? Yet things that seem diametrically opposed are not always so. It is true that majorities of Americans tell pollsters they favor comprehensive immigration reform, a path to citizenship for DACA recipients, and a return to pre-Trump refugee policies. It is also true that many believe there is an "invasion" under way and the Biden administration's border policy is failing. Similarly, many of us would naturally expect that temporary protected status should mean what it says — temporary — and yet we would look at individuals who are here under that status and welcome them to stay.

It is 1945. A rail-thin, boyish Frank Sinatra finishes a good take in a recording studio, the orchestra takes a break, and he heads out into the alley for a smoke. He arrives just as a mob of boys chases another boy into that alley, screaming threats, ready to beat him up. The singer intervenes, asking what was causing the commotion and noting the unfair odds, ten against one.

One of the ringleaders shouts, "We don't like him! We don't want him in our neighborhood or going to our school!" Now separated from the gang by the wispy Sinatra, their quarry fires back, "I've been living here as long as you!"

In these, the closing days of World War II, when the boys in the gang make clear they object to their target's religion, Sinatra compares them to Nazis. Being called a Nazi gets one of the boys angry, "Don't call me a Nazi! My father's a sergeant in the Army. He's been wounded even." I don't know if the term was used then, but with this exchange, Ol' Blue Eyes has reached a "teachable moment." He asks the boy being chased if his parents had donated blood at the blood bank. "Sure. My mother and my father both."

He turns to the gang. "You know what? I'll bet you some of his dad's blood helped save your pop's life. That's bad." The hook is in.

"What's bad about it?" The snarling antisemitic mob has now become a group of curious little boys.

"Doncha see? His father doesn't go to the same church as your father does. That's awful. Do you think maybe if your father knew about it at the time he would rather have died than take blood from a man of another religion? Would you have wanted him to die? Would your mom have wanted him to die?"

"No!"

"Look, fellas. Religion makes no difference. Except maybe to a Nazi, or somebody that's stupid. Why, people from all over the world worship God in many different ways. God created everybody. He didn't create one people better than another. Your blood's the same as mine. Mine's the same as his. Do you know what this wonderful country is made of? It's made up of a hundred different kinds of people. And a hundred different ways of talking. And a hundred different ways of going to church. But they're all American ways.

"Wouldn't we be silly if we went around hating people because they comb their hair differently from ours? Wouldn't we be a lot of dopes? My dad came from Italy. But he's an American. But should I hate your father because he came from Ireland or France or Russia? Wouldn't I be a first-class fathead?"

Frank tells this now rapt group of boys about a key battle in the Pacific theater of the war, and the teamwork that went into a US bomber sinking the *Haruna,* a Japanese battleship. "The pilot of that ship was named

Colin Kelly. An American and a Presbyterian. And you know who dropped the bombs? Meyer Levin. An American and a Jew. You think maybe they should have called the bombing off because they had different religions? Think about that, fellas. Use your good American heads. Don't let anybody make suckers outta you."

Sinatra then sings the gorgeous ballad "The House I Live In," backed by an unseen orchestra. That's also the title of this short film. The song is simple and direct, almost deceivingly so:

> *The house I live in*
> *A plot of earth, a street*
> *The grocer and the butcher*
> *And the people that I meet*
> *The children in the playground*
> *The faces that I see*
> *All races and religions*
> *That's America to me*

The reason I can watch this over and over and love it all over again is not in spite of but because of what I know about then and now. In 1945 many of the lyrics of this beautiful song were more aspirational than a reflection of daily life in America's streets and homes. The country had restricted immigration and naturalization from Asia for three-quarters of a century. The military that threw a Kelly and a Levin together in a bomber over the Pacific was still rigidly racially segregated. The blood transfusion Sinatra used as an example of how we are all the same under the skin came from blood supplies that in most places in America were still separated by race, a policy maintained until 1948. In the earliest days of the war, the American Red Cross began a nationwide blood drive in anticipation of military need. Black donors were simply turned away. In the face of criticism and controversy, the Red Cross and military began accepting "Negro" donors, then maintained a separate blood supply from Black donors and for Black recipients, "so that those receiving transfusions may be given plasma from blood of their own race."

The singer mentioned his Italian immigrant father to the boys, but a US Congress, panicked by the number of immigrants from Southern and Eastern Europe, had passed new laws back when the future star was in elementary school in Hoboken, New Jersey. The Immigration and Nationality Act of 1924 would have made it far more difficult for his mother and father to have made it to America in the first place.

Then there is the matter of the song itself, altered from the original to delete references to "my neighbors white and Black." To hear the song is to be reminded of who we thought we were, or who, as the ashes from World War II were still cooling across Europe and Asia, we liked to think we were.

The credits in the opening slides of the movie mention the song has music from Earl Robinson and lyrics by Lewis Allan. That loving vision of "all races and religions" was a product of the left side of the political spectrum. Robinson's work includes the patriotic cantata "Ballad for Americans" and the tribute to the slain labor organizer simply called "Joe Hill." The composer was later blacklisted for his left-wing sympathies in the McCarthy era.

The lyricist called himself "Lewis Allan," but that wasn't his given name. Abel Meeropol was the son of Russian Jewish immigrants, raised in the Bronx. He taught at DeWitt Clinton High School for seventeen years (counting James Baldwin among his students), while nurturing a sideline as a lyricist. Meeropol also wrote the words to the anti-lynching anthem "Strange Fruit," made famous by Billie Holiday. In later years, Meeropol and his wife adopted the two orphaned sons of Julius and Ethel Rosenberg, who were executed in 1953 after their conviction for aiding Soviet efforts to obtain the secrets necessary to build an atomic bomb.

If, rather than sniping at this short film for the things it leaves out, you embrace it as a vision of the America we could be, it has persistent power. Even today, as it approaches its eightieth birthday. The short film won an Oscar in 1946 and was entered into the National Film Registry of the Library of Congress for works deemed "culturally, historically, or aesthetically significant."

As I said, I am becoming a softy in my old age, suddenly seized, moved, by perfect little moments that seem to cut to the heart of the human condition and the American moment, even if they are very old. What I recognize right away in "The House I Live In" and the propaganda film series "Why We Fight" is how effective they are at reminding us of the best version of ourselves. I watched a lot of 20th-century propaganda movies while writing this book and thought a lot about what leaders say to their people and how they stress unity, even when it is cobbled together from disparate parts.

We were not nearly as diverse and divided a country in the 1940s as we would become in the 21st century. There had not been much immigration since the late 1920s. People were less mobile, and perhaps less inclined to believe the worst of people they were unlikely to meet. Small-town life was idealized. Citizen soldiers, from every walk of life, were extolled.

The talented Hollywood storytellers enlisted to tell us ennobling stories of ourselves and the war broke everything down to its essentials: why Nazis were bad, what made us good, and what made us strong. Of course they skipped over serious issues, starting with the racial divide. But the idealistic notes that they hit for the purposes of propaganda still ring true.

The people who describe themselves as "realists" when it comes to immigration talk about the world as if every patch of ground is sloping, and all of it is slippery. Let people in, they argue, and the world would simply pour in, overwhelming the US. They simply cannot believe a few basic propositions: That people love their home countries, their families, their languages, and their way of life. That leaving them all behind is really hard. And, as the people I talked to about the roads they took to becoming Americans said, again and again, making it in America is even harder. Yet the America held in imaginations, everywhere, remains powerful.

When I talked to the young Lebanese priest Fr. Halim Shukair, now in Dearborn, I asked him what I asked almost everybody you met in the pages of this book: "Are you an American?" By this time he had his green card, making him a legal permanent resident, for all of two months. He dates the tug of America to a much earlier time in his life. He grew up next to the American University in Beirut, where his father, grandfather, brother, an uncle, and an aunt were all graduates. He listened to American pop music. His playground was the campus of the American University of Beirut, which "shaped me, and shaped my family in liberal thought," which he valued especially during the dark years of the Lebanese Civil War, since the university had "created a very diverse neighborhood around it, different from all Lebanon with all the fighting that has been between Muslims and Christians and all the hatred." He mused that there were ways he was already an American before he even came here, that "it was in my DNA."

His time in Dearborn, among a yeasty and ecumenical group of Christians and a large number of recent Muslim immigrants from different countries, leads him to another question: "Are we to be Arabs in America or American Arabs?" I asked him to explain the difference. As he answered you could almost hear him thinking through what he wants to see in his new hometown.

"Yes, we have an identity as an immigrant. As an Arab Christian, as Middle Eastern. We have a great thing in our culture. We need to keep what we are proud of, but we also need to be open. This country will give us a lot of things we don't have in our culture, like how to live in a diverse community, not to be in a bubble."

It sounds to me like Fr. Shukair is looking for the new immigrant "sweet spot" between the old country and the new home. "We have all this opportunity. We need to give to our children the chance to have a healthy generation. If we were still living with all the thinking that is in our countries that we left, we will stay in our little town. We are going to build a generation of healthy Americans-to-be, and I believe we shouldn't be Arab in America but American Arabs." A little thing, this slightly different nomenclature, and yet a huge thing.

The people who told me their stories over the last several years had done a very difficult thing. They had struggled and found their own mix of what they retained about who they were and what they had become. So many of them, when telling me about getting settled here and figuring out how to move ahead in America, either in the context of a specific story or as an aside or stray thought, said, "It's so hard," or "It's very hard."

Yet for all the struggle, another emotion was common: gratitude. Our storytellers were grateful for opportunities, for dumb luck, for the ability to trade a place where hard work would rarely change their circumstances for a place where hard work was transformative. At the same time, the gratitude, while real, is seasoned with an eyes-open recognition of the shortcomings of the place. We are grown-ups, after all. We can keep two thoughts in our heads at the same time.

Immigrants do not have a monopoly on contested or contradictory thought. Prof. Mae Ngai, the daughter of Chinese immigrants and now an immigration scholar at Columbia University, argues that the things native-born people often hold in their heads about immigrants and immigration are untrue. "It is a common complaint that people have against immigrants, about the competition. But immigrants rarely compete head-to-head with native-born people. Usually they work in segmented labor markets." During the period of high anxiety about the arrival of Asian workers, Ngai said, "Chinese rarely competed with whites, especially with skilled workers, because they were excluded from those positions."

Ngai said the idea of unfair labor competition, mixed with nativism and short-term economic disappointment, gets the attention of policymakers. "Immigrants don't take away steelworkers' jobs or autoworkers' jobs. They work in other areas. So the idea does not bear close scrutiny.

"But it's a convenient way to get people riled up about their own circumstances and point the finger at a group of people that is not responsible." Ngai credits the changes in the way the law regards the rights of immigrants and their descendants—based on the 14th Amendment to the US Constitution—to a son of Chinese laborers in California named Wong Kim Ark.

He was born in San Francisco in 1873, years before the Page Act of 1875, and the Chinese Exclusion Act of 1882, made it nearly impossible for Chinese immigrants to settle in the US or become citizens. Wong Kim Ark was raised in California, but when he was in his teens, his parents decided to return to China. He married and decided to return to the United States in 1890.

He was admitted on the basis of his birth in the US. But then he returned to Guangdong Province to bring his wife to California in 1894. The next time he tried to return to the US, the following year, he was barred from reentry. The Collector of Customs of the Port of San Francisco argued that as the child of Chinese citizens, Wong Kim Ark's place of birth was irrelevant. With the help of a Chinese civic association in San Francisco, the young California native challenged the ruling, which eventually went all the way to the Supreme Court.

It took until March 1898 for Wong Kim Ark's legal saga to end. The Supreme Court ruled that any person born on US soil is an American citizen under the Citizenship Clause of the 14th Amendment, added to the Constitution thirty years earlier to guarantee American citizenship to millions of former slaves. Ngai is clear about why the high court found for Wong Kim Ark: "They did it not because they had any love for Chinese Americans. They did it because they knew that if they tinkered with the meaning of the 14th Amendment, they would jeopardize the citizenship of all the children born to European immigrants.

"Thank Wong Kim Ark for finally pushing this under the Supreme Court's nose in a way that they couldn't avoid: *jus soli*, the right of the soil, that comes from being born on American soil." You may be hearing a lot more than you ever expected to about Wong Kim Ark and the 14th Amendment in the coming years. In the 21st century many American politicians have become incensed about "anchor babies" and "illegal aliens" crossing the border to give birth. Birthright citizenship may have been settled in 1898, but the Supreme Court might think differently today.

In 2023, Florida governor Ron DeSantis sought ways to run to Donald Trump's right on immigration. During the years when immigrants were telling me their stories, the tumult in many countries continued to drive desperate people to stream toward the US. This country did not ask them to come. Across multiple presidential administrations, it specifically asked them not to try. They came anyway. Thus, the problems of faraway places became a persistent part of our national debates, a cudgel to use against opponents and immigrants themselves.

Los Angeles, Chicago, and New York are home to millions of immigrants, legal and illegal. New York alone has almost six hundred thousand undocumented people inside its five counties, the equivalent of an entire Milwaukee inside the already crowded city limits. Giant Los Angeles County has an estimated nine hundred thousand undocumented residents, equivalent to the population of Charlotte, North Carolina, inside its borders. Fueled by the myth that cities like New York and Los Angeles, and liberal enclaves like the island of Martha's Vineyard off the coast of Massachusetts, are somehow removed or insulated from the real problems of unauthorized migration, Governors Greg Abbott of Texas and Ron DeSantis of Florida sent newly arrived migrants north and west: to Los Angeles, Chicago, Washington, DC, Martha's Vineyard, and New York.

These stunts are meant to give malicious pleasure to people who think "Democrat-run cities" are full of starry-eyed idealists unacquainted with the real world of undocumented immigration. These politicians want other Americans to see the problem as they do, as an opportunity for partisan combat. As an added bonus, they believe stunts like loading asylum seekers on buses will expose the hypocrisy they imagine in others. Inconvenienced only slightly by the fact that Florida has no land border with foreign countries, Gov. DeSantis sent representatives to Texas to lure people seeking asylum onto a chartered plane to send them winging to Martha's Vineyard.

The refugees, now in a small beach resort, did not end up living in the streets, neglected by imaginary liberals unaware of what the US faces as its southern border. Churches sprang into action with shelter and food. The asylum seekers were transported to the Massachusetts mainland from a small island that lacked the social service infrastructure to serve them, into the hands of agencies with the staff and resources to get them help. The public employees involved in Massachusetts (and Chicago, Washington, DC, New York, and Los Angeles) deserve no special accolades. They did what they're supposed to do. Their agencies performed the work they were created to do.

The politicians who took real people and turned them into *things* have earned some criticism. Desperate people mixed in with people just looking for a better shot at a decent life should never be treated as political pawns. They are people. They would have preferred that life in the places they know best was not miserable and dangerous. They took a tremendous gamble with their futures. The US government has said publicly, here at home, and back in their countries, that it does not want them — but they were so desperate, they came anyway.

When the problems of other places become American problems, the country that has told the rest of the world for two centuries that it is both different and better has choices to face. Being "the same" and "no better" are both choices on that list. Yet most Americans appear inclined to help, not to turn their backs.

There is no "open border," unlike in the first century of our existence as a nation. In 2022, the US deported more people than in 2021. In 2023, deportations were up sharply from 2022. Years of data make it clear that people given "parole," that is, released pending an immigration hearing, show up for their hearing rather than disappearing into the streets of America. It only makes sense: if you don't show up for your hearing, you will be deported if found, and it will be impossible for you to eventually live legally in the United States.

Immigration opponents accuse the federal government of leaving our borders wide-open. Yet open borders are not patrolled by tens of thousands of federal agents or wired for hundreds of miles with infrared cameras and motion-sensing detectors, and blocked by fences and walls. Tons of drugs and thousands of weapons are not intercepted, nor are gang members and human traffickers arrested, along open borders.

There is no "invasion." Invaders do not surrender to authorities in an effort to get into the cumbersome, slow, and unpredictable immigration system. The hundreds of thousands of people who have been caught in recent years trying to sneak into the United States, only to be deported, might find it a strange kind of invasion.

People seeking illegal entry are being deported. Asylum seekers are being processed. Post-pandemic, about a million people a year are becoming naturalized American citizens. A million people a year are becoming lawful permanent residents, the legal name for what we popularly call green card holders, even though the card is no longer green. The permanent residents come in a variety of ways, about a third with employment-based visas, about a quarter with the help of a close relative under family unification preferences in current law, and one of every fifteen or so coming under the diversity lottery for visas.

Recent trends in American diversity show no signs of slowing down. The top five countries of origin for green card holders are India, Mexico, China, Cuba, and the Dominican Republic. The children of those new legal residents are already in an elementary school near you or will soon be born as American citizens in your local hospital.

We have lived with immigration's ongoing mutual benefit for centuries. Yet it appears we have to relearn its surprising gifts to our country generation after generation. By now you have crossed the border with Socorro, and Jaime. You've walked into the bakery business with Andrew, waited tables with Deborah, gone back to Lebanon from California only to give the US another shot with Nelly, and watched a kid who's been a permanent resident for just a few months explain to puzzled Koreans why he really doesn't know very much about America, alongside Samir. You've watched a proud declaration of love for American values from

Imam Ossama, and carried gurneys loaded with frightened COVID patients with Jesus.

The immigrants are flexible, rolling with every punch America dishes out, and becoming hermit crabs in a complicated country. Becoming *what?* The hermit crab, as it develops, creates a home by taking up residence inside whatever cast off shell is available and fits. All up and down the economy, in every kind of American community from the biggest cities to the smallest rural settlements, immigrants make economies work. They are making homes for themselves, like the Dominicans of Hazleton, Pennsylvania, in whatever next place fits.

For all the efforts in recent years to cast suspicion on motivation, acculturation, and their desire to become "us," modern immigrants continue the alchemy of America, continue the amazing work of transformation. Their children—a real estate agent in Texas, a business consultant in San Francisco, an immigration attorney in Boston, a college professor in New York, a kid scooting around a dinette in a Queens apartment—don't have to become us. They are born one of us on day one.

You don't have to be a softy to get a little catch in your throat when you hear these words. We have been good at this. A lot of places in the world have not. America 2.0 is coming, ready or not. We can make this easy, or we can make it harder. Or we can just make it American, by being true to our ideals.

The town I live in
The street, the house, the room,
Pavement of the city
Or a garden all in bloom
The church, the school, the clubhouse
The million lights I see
But especially the people
That's America to me

Acknowledgments

My thanks go to all the people who agreed to tell me their stories, sometimes even against their better judgment, so that their fellow Americans would understand a little more about the immigrant experience in recent decades.

Thanks to the people who opened their doors at a time of tremendous wariness and suspicion, overcoming well-founded worries about a pandemic that made our hometowns scary, for a time.

Thanks to the immigration attorneys who helped me understand the constantly shifting intricacies of American immigration law as written and practiced.

Thanks, again, go to Bruce Nichols, my first editor, twenty-five years ago, who helped make me an author.

Thanks to my transcriber, Deb Reeb, who got the hang of a dozen different accents when listening to hour after hour of interviews from the field.

Thanks to African Communities Together, for their advice, resources, scholarship, and service to one of the country's newest immigrant populations.

Thanks to all the people who heard what I was up to and passed along tips and recommendations, phone numbers and names.

And finally, thanks to all the brave, risk-taking, adventurous people who are writing this newest chapter in American history. You have joined a four-hundred-year-long procession, and in the same moment, made something new. You are home.

Appendix

A Statistical Survey of US Immigration and Attitudes

A Selected Set of Statistics and Polling Data on the New Americans

PART ONE

A Demographic Portrait

States with the Largest Immigrant Populations (in millions)

California	10.5
Texas	5.1
Florida	4.6
New York	4.4
New Jersey	2.1

(Source: Migration Policy Institute/US Census Bureau)

Ten States with the Highest Percentage of Foreign-Born Residents (by percentage)

California	26.6
New Jersey	23
New York	22.3
Florida	21.2

Hawaii	18.8
Nevada	18.4
Massachusetts	17.6
Texas	17.2
Maryland	15.9
Connecticut	15.2

(Source US Census Bureau)

US States with the Lowest Percentage of Foreign-Born Residents (by percentage)

West Virginia	1.6
Mississippi	2.1
Montana	2.2
Wyoming	3.4
South Dakota	3.5
Alabama	3.5
Kentucky	4
Maine	4.1
Missouri	4.1
Vermont	4.2

(Source: Statista.com)

States with the Fastest-Growing Foreign-Born Populations 2010–21 (by percentage)

North Dakota	103
Delaware	41

South Dakota	39
Idaho	32
Kentucky	29
Washington	29

(Source: Migration Policy Institute)

US Cities with the Largest Foreign-Born Populations

City	foreign-born	% of pop
New York City	2,996,580	35.7
Los Angeles	1,521,119	39.7
Houston	644,167	28.5
Chicago	588,480	20.6
San Jose	367,711	38.1
Phoenix	346,430	21.7
San Diego	325,819	24.9
Dallas	322,072	24.8
San Francisco	278,369	34.1
Miami	244,352	56.4

(Source: 2020 US Census)

Top Birth Countries of Foreign-Born US Residents, 1850 (by percentage)

Ireland	42
Germany	26
Great Britain	17
Canada	7
France	2

(Source: US Census Bureau)

Top Birth Countries of Foreign-Born US Residents, 2020 (by percentage)

Mexico	14
India	13
China	7
The Philippines	4
Dominican Republic	3
Cuba	3

(Source US Census Bureau)

How New Arrivals Legally Entered the US in Fiscal Year 2021 (by percentage of 740,000 total)

Immediate relatives of US citizens	52
Family-related immigrants	9
Employer sponsored/skills-related	26
Refugees/those granted asylum	8
Diversity lottery	2

(Source: Migration Policy Institute)

Languages Spoken at Home by US Households (by percentage)

People who speak a language other than English at home	21.7
People who say they speak English "less than well"	8.2
People who speak Spanish at home	13.3

(Source US Census Bureau)

By US State, Most Commonly Spoken Language *Other Than* English or Spanish

VERY interesting data…take away English *and* Spanish, and the most common languages are:

Cantonese and Mandarin	WA, OR, ID, CA, UT, CO, KS, MO, AL, NC, VA, WV, PA, DE, MD, NJ, NY
Vietnamese	GA, MS, TX, OK
French	LA, VT, NH, ME
Portuguese	MA, RI, CT
German	ND, IA, SC, KY
Arabic	TN, MI
Hmong	WI
Polish	IL
Haitian Creole	MN, FL
SW Pacific Island languages	AR, HI
Navajo	AZ, NM
Pennsylvania Dutch	IN, OH
Yupik	AK
Tagalog	NV
Dakota	SD

(Source US Census Bureau)

Percentage of US Population That Is Foreign-Born, by Census Year

1850	9.7
1860	13.2
1870	14.4

1880	13.3
1890	14.8 (historic high)
1900	13.6
1910	14.7
1920	13.2
1930	11.6
1940	8.8
1950	6.9
1960	5.4

(Immigration and Nationality Act of 1965 signed)

1970	4.7
1980	6.2
1990	7.9
2000	11.1
2010	12.9
2020	13.6 (highest percentage since 1910)

(Source US Census Bureau)

Levels of Education of US-born, Immigrant, and Recent-Immigrant Adults (by percentage)

Bachelor's Degree or Higher

Recently arrived immigrants	47
Immigrants	34
US-born	35

Some College, or Associate's Degree

Recently arrived immigrants	14
Immigrants	19
US-born	30

High School Diploma or GED

Recently arrived immigrants	19
Immigrants	22
US-born	27

9–12th Grade

Recently arrived immigrants	7
Immigrants	9
US-born	5

(Source: Migration Policy Institute using data from US Census Bureau American Community Survey)

Comparing Household Income of Immigrant and Native-born workers

(Migration Policy Institute from US Census Bureau)
Median household income, immigrant-led household $69,622
Median household income, native-born led household $69,734

Children with at Least One Immigrant Parent

1990 8,194,000 born in US: 77
2021 18,021,000 born in US: 87.9

(Migration Policy Institute from American Community Survey)

PART TWO

Public Opinion About the New Americans

The Public Religion Research Institute (PRRI) regularly surveys American opinions on a range of questions of tolerance. Here are some recent findings:

Do you agree with the following statements?

God intended America to be a new promised land where European Christians could create a society that would be an example to the rest of the world.

Republicans	49
Independents	26
Democrats	18

Newcomers threaten traditional American customs and values.

Republicans	69
Independents	37
Democrats	17

Immigration is a critical issue in the 2022 elections.

One among many issues	47
Critical	40
Not that important	12
Republicans	63
Independents	35
Democrats	23

There should be a pathway to citizenship for undocumented immigrants.

Republicans	40
Independents	58
Democrats	77
All Americans	57

Children brought illegally to the US by their parents should be allowed to apply for citizenship or permanent residence status.

Republicans	18
Independents	42
Democrats	66
All Americans	41
White evangelical Protestants	21
Hispanic Catholics	55
Black Protestants	57

The Pew Research Center also regularly undertakes opinion polls on a wide range of issues. Here is a recent finding on the importance of taking in refugees:

Taking in civilian refugees from countries where people are trying to escape violence and war should be a _____ goal for immigration policy in the United States.

Not at all important...

Republican/Lean Republican	13
Democratic/Lean Democratic	4

Not too important

Republican/Lean Republican	28
Democratic/Lean Democratic	11

APPENDIX

Somewhat important
Republican/Lean Republican 45
Democratic/Lean Democratic 44

Very important
Republican/Lean Republican 13
Democratic/Lean Democratic 41

For more, visit:

Pew Research Center
https://www.pewresearch.org/about/terms-and-conditions/

Public Religion Research Institute
prri.org

Migration Policy Institute
migrationpolicy.org

US Census Bureau
census.gov

INDEX

INDEX

INDEX

INDEX

Olopade, Olofunmilayo "Funmi," 124, 131–136, 149–150
Olopade, Sola, 132, 134–136, 150
Omar, Ilhan, 234–235
"open border" claim, 271–272
opportunities, for second generation in the US, 34–35
Ortega, Daniel, 233
Orthodox Jews, 50–51
Ozawa, Takao, 92
Ozawa v. United States, 91–92

Page Act of 1875, 269
Palestinian immigrants, 95
particularism, 75–76
passports, US, 180
patriotism, 26, 85, 232, 253–254
Pennsylvania
    Hazleton, 237–239
    immigrants settling in, 80
    Philadelphia, 6, 77–82
    Pittsburgh, 5
Pew Research Center, 184, 185, 209
Philadelphia, Pennsylvania, 6, 77–82
Pittsburgh, Pennsylvania, 5
Polish immigrants, 47, 77
political parties
    need for change in, 85–86
    "the White Christian Party," 240
political power
    immigration to shift balance of, 5
    in resource deployment, 76
politics
    immigrants' distrust of, 202–203
    immigration as exploitable issue in, 240, 270–271
    leveraging cultural anxiety in, 239–240
    in Michigan, 221–223
    race issue in, 142–143
Poway, California synagogue shooting, 253
prejudice, 74–76, 82, 101–104
presidential power in immigration policy, 152–153
Presley, Ayanna, 234–235
The Problem with Apu (documentary), 246

Qian, Nancy, 203–205
Queens, New York City, 186–190, 193–195
quota system
    as 1964 election issue, 19

end of, 11, 19 (*See also* Immigration and Nationality Act of 1965)
post-WWII unused slots under, 16

R-1 visas, 100
race
    American promise dependent on, 86
    Census Bureau choices for, 128–129
    cultural arguments based on, 9
    definitions of "white," 90–96
    as flexible, 79–80
    and prejudice, 74–76
    scientific and pseudoscientific studies of, 8–9, 92
    struggle in US over, 128
racial consciousness, 27–28
racial identity, 94, 244–245
racism, experience of, 138, 142–143
Raspail, Jean, 250–251
Reagan, Ronald, 133, 232
reasons for immigration, 37, 38, 79
refugees, 153–183
    Afghan, 159–171
    Americans' attitudes toward, 181–183
    "boat people," 172–174
    and border enforcement, 87
    congressional division about, 168–169
    Cuban, 19
    exclusion of vs. generosity toward, 168
    fear of bad actors among, 155–157
    as immigration law priority, 42–48
    and Jackson-Vanik Amendment, 48–49
    jobs for, 167
    naturalization of, 272
    post-World War II, 16
    quotas for, 154–155
    religious minorities, 155
    restriction on, 140
    suspicion of, 43
    temporary protected status for, 261–262
    transported to other areas, 270–271
    Trump's portrayal of, 235
    at US borders, 181
    US Refugee Admissions Program, 153–154
    Vietnamese, 168, 171–179
religious identity/affiliation, 90–122
    of Arabic-speaking immigrants, 108–111
    attitudes toward Muslim immigrants, 101–104
    and attitudes toward refugees, 181–183

INDEX

About the Author

RAY SUAREZ is a writer and broadcaster who currently hosts the weekly foreign affairs radio program and podcast *On Shifting Ground.* He was the chief national correspondent for *The PBS NewsHour,* host of NPR's *Talk of the Nation,* and a reporter in Chicago, Los Angeles, London, and Rome. His books include *Latino Americans* (Penguin, 2013), *The Holy Vote* (Harper, 2005), and *The Old Neighborhood* (Free Press, 1999). He lives in Washington, DC.